FLY FISHING

THE GREATER

YELLOWSTONE
BACKCOUNTRY

BRUCE STAPLES

STACKPOLE
BOOKS

Guilford, Connecticut

Published by Stackpole Books
An imprint of Globe Pequot
Trade Division of The Rowman & Littlefield Publishing Group, Inc.
4501 Forbes Boulevard, Suite 200, Lanham, Maryland 20706

Distributed by NATIONAL BOOK NETWORK
800-462-6420

British Library Cataloguing in Publication Information Available

Library of Congress Cataloging-in-Publication Data

Names: Staples, Bruce, author.
Title: Fly fishing the greater Yellowstone backcountry / Bruce Staples.
Description: Guilford, CT : Stackpole Books, 2017. | Includes bibliographical
  references and index.
Identifiers: LCCN 2017034319 (print) | LCCN 2017036200 (ebook) | ISBN
  9780811766821 | ISBN 9780811716208 (pbk.)
Subjects: LCSH: Fly fishing—Yellowstone National Park Region. | Fly
  fishing—Yellowstone National Park Region—Guidebooks. | Yellowstone
  National Park Region—Guidebooks.
Classification: LCC SH464.Y45 (ebook) | LCC SH464.Y45 S73 2017 (print)
| DDC
  799.12/4097875—dc23
LC record available at https://lccn.loc.gov/2017034319

♾ TM   The paper used in this publication meets the minimum requirements
of American National Standard for Information Sciences—Permanence of
Paper for Printed Library Materials, ANSI/NISO Z39.48-1992.

Printed in the United States of America

CONTENTS

PART 3: Southwestern Montana. 123

PART 4: Northwestern Wyoming 175

PART 5: Fly Patterns.................................. 233

ACKNOWLEDGMENTS

have spent three decades visiting different waters within the Greater Yellowstone Area. Yet, because of the vast amount of trout water hosting (six species of salmonids, including grayling) in the area, many waters remain on my "to visit" list. Thus I called on other fly fishers to contribute the benefit of their experience to this book. I also asked fly fishers who have more experience than I on certain waters to contribute rather than write from my lesser experience. Each author is credited for their contribution. I am indebted to all of these contributors and want the reader to know of their generosity and fly fishing expertise: Boots Allen, Charles Barnes, Dave Brackett, Dr. Joe Burke, Doug Gibson, Kelly Glissmeyer, Lorenzo "Buck" Goodrich, Steve Hyde, Bob Jacklin, Mike Lawson, Larry Lewis, Bill Liebegott, Gregg Messel, Dr. Harley W. Reno, Leon Sanderson, Tim Tollett, Tim Wade, and Satoshi Yamamoto. Other than contributions from these persons, I author all others.

I thank Dave Delisi, the Woodson Ranch Outreach Coordinator, for providing information on the Ruby Habitat Foundation. Joe Deromedi of the Wyoming Game & Fish Department provided information on the Wind River drainage. Jimmy Gabettas suggested experienced fly fishers with whom I should communicate for information on certain waters.

To Dr. Roger Blew I express much appreciation for the flights that gave opportunities for aerial photography. Mike Carlson provided detailed information on fishing some western Wyoming waters. I thank photo contributors, and I also thank those fly tiers who made contributions to the chapter describing new fly patterns. Once again, working with Jay Nichols was informative and a pleasure.

FOREWORD

I began fly fishing in the early 1970s and took up fly tying a few years later. In the beginning I concentrated my efforts on the fabled waters of the Greater Yellowstone Area, as any fly fisher would. These included such streams as the Firehole, Yellowstone, and Madison Rivers; the South Fork reach of the Snake River (from now on referred to as South Fork reach); and the Henry's Fork. As time passed, I realized that the Greater Yellowstone Area hosts a superb variety of quality waters of lesser renown. Having always enjoyed discovery, I turned increasingly to visiting remote and lesser-known waters. So came visits to Fall River Basin, Shoshone Lake, Slough Creek, and the upper Yellowstone River; early-season visits to Heart Lake Basin, where I experienced the best inland trout fishing of my life; and other waters within Yellowstone National Park. With these came visits—too numerous

In the first few decades of the mid twentieth century the South Fork of the Madison River was considered the best stream in the Greater Yellowstone Area on which to encounter grayling. Brown and rainbow trout have now replaced the grayling and cutthroat trout.

JOHN JURACEK PHOTO

vii

to identify here—to waters in southeastern Idaho, southwestern Montana, and northwestern Wyoming.

Certainly in this quest, I have come to have favorite fly fishing locations, particularly meadow streams. Perhaps this comes from my early days fishing the Harriman State Park reach of the Henry's Fork in its less-crowded past. I revel in the stair-step meadows of Fall River, Slough Creek, and Bechler River, all in Yellowstone Park. I feel the same about the meadow streams of southwestern Montana's Centennial Valley and eastern Idaho's upper Blackfoot River, along with numerous small streams. My quest for discovery in the fly fishing world continues, and I will share my accumulated knowledge with anyone having the same or better environmental values than I possess.

As my fly fishing experience and knowledge grew, so did my concern for the fragile status of cutthroat trout. Certainly, others have the same concern. For example, Jimmy Gabettas, owner of Jimmy's All Seasons Angler, in Idaho Falls and authority on fishing Greater Yellowstone waters, offers: "The presence of cutthroat trout may be an underlying reason for many fly fishing visits to our Greater Yellowstone Area. I feel almost duty-bound to act to protect not only them, but their habitat." So I am not alone in having reverence for cutthroat trout, the sole native trout, albeit in different subspecies, in the area. How their diversion into subspecies came about fascinates me. To me their beauty as a salmonid is second to only grayling. These two fish, along with the Rocky Mountain whitefish, are the sole native salmonids in the Greater Yellowstone Area, excepting the lake trout population of southwestern Montana's Elk Lake.

Three subspecies of cutthroat trout are native to the Greater Yellowstone Area. How this speciation came about because of regional geologic events is fascinating. Encountering cutthroat trout of the different subspecies becomes a goal of many fly fishers visiting the area. JOHN JURACEK PHOTO

The headwaters of eastern Idaho's McCoy Creek offer stunning scenery as well as undisturbed fishing for Snake River fine spotted cutthroat trout.

Yes, I hear all the chat that "cutties" do not put up a spectacular fight compared to some exotic salmonid species introduced to the area. But I wonder if persons making such comments have encountered the westslope cutthroat that is being reintroduced to certain waters, or the Yellowstone or Snake River fine–spotted cutthroat trout in Heart Lake Basin. I would rather catch a 5-pound cutthroat than a 5-pound rainbow or brown trout for one simple reason: Much fewer cutthroat trout of that size exist. More important than judging fighting qualities is accepting the fact that cutthroat trout numbers are shrinking because of environmental changes that negatively impact the cutthroat's natural equilibrium and because of competition from introduced exotic species. I have also come to realize the cutthroat's economic value, as nowhere else on earth other than the Rocky Mountains does it exist in self-sustaining numbers. If it disappears, one of the compelling reasons for fly fishers to visit the Greater Yellowstone Area vanishes. Thus I support all efforts to preserve the cutthroat as well as the even more endangered Montana grayling. I encourage all fly fishers to do the same.

I support the presence of exotic salmonids in the Greater Yellowstone Area. I admire the sporting qualities and beauty of brook, brown, lake, and rainbow trout, but I question their presence in waters where they appear to diminish the number of native salmonids. They certainly, however, fill a void in waters that have changed to the point where native salmonids can no longer sustain themselves.

Very large trout occupy several Greater Yellowstone Area small streams. Heart Lake Basin's Beaver Creek, shown here, is an example.

INTRODUCTION

Defining the Greater Yellowstone Area can be subjective, but Yellowstone National Park surrounded by Bridger-Teton, Caribou-Targhee, Custer-Gallatin, and Shoshone National Forests and Grand Teton National Park are certainly at its core. Beaverhead-Deerlodge National Forest is adjacent to these on the west. Therefore, most of the waters addressed in this book are within these public lands. Beyond this core lies a mixture of public and private land, the extent of which can be included in the area for the purpose of fly fishing.

In the world of cold water fly fishing, trout reign supreme. Combine their popularity with the fact that the number of quality waters for enjoying these fish is diminishing throughout the country, and the result is more enthusiasts on fewer waters available to the fly fishing public. Nowhere in the country is this more true than in

The Greater Yellowstone Area abounds in beautiful but distracting scenery. Take time to enjoy and appreciate such surroundings, and upon leaving them consider taking part in the actions to preserve them for future generations. JOHN JURACEK PHOTO

Duck Creek, within Yellowstone Park, is a classic meadow stream. Above its meadow reach it flows through prime bear country, and thus should be visited with caution. JOHN JURACEK PHOTO

the Greater Yellowstone Area, the region where the most remaining high-quality wild inland salmonid populations can be accessed and enjoyed. On many rivers outside Yellowstone National Park, which limits motorized boat fishing to Yellowstone and Lewis Lakes, this increase is mostly due to the explosion of fishing from boats, particularly on larger waters. But the decline in quality fly fishing experiences does not have to be the case for fly fishers on Greater Yellowstone waters. That is simply because waters renowned in the minds of so many fly fishers, and therefore most visited, are only a portion of quality waters the area hosts. In this book, I reveal the many quality waters—moving and still, large and small—in this region that are alternatives to the famous ones. Many of the lesser known waters included in this book have scenery and fishing that rival or exceed adjacent famous waters. While they almost guarantee less crowded conditions, informational resources on them, up until this point, have been in short supply.

With respect to salmonids species, many area waters, renowned or not so well known, are refuges for Snake River fine-spotted, westslope, and Yellowstone cutthroat trout, the sole historic trout natives to much of the Greater Yellowstone Area. Populations of these cutthroat species have diminished in renowned waters such as the Snake River, Yellowstone Lake, and the Yellowstone River, but in many less-famous waters, Yellowstone and Snake River fine-spotted species reign supreme. The same does not hold true for westslope cutthroat trout, which, like grayling, were nearly eliminated from the area. Reintroduction of the westslope in Yellowstone National Park waters and in certain waters in the southwestern Montana part of the Greater Yellowstone Area is in progress. Let's hope they can obtain a foothold. Efforts to do the same for Montana grayling, also native to many area waters, have met with mixed success.

Greater Yellowstone fishing clubs not only act to protect salmonid habitat but hold outings to remote quality waters. Here Snake River Cutthroat members assemble during a lower Blackfoot River outing. Becoming a member in a club such as this cements friendships and serves as a platform to exchange fishing information in addition to taking part in actions with the goal of preserving regional coldwater fisheries.

Of the native salmonids present in the area, the Rocky Mountain whitefish seems to have best weathered the alteration of area waters and the introduction of exotic salmonids and non-salmonids. Receiving minimal respect from most fly fishers (eastern Idaho natives apply the term "stiffie" or "stiff," while some Montanans call them "whistlers"), they should get more credit for taking a well-presented dry fly or nymph then putting up a dogged fight. Credit should also apply for being able to maintain their population through environmental change and the introduction of exotic salmonids better than the other native salmonids.

Before discussing the alternative quality waters, it seems appropriate to overview the more famed waters. We will do this in terms of how and why they have gained such renown. Numerous works are available on strategies for fly fishing these waters, as well there should be, and the best span almost a century of experience. These waters remain extremely worthy of a visit, and there are surely times when they can produce an unforgettable quality fishing experience.

Famed Waters Overview

Since at least the beginning of the 20th century, such Greater Yellowstone Area waters as the Henry's Fork, the Madison River, Yellowstone Lake, and the Yellowstone River were known to be exceptional coldwater fisheries for Montana grayling in certain waters, cutthroat trout, and Rocky Mountain whitefish. In the upper

Expect plenty of company when fishing the fabled Firehole River. Like all Park waters, bad weather and shoulder seasons offer a chance to fish without the crowds. JOHN JURACEK PHOTO

Madison River drainage, upper Gallatin River drainage, upper Ruby River, and Centennial Valley waters, Montana grayling accompanied westslope cutthroat. Both species were absent in the Henry's Fork, the Snake, and the Yellowstone River drainages, each hosting Snake River fine-spotted cutthroat or Yellowstone cutthroat trout. Below physical barriers, Rocky Mountain whitefish accompanied these cutthroat, except within the Henry's Fork. To the east, the same two salmonids populated the Shoshone River and Clarks Fork of the Yellowstone River drainages. Yellowstone cutthroat were the only salmonids native to Yellowstone Lake.

Within Yellowstone National Park between the Yellowstone River drainage to the east, the Madison and Gallatin River drainages to the north and west, and the Fall River Basin and upper Snake River drainages to the south lay a land devoid of salmonids because of barriers established through volcanic action. Many of these physical barriers are the spectacular waterfalls we enjoy today. By the late 19th century, stocking of salmonids by the U.S. Fish & Wildlife Service (formerly the U.S. Fish Commission) began in this area. In 1889 brook trout were introduced into the Firehole River. They soon flourished and by the 1920s were accompanied by brown and rainbow trout introduced in its drainage. They, too, flourished to the point that rainbow trout is the dominant salmonid within the drainage, so by the 1930s the Firehole and Gibbon Rivers, easily approached by road, were added to the list of exceptional coldwater fisheries.

As the early 20th century progressed, political pressure from eastern fly fishers and fisheries professionals dictated that brook, brown, and rainbow trout be introduced in other waters of the once salmonid-free area. Lake Michigan lake trout and brown trout were released in the upper Lewis River drainage. Shoshone and

Lewis Lakes were chosen for the lake trout because they were considered to be an appropriate refuge for these Great Lakes fish. Both species flourished to the point where commercial angling took place on each lake in order to supply Yellowstone Park eateries with wild trout.

Through downstream drift and later planting, the Lewis River and the Snake River down to Jackson Lake became primarily brown trout fisheries. Likewise, rainbow and brown trout took the Madison River over from westslope cutthroat and Montana grayling because of downstream drift from waters in the park. Both exotics flourished in Hebgen Lake after it was filled in 1917. Hebgen Lake was also the death knell for the native salmonids in upstream tributaries such as the South Fork of the Madison River, Grayling Creek, and Duck Creek. Into the first decades of the 20th century, the South Fork of the Madison River was considered by many anglers to be the best grayling stream in the Greater Yellowstone Area. Now it hosts brown and rainbow trout and Rocky Mountain whitefish. Escaping from private fisheries, rainbow trout began hybridizing with Henry's Fork cutthroat until cutthroat-rainbow hybrids (cuttbows) dominated prior to the mid-20th century. Later in the century brown trout were introduced in the Henry's Fork below lower Mesa Falls and in the South Fork reach as well as some of its tributaries. So whether through downstream drift or planting, we have the salmonid makeup of today in many Greater Yellowstone waters.

In most cases the quality of area fisheries remained after exotic salmonids took hold. But in the early 20th century, only the well-healed angler could afford to fish these waters. It was the affordable automobile and a developing infrastructure that first allowed the middle-class angler to reach the Greater Yellowstone region. As

Few waters are as renowned as the Harriman State Park reach of the Henry's Fork. Famed for massive and varied mayfly emergences, abundant terrestrial insects, wildlife presence, and large, vigorous cuttbow trout, the reach attracts crowds of fly fishers through most of the season.

these anglers visited the area in increasing numbers, beginning just before mid-20th century, they sought information on where and how to fish within it. In those days Dan Bailey, Don Martinez, and Bob Carmichael ruled the fly fishing retail roost and catered to visitors. Outdoor magazines and newspapers were the main media. Thus when outdoor writers such as Ray Bergman and Joe Brooks came to the area, Bailey, Martinez, Carmichael, and Yellowstone Park Ranger Scotty Chapman, known to be experts on where and how to fish the area, were consulted.

Naturally, owners of fly fishing retail establishments would send the inquiring writer to waters that would most likely benefit their businesses. Thus with roads paralleling or adjacent to much of them, the Firehole, Gallatin, Madison, and Yellowstone Rivers; the Snake River in Jackson Hole; the Henry's Fork; and Hebgen, Henry's, and Yellowstone Lakes were suggested and targeted. And the writer, perhaps on a tight schedule, subject to whims of area weather, and unsure of available transportation home, found it most convenient to drive to these superb waters to acquire information for articles to be offered to outdoor magazines or newspapers. Perhaps that writer did not visit these waters at all but took information directly offered by Bailey, Martinez, Carmichael, or Chapman to fashion his piece.

As the century passed its middle, a few more waters such as Slough Creek and the Gros Ventre River, the lower reaches of each being adjacent to passable roads, became featured in media that now included television. With the advent of television, the fly fisher aspiring to fish the Greater Yellowstone Area could now observe more of its natural beauty as well as observe firsthand its superb fishing opportunities. This ability is now enhanced through the Internet. Today rivers such as the Firehole, Gallatin, Madison, Yellowstone, North Fork of the Shoshone, South Fork reach, and Henry's Fork are among the most discussed and visited streams in the fly fishing world, and rightfully so. In fact, so popular is the South Fork reach, that restrictions may be forthcoming to lessen social problems created by overcrowding at some locations. Thus to the present day, area fly fishing retailers promote the angling quality of these renowned waters on which the success of their businesses relies. These businesses are also in the forefront of protecting their habitat and hosted fishery. Doing so is understandable especially when success so much depends on satisfying customers during the relatively short fishing season spanning from late spring to early autumn.

Backcountry Waters Overview

In the last several years, the number of anglers requesting visits to quality remote fly fishing locations in the Greater Yellowstone Area has grown dramatically. Increasingly we in the local fly fishing industry hear something like "Hey, I had good day on the Madison, but I sure got crowded when fish became active. Can you send me to a place where there are not so many people fishing?" I advise visiting anglers to visit the famous waters—they are most certainly worthy of attention—but leave time and bring resources to try some of the lesser known, high quality waters in the area. You will end up with a greater appreciation for what the area offers from a fly fishing standpoint as well as enrich your experience.

Wind River Lake, near the head of the Wind River, is adjacent to US Highway 26/287 on the east side of Togwotee Pass, making it easily accessible. Stopping to fish from its shoreline during sunset gives witness to a beautiful alpenglow display. Nearby streams combine to form the Wind River, which eventually becomes the Bighorn River.

A common question when recommending off-the-beaten-path waters to fly fishers is: "Why should I spend time walking when I could drive to a river or lake and be fishing quickly?" It is true that some of the waters I cover in this book require considerable effort to approach, but others not so much. Be assured that there are reasons why the time spent getting there does not necessarily detract from the time spent fishing. These reasons can be a key to enjoying so many quality waters that require some physical effort to reach. Explanation is in order and follows: The Greater Yellowstone Area is high country. The atmosphere here is thinner and drier than in lower elevations, meaning that heat radiates outward through it more quickly. For example, I have seen July water temperatures in the Bechler River in the mid-40 degrees F (all temperature references are in degrees Fahrenheit) at nine in the morning. That's cold enough to chill your beer and to discourage wading wet! Thus it takes waters, particularly moving waters not influenced by a shallow upstream reservoir, at these temperatures longer to heat back up to a level where most aquatic insects are active. In its meadow reach at that time of year, Bechler River water temperatures typically rise to the mid-50s by mid-afternoon. During lower-than-normal water conditions, they can reach as high as the low 60s in July and August.

Of course, cooler weather can change this thermal progression. Therefore, during the middle of the fly fishing season (June into September), when most visitations take place and aquatic insects are most active, with the exception of late-summer

This typical dwelling for herders that come from a variety of South American and European countries indicates another legitimate backcountry use outside of Yellowstone and Grand Teton National Parks. Most Greater Yellowstone national forests have grazing allotments that are used from June into September. Consider stopping by to converse with an occupant. Doing so could enrich your visit to the Greater Yellowstone Area.

Established trail systems in the national parks and national forests of the Greater Yellowstone Area provide access to much backcountry. This sign at the Bechler River Ranger Station offers a tantalizing number of choices to fish beautiful, unspoiled waters as well as many scenic wonders that beg to be photographed.

Trico activity, certain spinner falls and streamer presentation, being on the water early is not always necessary for success. The same applies to many terrestrial insects and aquatic insects finishing their life cycle on land: Cooler early-in-the-day air temperatures take more time to reach levels where these insects become active.

Understanding the impacts of these atmospheric conditions is most important when one considers fishing these off-the-beaten-path waters where few if any alterations by man has impacted their natural physical characteristics. Paying close attention to oncoming weather before visiting a backcountry water can pay dividends in terms of angling success. Such is not always the case with some of the area's renowned and easily approachable waters. That is because outside Yellowstone National Park, several waters below impoundments are tailwaters for many miles and are thus impacted by the temperature of the stillwaters above, particularly if those stillwaters are shallow. When a natural temperature profile changes, impacts on aquatic insect behavior take place that greatly affect resident salmonid feeding behavior.

A good example is the difference in time when Green Drakes emerge. The famed emergence in the Harriman State Park reach of the Henry's Fork peaks around mid-morning, usually in mid-June, because water in the relatively shallow Island Park Reservoir, a few miles above, has not radiated heat as fast as moving water below, resulting in a warmer inflow. The same Green Drake emergence peak from Fall River Basin waters, not far to the east in Yellowstone Park and without any upstream impoundments (except for a minor and intermittent inflow to Fall River from Grassy Lake Reservoir), is around mid-afternoon when water temperatures reach the low 50s. The same applies to this emergence on the Lewis River between Lewis and Shoshone Lakes and the stretch in the meadow below Lewis Lake. Because both lakes are deep and cool, the Green Drake emergence on these water takes place weeks later than on the Henry's Fork. To a lesser extent, the same applies to other *Drunella* mayflies. Compare the time of emergence of these insects in waters such as the South Fork reach to its tributaries Bear, Big Elk, Palisades, and McCoy Creeks, for example.

The point of this discussion is that there is ample time, in many cases, to enjoy a leisurely journey to many off-the-beaten-path places and perhaps a hearty breakfast or even lunch before the best fishing on these waters is available. Take time for photography or on-stream observations that may aid in having successful fishing later in the day as well as enhance the quality of the visit.

Large cutthroat trout can be encountered in many Greater Yellowstone backcountry waters, regardless of size. Even though competition and degradation have reduced their range, much of the area remains their bastion. This book will reveal many quality waters to visit if your quest is to encounter them.

Water Types and Fishing Strategies

The Greater Yellowstone Area contains water types hosting salmonids from large lakes to tiny ponds and from major rivers to small creeks. All range throughout the elevation profile from around 4,500 to just under 10,000 feet. Within each of these types are physical similarities that can be addressed in the general sense. These similarities provide information for an overall fishing strategy for a given water type. Thus to minimize repetition, we discuss the interaction of physical character, common hosted life-forms, and strategy here. Where there are significant differences, natural or man-made, within a given water type that influence strategy, we pinpoint such in the discussion on individual waters. Because we are discussing backcountry waters, visitations are fewer than on waters adjacent to roads and habitation. Therefore, information on life-form activity is less complete than on much-visited waters any time of the season. It is thus in the best interest of the fly fisher to include a variety of tackle in order to meet any angling condition during a backcountry visit, and any area fly shop worth visiting should feature nearby backcountry waters information that will help in the selection of fly patterns and tackle.

The numerous stillwaters in the area vary from beaver ponds to lakes encompassing several square miles; most are natural, some are man-made. The higher in elevation the water, the later ice-out occurs, the shorter the growing season, and the later aquatic insects mature. Usually the maturation sequence of major aquatic

Meadow streams of quality, small and large, abound in the Greater Yellowstone Area. No other area can likely match its number of such streams. Examples range from the small but well-endowed with cutthroat South Fork of Tincup Creek, Torrey Creek (below), to the majestic and pristine Bechler River hosting cuttbows ranging to several pounds.

Smaller waters abound in the Greater Yellowstone Area. Many offer a measure of tranquility not found on the fabled waters. JOHN JURACEK PHOTO

insects in still waters begins with dragonflies and then moves on to damselflies, then Speckled Dun mayflies, then Tricos, all overlapping in varying degrees. On nearly all stillwaters, midges emerge throughout the season and scuds, leeches, and minnow species are present. Caddisflies, mayflies, and stoneflies follow a usually predictable life cycle. Less-numerous food forms are available but will be discussed later only when significant. Therefore, the wise fly fisher takes sinking lines of various speeds, an intermediate line, and a floating line to meet any situation of fish feeding on various life-forms. Likewise, fly patterns imitating the complete life cycles of major life-forms should be included in the accompanying fly box. Depending on the size of the fish, lightweight to medium-weight rod-reel combinations are appropriate for fishing stillwaters.

Streams are more numerous and physically varied in the backcountry than stillwaters. Therefore, there is no overall strategy for fishing them. Strategy formulation must be directed to water type rather than the stream as a whole, and it is important to realize that most area streams have varied water types within their reach. Also, early-season visits must take into account runoff impacts. All Greater Yellowstone streams are subject to effects of runoff, even those located below a large stillwater body because runoff deepens and cools the lake, making outflow cooler.

The diversion of water from the lower reaches for agricultural purposes is common in many of the streams we will discuss. Diversion usually occurs from the late spring to late summer growing season and lowers and warms water enough to impact both fish and insect activity.

We begin with developing a general strategy for low-gradient reaches such as in meadows or flat areas. Some of these streams originate as spring creeks. Most have substrate of either silt, sand, or fine gravel, or combinations of each. Typically fish reside in deeper holes and runs here, but move to shallower waters or sheltered banks or toward the surface to feed. On most of these streams, runoff ends around the first of July and the general progression of aquatic insect emergences begins with March brown mayflies, *Isoperla* stoneflies, Pale Morning Dun (PMD) mayflies, damselflies, and Gray Drake mayflies. Where riffle-and-run or freestone reaches are adjacent, Giant and Golden Stoneflies are blown in by winds. Soon the may-fly emergence sequence continues with afternoon Green Drakes, evening Brown Drakes, *flavilinea* on some waters, then overlapping Trico, Mahogany Dun, and Blue-Winged Olive (BWO) mayflies later in the season. By early July terrestrial insects become important and increasingly so through summer, until frosts become deeper in early autumn. Leeches, burrowing annelids, minnows, some caddisfly species, and in well-vegetated parts scuds are always present.

A riffle-and-run sequence comes about as a stream's gradient increases and flow structure becomes more turbulent. Gravel, rocks, or coarser sediments make up the usual substrate in riffles, and surface turbulence is caused by this uneven substrate over which water flows. Pools, larger pockets, and deeper calm areas in these streams usually have finer substrate such as silt or sand. Streams consisting of silt or sand substrate alone do not develop the riffle-and-run feature. Meandering streams with a relatively coarse bed tend to develop a riffle-pool sequence with pools in the outsides of the bends and riffles between one meander and the next. Most erosion occurs in the deep areas and outsides of bends due to forces from the mass of running water but is compensated by settling of materials from upstream erosion. Eroded material can deposit in the riffle areas below as well.

Aquatic life-forms in riffle-and-run reaches vary from those in meadow reaches. Deep pools and runs can host much of the same substrate as low-gradient streams, but riffles and their coarser substrate tend to host more caddisflies and stoneflies and different mayfly species. Widespread mayfly species such as BWOs, PMDs, Mahogany Duns, and Tricos can occur in these waters as well as in lower-gradient waters; however, other mayfly species can vary in number. The October Caddis is widespread in the area's riffle-and-run reaches and present somewhat in lower-gradient streams. Annelids, crane flies, midges, and minnows are present in good numbers. Thus patterns to simulate all these life-forms in their various life cycles, where appropriate, should be considered. The presence of crawdads is a tip-off that a water body, still or moving, is high in dissolved calcium bicarbonate, so vital in building exoskeletons. Rarely are freshwater mussels present.

Flows vary seasonally in a freestone stream based on the water supply. In the summer, freestone streams grow warm and have reduced flow after snowmelt inflow has diminished. Those having springs supplying most of their water do not vary seasonably as much in flow as streams having higher amounts of water from snow-melt unless the water table drops significantly. Freestone streams generally flow over denser sedimentary rock or hard, crystalline rock. Many freestone streams in the Greater Yellowstone Area are supplied by runoff from snowmelt. While reaches of these are common, few streams are freestone throughout their entire length. Many higher-gradient streams are combinations, with riffle-and-run or even meadow reaches. This is true of streams that flow through lengthy deep-canyon reaches of gradient, such as the Clarks Fork and Fall and Lewis Rivers. Aquatic

Mid- to late summer means many Greater Yellowstone streams, such as the Gros Ventre River, shown above, drop to base flows. On reaching base flows, the streams tend to warm, meaning fish are likely to be more active during a few hours following sunrise or at twilight as the water cools.

insects here are more likely to be caddisfly and stonefly species, as in riffle-and-run streams, with annelids, crane flies, and minnows present. Both riffle-and-run and freestone streams call for light (such as 2-weight) to medium (5- or 6-weight) tackle, depending on the size of the stream and the salmonids it hosts, with floating and sink-tip lines.

The term *spring creek* refers to origin and implies a subterranean source that provides a constant flow of low water temperature. Spring creeks, or better stated *spring creek reaches*, are numerous in the Greater Yellowstone Area. They too can acquire a runoff component, and commonly a stream of such origin changes physical characteristics, such as becoming a riffle-and-run, high-gradient, or meadow stream on descending from higher elevations.

Relative humidity is a major variable impacting the emergence density of aquatic insects. In the Greater Yellowstone Area, relative humidity less than 20 percent during the daytime is common during the angling season. Thus during afternoon hours, the atmosphere is at it driest, especially in mid to late summer, resulting in fewer insects of a given species emerging. Simply stated, insects do not dehydrate as quickly in humid air as they do in drier air. Therefore, the more humid overlying air is, the denser an emergence is likely to become, all other variables being equal. During these times rainfall can bring relative humidity up to concentrations more suitable for aquatic insect emergence.

Perhaps the most dramatic rainfall effect is from thundershowers, which are common in the area during summer. When a thundershower approaches, relative humidity increases but air temperature begins to drop. During the shower, relative humidity rises as precipitation cools the atmosphere. But as the shower passes and winds die, relative humidity remains near its highest until the air begins to warm. This is when aquatic insects in season take advantage of these optimal atmospheric conditions to emerge in bulk. The result can be some of the fastest dry fly fishing, and this condition can take place several times during the summer season.

Relative humidity has a lesser impact on terrestrial insects than air temperature, which dominates in bringing on their activity. Prevailing weather conditions determine when air temperatures rise to a level where these insects become active. During fair weather, air temperatures usually rise by midday to bring on most activity in terrestrial insects and therefore availability to foraging fish.

Precautions

Certain aspects, natural and otherwise, must be considered before venturing into the backcountry. Fishing regulations vary by state. Yellowstone National Park, which spans Wyoming, Montana, and Idaho, has its own regulations. This is not the case with Grand Teton National Park, which is entirely in Wyoming and therefore subject to Wyoming fishing regulations. Access to private land varies by state in the Greater

If it were not for Wyoming Game & Fish purchasing public access areas or establishing access agreements, many Wyoming waters flowing through private lands would essentially be locked up. By law, adjacent landowners own stream bottoms in Wyoming, and wading such streams is illegal without landowner permission. In the same manner, boating anglers cannot disembark from their boats to contact stream bottoms or banks without landowner permission.

The lower reaches of many rivers, such as the lower Gros Ventre River, become dewatered during the agricultural season because agricultural water rights precede the establishment of national forests, thus reservoirs are present in many locations. Some of these have become famed and productive fisheries. Diversions from streams abound in lower reaches, and these can impact late-season salmonid populations.

Yellowstone Area. For example, access restrictions in Wyoming greatly impact both wading and float fishing. A full understanding of access laws is essential.

The best way to determine up-to-date access laws, locations of public fishing access sites (particularly for Wyoming), and fishing regulations is to go to the state or park websites: Idaho Department of Fish and Game, https://idfg.idaho.gov/fishing; Montana Fish, Wildlife & Parks, http://fwp.mt.gov/fishing; Wyoming Game & Fish Department, https://wgfd.wyo.gov/fishing; Yellowstone National Park, https://www.nps.gov/yell/planyourvisit/fishing.htm.

There is a particular reason for paying close attention to Yellowstone National Park fishing regulations. Park fishing authorities reserve the right to close any water during the fishing season if the water temperature rises to a level where resident salmonids are in danger from reduced dissolved oxygen. For example, in 2007 fishing in all park waters was restricted to early morning and evening hours because of unusually hot and dry conditions. Montana Fish, Wildlife & Parks is adopting this practice through "hoot owl" closures. Therefore, checking the appropriate website for any stream or stillwater closures just before a visit is prudent. Occasionally park and state wildlife authorities will also close certain lands temporarily to protect habitat or wildlife. These will be posted on the respective websites. Protecting Greater Yellowstone wildlife has obvious economic benefits when one considers that the greatest accessible concentration of wildlife is hosted here. Protecting against invasive species is also a major effort. Montana now requires that all anglers, resident

In the drying climate of the Greater Yellowstone Area, forest fire season holds potential restrictions to backcountry access. Late summer into October is the time of greatest fire danger. Especially during this time, it is prudent to adopt actions recommended by agencies overseeing public lands. Reporting the presence and extent of any observed fires helps to limit potential damage not only to lands but also to waters and their fish populations.

and non-resident, obtain an invasive species sticker in addition to a fishing license. Prevention procedures and information can be found on the websites listed above.

Seasonal road closures in the area can also impact fishing plans. Depending on the severity of the previous winter or a late spring, backcountry roads can easily open later than normal. Likewise, autumn snows can close roads earlier than normal. Occurrences such as landslides and downed timber can cause temporary closures. The best way to search for closures and detours is to go to the highway department websites for each state and for Yellowstone Park. For roads maintained by the USDA Forest Service (USFS) or the Bureau of Land Management (BLM), go to their websites for public information telephone numbers or current road closures. Also be aware that unstable soils abound in many locations within the area. Heavy rainstorms can erode these soils, sending enough sediment into streams and even stillwaters to cloud them for days. Parts of the Clarks Fork of the Yellowstone River, Lamar River, Shoshone River, and Snake River drainages are particularly prone to this condition.

Most of the Greater Yellowstone Area is high country where weather can change in an instant. Snow can materialize every month of the year, even at elevations of 4,000 to 5,000 feet. Thunderstorms can drop air temperatures 30 degrees in a matter of minutes. Late- and early-season snow squalls can drop air temperatures even further. Add wind to any of these events and wind chill can even become life-threatening, especially when a person is wet. It is therefore wise to anticipate these events and prepare accordingly. Hooded rain gear supplements waders. Add to this a compact means to start an emergency fire, packable insulating clothing, and high energy food items. Polarized sunglasses with side protectors are a must. Natural potable water is becoming rare, even in the Greater Yellowstone backcountry. Carrying potable water is a solution, but better yet is carrying a portable water purifier, which guarantees a supply in case of emergency.

Portable electronic distress beacons are becoming increasingly popular, and for good reason. Phone numbers, e-mails, or text messages can be programmed into it and the GPS location of the sender determined. When such a communication is activated, the device beacon sends the message and GPS location to a satellite, which relays this information to a selected destination. Such a device, usually kept in service by subscription, can be a lifesaver for a person in backcountry trouble. These devices can be found at sporting goods or outdoor activity stores or online. Whether an individual carries one of these devices or not, it is prudent to inform authorities such as a park or Forest Service ranger, or even an angling retailer, of your plans to visit a backcountry angling location. Also consider that cellphone service may not be available in certain backcountry locations.

Give particular respect to landowners that allow access to waters on their property. Actions such as removing trash, closing gates, and reporting property damage and livestock abuse can gain landowner confidence and give further permission to trespass. Simply meeting with landowners to provide personal identification and sending them communications expressing appreciation and offering thanks for allowing trespass can guarantee additional access.

So many times I hear the comment: "That's bear country, and I am not going there." When I respond that I'm more likely to have a bad highway encounter while driving to any fishing destination than a bear encounter once there, I receive a blank stare. This stare indicates familiarity has taken over because highway incidents are commonplace, whereas bear encounters are rare and therefore incite fear of the unknown. Yes, much of the Greater Yellowstone Area is bear country, but there are measures that certainly decrease chances of an encounter. I subscribe to these in an almost fanatic manner.

First, when huckleberries (early August) and hawthorn berries (late August to early September) ripen, I completely avoid certain areas. Second, I make noise to advertise my presence. This nearly guarantees that a bear on hearing the noise will take heed and leave my vicinity. Conversation with a fishing companion can suffice, as can whistling or singing, but my favorite action, especially when alone, is to carry a portable claxon horn and use it at intervals. Lightweight, compact, and inexpensive, these horns easily fit in a vest or shirt pocket. They are available in almost any marine supply shop. The noise they make is unearthly and carries for a good distance, even in timber, and easily carries over the noise of a rushing stream.

Electronic media such as Google Earth and Google Maps help in locating remote gems such as this meadow stream, an example of the numerous accessible meadow streams of the Greater Yellowstone Area. This one hosts Yellowstone cutthroat trout approaching 30 inches in length. A well-maintained road is nearby, but most fly fishers migrate to nearby well-known waters.

Here is the lowest downstream of Fall River's tier of meadows in Yellowstone National Park. Nearest road is a mile or so away, so bushwhacking must be applied to reach it.

Next in importance is to have bear spray conveniently available, although a noise device such as a claxon horn reduces the chances of needing to use bear spray. Certainly an encounter at a distance is more desirable than one up close. There are many brands of spray on the market, but the best choice may be made by inquiring which one is favored by land management agencies or fish and game departments for equipping field personnel. Of course, one never approaches a bear, buffalo, coyote, elk, moose, or wolf. The best place to learn about backcountry behavior where wildlife is involved, including during overnight stays, is the Yellowstone Park website.

So much for "mega-wildlife"—now for "micro-wildlife." In season, mosquitoes can be ferocious enough to equal fear of bears in keeping persons out of not only the backcountry, but many parts of the area. Mosquito season here begins in early June and lasts well into July, especially in wetlands. Repellent heavy in DEET is a powerful deterrent for mosquitoes as well as for deer ticks, though it acts as a solvent on the surface coating on most fly lines. Citronella-based compounds have no effect on these insects. Problems from either of these insects can also be reduced through the use of clothing that provides appropriate coverage. Not to be outdone, horse-flies take over as pests when mosquitoes pass their peak and the countryside dries. Clothing thick enough not to be penetrated by their bite is the best deterrent here.

Clothing that provides a shield from intense sunlight is also necessary. High country such as the Greater Yellowstone Area means a thinner atmosphere and more intense ultraviolet radiation. Such clothing should be supplemented with sunscreen having an SPF rating greater than 30.

How to Use This Book

Each featured water begins with an overview followed by six specific categories:

Access: Identity of roads and principle trailheads that access the water. In cases where more than one access route to the water is available, I give the most direct or most convenient.

Coordinates: GPS coordinates are given for the most convenient access points. For certain streams a number of coordinates are given for access points leading to on-stream locations of high fishing quality. Internet sites are available in which GPS coordinates can be converted to DMS coordinates.

Equipment: Though often a personal choice, I provide my recommendations for line weights, line types, and fly patterns. Fly patterns, so dependent on personal preference and therefore generalized, are given to simulate food forms in the subject waters. For all mayflies and caddis recommended, you should carry patterns that imitate the complete life cycles of these insects.

Nearest facilities and services: Nearest town where accommodations, eateries, and rental, retail, and medical services are available. Campgrounds, rental cabins, and lodges are given when available and convenient.

Information resources: Federal, state, and municipal agencies; visitor centers; and ranger stations are identified from which accessibility and usage information such as public access sites and travel conditions can be obtained. Pertinent United States Geologic Survey (USGS) flow station gage numbers (where available) and USGS 7.5-minute (1:24000) topographic maps are identified.

Salmonids present: Salmonids, native and non-native, are almost exclusively the only sportfish in the area. Brook, brown, cutthroat, cuttbow, golden, and lake trout, grayling, kokanee salmon (infrequently), and Rocky Mountain whitefish make up the resident salmonids. Their species distribution here varies from water to water as given in the following descriptions. Some waters host only one salmonid species, while others host various combinations of these. Only a few waters, mainly reservoirs, host introduced (exotic) sportfish other than these.

Much of the information included can be used to begin Google Earth and Internet searches. For example, the identified nearest towns can be the sources for information on services and weather forecasts.

Adding hard copy maps for each water would require too much space for the size of this book. Better quality mapping can be obtain through the internet. For example, combing use of Google Maps with that of Google Earth results in detailed and quality information that can reveal the path to and character of nearly any water in the Greater Yellowstone Area. In supplement, 7.5-minute topographic sheets produced by the United States Geological Survey (USGS) can add further detail.

PART 1

YELLOWSTONE NATIONAL PARK

For over 100 years, Yellowstone National Park waters have been the subject of numerous books and magazine and Internet features. Most of these focus on the major rivers and lakes adjacent to the park road system. In terms of miles of stream and acres of stillwaters, excluding Yellowstone Lake, these famed park waters are only a fraction of those located in the backcountry. Howard Back's *The Waters of Yellowstone with Rod and Fly*, published in the 1930s, hinted at the area's backcountry waters. Nate Schweber's recent book, *Fly Fishing Yellowstone National Park: An Insider's Guide to the 50 Best Places* (Stackpole Books) expanded the look

Unidentified pond in Yellowstone National Park. Beaver ponds are mostly encountered on smaller streams in the park. They can, however, host surprisingly large trout. JOHN JURACEK PHOTO

at park backcountry waters. But Yellowstone Park and its immediate surroundings host many more superb waters than those described in these books.

A map of any detail reveals that the Continental Divide runs nearly diagonally northwest to southeast across the park. On the Atlantic side of the divide, all waters, whether from the Madison, Gallatin, or Yellowstone system, ultimately contribute to the Missouri River drainage. On the Pacific side of the divide, whether from the Henry's Fork or Snake River system, all ultimately contribute to the Columbia River drainage. About two-thirds of the park's land surface is on the Atlantic side of the divide, with the lesser amount on the Pacific side. However, the amount of backcountry waters in terms of stream miles is nearly equal, while the acres of stillwaters, again excluding Yellowstone Lake, is greater on the Pacific side of the divide.

First we will discuss the two major drainages on the Pacific aside of the Continental Divide, then do the same for the Atlantic side. The waters in the upper Yellowstone drainage are recovering from the ravages of whirling disease and the effects of the illegal introduction of lake trout in Yellowstone Lake. The worst impacts of whirling disease have passed, efforts to control lake trout in the lake are making headway, and the Yellowstone cutthroat population is increasing. However, the road to recovery remains long, and it is in the best interest of Yellowstone cutthroat trout in their biggest bastion to minimize actions that slow their progress, even though such actions as sportfishing are seemingly minor.

Boundary Creek is the farthest west of quality Fall River Basin drainage waters and hosts a good number of trophy-size trout. Overshadowed by the adjacent Bechler River, to which it is confluent, it nevertheless should be considered a destination. In addition to its excellent trout population, its lengthy meadow reach offers solitude, scenery, and primitive campgrounds that are ideal bases from which to fish.

Cave Falls is the barrier waterfall for all Fall River Basin streams in Yellowstone Park. Just a quarter mile above, the confluence of the Bechler and Fall Rivers is a major landmark. Just below, the Fall River begins its descent into a lengthy, isolated canyon. The Cave Falls vicinity is easily approached, as Cave Falls Road terminates alongside it. The river offers cuttbow trout ranging to medium size.

The Pacific side of the Continental Divide contains a smaller portion of the park road system than the Atlantic side. Only one major park road is on the Pacific side: the road from the south entrance northward, going over the Continental Divide to West Thumb Junction. A small portion of the Snake River, the Lewis River above its canyon, and Lewis Lake are adjacent to this road. In addition, a small portion of West Thumb Junction–Old Faithful Road spans the DeLacey Creek drainage that feeds into Shoshone Lake. None of these waters are as renowned as those on the Atlantic side. However, most of quality remote waters in the park are on this side of the divide.

If ever there were a fly fishing heaven on earth, Fall River Basin would be it. Creeks, lakes, and rivers in a totally natural or near-natural state adorn the basin. The best of these from a fly fishing standpoint are protected forever through being situated in the southwest corner of Yellowstone National Park. The miles of undisturbed meadow streams here are the longest of any drainage in the Greater Yellowstone Area, and perhaps anywhere in the United States, with all major basin streams making contributions to this water type.

Originally thought to be barren of salmonids, these waters were planted with Yellowstone cutthroat trout in the early 20th century. Downstream barrier waterfalls had blocked entry of salmonids from below. To this day, Rocky Mountain whitefish do not inhabit Fall River Basin waters in the park. The Yellowstone cutthroat trout flourished for a while, until hybridization with rainbow trout from an unidentified source took place in much of the basin waters. If Snake River Plain irrigators and their congressional representatives had had their way back in the 1920s, Bechler

Bechler Meadows with Grand Teton presiding. The meadows provide an unusual view because the viewer looks down the main axis of the range. From the flat meadow and adjacent forest, foothills rise to the main peaks towering above the southern horizon.

Meadows would have been submerged in shallow water by a low dam at Rocky Ford. To the benefit of the park, the wildlife, and the public, eastern states conservationists and their congressional representatives stepped in and quashed the proposal. Considering public opinion today, such a proposal would be a laughingstock at best.

Henry's Fork Drainage

BECHLER RIVER

It is a visual reward to see Bechler Meadows after the monotonous 3.5-mile walk through the jack pine forest to Boundary Creek. The minimum half-mile walk to the river, which holds large, vigorous cuttbows, reveals scenery having few equals in the Greater Yellowstone Area.

Access: Cave Falls Road off Mesa Falls Scenic Byway (Idaho Highway 47) to Bechler Ranger Station Road and Bechler River trailhead

GPS Coordinates: 44.149694, -111.0445715

Equipment: 5- or 6-weight system with floating and sink-tip lines; caddisfly, PMD, Brown Drake, Giant Stone, Golden Stone, Gray Drake, Green Drake, Trico, and Yellow Sally patterns, and streamer, terrestrial insect, and traditional attractor patterns

Nearest facilities and services: Ashton (Idaho), Bechler Ranger Station, USFS Cave Falls Campground, Three Rivers Ranch

Information resources: Yellowstone National Park; USGS Flow Station Gage 13046995; Bechler Falls, Cave Falls, and Trischman Knob USGS topographic maps

Salmonids present: Cutthroat, cuttbow, and rainbow trout

Several years ago I pulled into the Bechler Ranger Station on the first day of July with the purpose of fishing the river and Boundary Creek in the meadows. It had been a cool spring after a winter featuring massive snowfalls in the region, but a few days before I arrived, air temperatures on the Pitchstone and Madison plateaus reached the low 80s. As I geared up, Dunbar Susong, chief ranger in those days, came over to offer what I thought would be his usual welcoming greeting. I answered in the affirmative to his inquiry about going fishing in the meadows.

"Where's your canoe?" he asked, then added, "Be careful, the meadows are flooded into the timber with cold water."

I had to see what he described, so geared up for fishing, I walked to the primitive campground on Boundary Creek. What confronted me there was a mile-wide sheet of moving water. Snowmelt from the plateaus above thundered down through Cascade Corner canyons to inundate the meadow with ice water. I could not see adjacent Boundary Creek, but tried to cross it to get to the Bechler River. I gave up after discovering the creek at the ford was running at a depth up to my chest. Having measured a water temperature in the low 40s, I thought the better and headed back out to fish somewhere on the Henry's Fork. A week later on the Bechler River and Boundary Creek, the season for presenting dry flies was near its start. Yes, this was runoff in the extreme, but I include this story to emphasize that not considering weather and snowpack conditions can ruin an early-summer visit to fish in Fall River Basin.

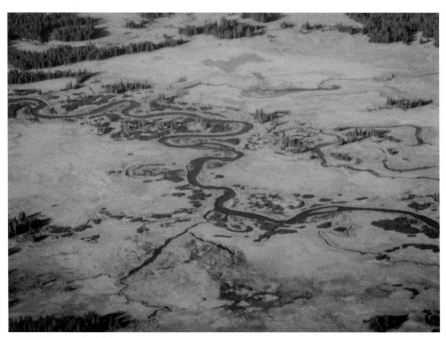

Fall brings a golden color to Bechler Meadows and reduces the river to base flow. This is the time of year terrestrial insects are an important food item for trout residing in the river. For the fly fisher visiting at this time, bringing ant, hopper, and beetle patterns is almost a requirement for fishing success.

The Bechler Soldier Station is the gateway to Fall River Basin waters. It began in the early 20th century as a base for US Army soldiers assigned to fight poaching and illegal grazing activities in the basin. By 1916 park rangers replaced the army and to this day perform actions that protect the park and its visitors.

During years of light snowfall on the plateaus above, and under usual weather conditions, the Bechler River and other basin streams may be in dry fly shape by mid-June, and for a time fish feed on the surface in good numbers. Problems come later in the summer when waters drop to base levels early and water temperatures climb as high as the middle 60s on sunny afternoons. Because these streams in their meadow reaches move slowly, trout subject to these conditions, especially larger individuals, avoid the surface and congregate in the deeper waters where higher dissolved oxygen concentrations provide more comfort. With shorter daylight hours and the cooling atmosphere late in the summer, water temperatures do not rise to the midsummer extremes, and so more fish feed on the surface.

The quickest route to fishing this meadow reach is through the Bechler River Trail from the ranger station. This route goes 3.5 miles to the edge of the meadows at Boundary Creek then traverses another 1.5 miles through the meadows to Bechler Ford, where another primitive campground offers a base from which to fish. Above and below this location is 7 miles of river meandering in one of the most breathtaking settings in the park. Here in a totally natural state the river varies from shallow flats to deep runs and holes at every bend, some deep enough to engulf a bus.

A 1-mile section of challenging water lies above the meadow where the river flows through the pine forest. The stream gradient here is the same as in the meadow, but the challenge comes from the accumulation of downed timber that clogs holes with snags and tree trunks. In some places the combination of these are thick enough to walk over, and in others an impediment to casting both wet and dry flies.

Bechler Meadows in the late June purple camas bloom. Traversing the meadow during early summer offers a near-field beauty to complement the distant beauty of plateaus and mountains. Camas bulbs provided Native Americans with an important food source up to the end of the 19th century.

For certain, this overhead cover shelters an abundance of large trout. Tie into one of these large individuals and a combination of luck and skill is the only hope for landing it!

Above this section, the stream gradient increases and fewer large trout are present. These characteristics remain up to Colonnade Falls, the beautiful double falls of 60 and 40 feet that are the barrier for cuttbow trout. Above, Yellowstone cutthroat trout are the only salmonid residents in the 6 miles of river now held in the strikingly beautiful Bechler Canyon. Above is the Three Rivers location, where the Bechler River branches into its tributaries and the concentration of waterfalls is unequalled.

The other route from the ranger station to the river is a branch of the Bechler River Trail heading due east. After a 1.5-mile walk through monotonous jack pines, you'll reach a slow section of the river. Large trout reside here to challenge traveling fly fishers to try their skills. Wading is not easy here, as the deep runs span bank to bank with brief shallow areas and little room for backcasts. Above, the river changes in character to a riffle-and-run stream. After a nearly 2-mile walk along the river, Rocky Ford comes into view. Here, like a deep and slow-moving canal with ample casting room, few stretches of any river in the Greater Yellowstone Area are as alluring as what is in view above the ford. Above and around a bend in the river is the Boundary Creek confluence. Many of the largest trout in all of Fall River Basin reside in this half-mile section. Not far above is the lower end of Bechler Meadows, one of the most enchanting places to fish in the Greater Yellowstone Area.

BEULA LAKE
By Buck Goodrich

Beula Lake is my first choice for a stillwater in which to catch cutthroat trout. Few waters containing cutthroat up to trophy size can match the action Beula Lake can provide, making it a fly fishing treasure.

Access: Ashton–Flagg Ranch Road off US Highway 20 or John D. Rockefeller Jr. Memorial Parkway to Beula Lake trailhead

GPS Coordinates: 44.125604, -110.786322

Equipment: 5- or 6-weight system with floating and intermediate lines; caddisfly, damselfly, and Speckled Dun patterns, and leech, scud, soft-hackle, streamer, terrestrial insect, and traditional attractor patterns

Nearest facilities and services: Ashton (Idaho), Bechler and South Entrance Ranger Stations, Flagg Ranch Resort

Information resources: Yellowstone National Park; Grassy Lake Reservoir USGS topographic map

Salmonids present: Cutthroat trout

"Catch your age—it gets harder every year!"

That's my jest to fellow fly fishers visiting Beula Lake. Last season I turned 74 years old and through float tubing I caught my age during one visit, but it took until evening. I had barely enough energy left for the 2.5-mile walk out!

Beula (right) and Hering (left) Lakes host only Yellowstone cutthroat trout ranging to trophy sizes. Grassy Lake Reservoir (center background) hosts lake and rainbow trout. Beula and Hering Lakes require a 2.5-mile walk, while Grassy Lake Reservoir is adjacent to the Ashton–Flagg Ranch Road.

My jest is more serious than first appears because of the hungry cutthroat hosted there. If a fly fisher were to ask me where it would be possible to catch and release 50 trout in a day, this is where I would advise they go. I would recommend the same for a neophyte stillwater fly fisher. Because of their eager feeding nature, encountering these trout concentrates the lessons of hooking, playing, landing, and releasing trout.

It is believed that this lake was named by the 1872 Hayden Expedition after the Land of Beulah in John Bunyan's *Pilgrim's Progress.* Beula Lake lies at an elevation of 7,377 feet and covers 107 acres, and the maximum depth is 36 feet. It hosts abundant aquatic plant growth, which in turn harbors a vast quantity of insects, scuds, and leeches. Yellowstone cutthroat trout are the only salmonids hosted within. Shorelines teem with terrestrial insects during the summer, and daily afternoon breezes blow them onto the lake in abundance. There are two inlets to Beula Lake: Fall River at the southeast corner and the intermittent inlet on the southeast from Hering Lake. Originally both lakes were devoid of salmonids, but records indicate that trout were planted in Beula Lake and its tributaries between 1935 and 1944. Fish residing in the lake run up the Fall River to spawn. On finishing, they soon return to the more-hospitable lake. Juvenile trout rear in the river but also soon descend to the lake.

Beula Lake (and Hering Lake) lie just across the park's south boundary. The trailhead leaves Ashton–Flagg Ranch Road at the east end of Grassy Lake Reservoir in Caribou-Targhee National Forest, just inside the boundary with the John D. Rockefeller Jr. Memorial Parkway. The 2.5-mile walk into Beula Lake offers a view of the valley holding the Fall River on its way downstream. The trail was used as the fire line for stopping the 1988 fire from proceeding east. The west side of the trail was burnt and is now recovering its pine forest, while the east side of the trail is old timber. About half of the forest around Beula Lake, mainly the northeast and north sides, burned in the 1988 fire. The trail makes a short, steep pitch to the first of three primitive campsites on west shore of the lake. Backcountry permits are required for their use; these are most conveniently obtained at the Yellowstone National Park South Entrance. Potable water is not available at the lake.

Most Beula Lake fish inhabit shallow water when feeding. Arrive at the lake earlier than 9 a.m. The reason for this is twofold: First, the wind normally comes up from the southwest in early afternoon, meaning dry fly fishing is either over or reduced, and second, the premier aquatic insect emergence on the lake, that of the Cinnamon Caddis, begins about this time. On reaching the lake, bear to the right. Shortly, turn east into the narrow meadow and cross the intermittent inlet from Hering Lake. Continue east and begin watching the surface for cruising trout rising on the backside of lily pads and in water less than 3 feet deep. Once sighted, try for a precise cast in order not to spook the fish. The dry fly pattern that one uses seems relatively unimportant—it should just be of medium size. If the fish refuse these, a soft-hackle in the surface film seems to change their mind.

Continue stalking fish going east to the inlet, where the fish normally stack up to feed on food items coming into the lake. They may stop feeding on the surface when the wind comes up, so switch to a leech pattern to continue catching. You may not have to proceed further around the lake to catch your age! Continuing east past the inlet, one enters about 200 yards of shoreline having reeds and sunken logs, with trout cruising and sipping from the surface in about 3 feet of water. The area beyond the reeds and the sunken logs is shallow, with the best fishing water out about 50 yards from shore. At this point there is a drop-off, near which trout cruise in good numbers and usually provide fast action.

Beyond, going north around the lake, is where the 1988 burn reached the lake. Large sunken trees and deadfall make this area particularly difficult to wade and walk through. The outlet, which is the main branch of the Fall River, is at the northwest corner. At the outlet, lily pads and reeds abound, providing cover for some of the largest trout in the lake. Water is deeper here, making fishing from a floatation device ideal. Interestingly, my tactics also work on Riddle Lake on the other side of the Continental Divide about 10 miles to the northeast. The walk into this lake from the South Entrance Road trailhead is flatter than that into Beula Lake and shorter by a half mile. But the fish in Riddle Lake run smaller, and less of the shoreline can be approached for fishing.

BOUNDARY CREEK

This beautiful meadow stream provides solitude and surprisingly large trout, especially where it enters Bechler Meadows.

Access: Cave Falls Road off Mesa Falls Scenic Byway to Bechler Ranger Station Road, then 3.5 miles on Bechler River Trail or 5 miles on Boundary Creek Trail
GPS Coordinates: 44.150014, -111.0445683
Equipment: 5-weight system with floating and sink-tip lines; caddisfly, PMD, Brown Drake, Giant Stone, Golden Stone, Gray Drake, Green Drake, Trico, and Yellow Sally patterns, and streamer, terrestrial insect, and traditional attractor patterns
Nearest facilities and services: Ashton (Idaho), Bechler Ranger Station, USFS Cave Falls Campground, Three Rivers Ranch
Information resources: Yellowstone National Park; Bechler Falls USGS topographic map
Salmonids present: Cutthroat, cuttbow, and rainbow trout

Boundary Creek, a superb meadow stream, is so named because much of its reach, as it flows southerly, nearly parallels the west boundary of Yellowstone National Park. After entering Bechler Meadows, it meanders southeasterly to reach the Bechler River just below the meadows. Just above the meadows, Boundary Creek splits into its east and west forks. In its fairly brief low-gradient section, the east fork holds cuttbows that reach trophy size. Farther upstream are hot springs and a primitive campground, both popular with folks enjoying geothermally warmed water. Around the springs, a panoramic view of Bechler Meadows to the south with the Grand Teton Range in the background can be enjoyed. Above the springs, there is little of interest to the fly fisher.

The West Fork is different. Above its low-gradient reach, also where trophy hybrid trout (cuttbow) reside, 150-foot Dunanda Falls forms an upstream barrier for cuttbows. Above it, Boundary Creek hosts only Yellowstone cutthroat trout and is fished infrequently. This location is also the western extent of Cascade Corner,

Boundary Creek is totally contained within Fall River Basin and hosts a good number of trophy-size trout. It is another nearly overlooked water compared to neighboring streams, so the solitude it offers is as good as it gets.

hosting the heaviest concentration of waterfalls in the Greater Yellowstone Area. This famed feature is bounded on the north by the Madison and Pitchstone plateaus.

It is the creek below the confluence of the two forks that is most interesting for the fly fisher. Here it enters Bechler Meadows and is in near isolation, the nearest road being about 5 miles to the south at the Bechler Ranger Station, and this is where the best access to this beautiful meadow stream begins. Trophy-size individuals are present in good numbers, and some of these easily exceed 20 inches. This part of the creek can also be reached overland from eastern Idaho's Snow Creek Road, but the miles of bushwhacking due east seems impractical compared to the relatively easy access from the ranger station.

The two major routes from the Bechler Ranger Station to reach Boundary Creek are given above. The Bechler River Trail is the more popular of the two, bringing the most anglers to its water. A popular primitive campground and horse camp sits on the edge of the meadow where this trail, by way of a suspension bridge, crosses Boundary Creek. Fly fishers use it as a base for fishing both the creek and the river.

About 1.6 miles above the ranger station, the Boundary Creek Trail branches left off the Bechler River Trail. After walking a few miles north on the Boundary Creek Trail, one reaches the meadows. Here 50-foot-wide Bartlett Slough, which can be high with cold runoff water through June, must be crossed. As one proceeds north on the trail, the creek and trail converge to meet at the primitive campground near the top of the meadow. Here the campground can be used as a base from which to fish the creek. For miles downstream, it can be fished in solitude.

By applying stealth as well as dry fly patterns through long drifts, it is not uncommon to experience days when 30 fish are landed, among these a number of trophy-size individuals. As an alternative to fishing down through the meadows, one can follow the trail upstream about a mile to where the forest impinges on the meadows and fish where the creek forks and beyond.

FALL RIVER

From freestone runs and canyon water to meadow reaches, this river offers amazing variety. An entire season could be spent fishing the river, with most of that time spent in solitude trying some sections inhabited solely by cutthroat trout and other sections inhabited by tackle-busting cuttbows.

Access: Ashton–Flagg Ranch Road off US Highway 20 to Fish Lake Road to the Winegar Hole Wilderness Area boundary trailhead

GPS Coordinates: Winegar Hole trailhead, 44.123379, -110.944490; Terraced Falls trailhead, 44.129007, -110.847630; Grassy Creek (Old Marysville Road) trailhead, 44.132138, -110.820234

Equipment: 5- or 6-weight system with floating and sink-tip lines; caddisfly, PMD, Brown Drake, Giant Stone, Golden Stone, Gray Drake, Green Drake, Trico, and Yellow Sally patterns, and streamer, terrestrial insect, and traditional attractor patterns

Nearest facilities and services: Ashton (Idaho), Bechler and South Entrance Ranger Stations, USFS Cave Falls Campground, Three Rivers Ranch

Information resources: Yellowstone National Park; USGS Flow Station Gage 13046995; Bechler Falls, Cave Falls, and Grassy Lake Reservoir USGS topographic maps

Salmonids present: Brook, cutthroat, cuttbow, and rainbow trout

Of the Fall River Basin's major streams, Fall River is the most complex. No doubt it is one of the most complex in the Greater Yellowstone Area due to its brawling cascades, freestone reaches, lakes, major waterfalls, minor waterfalls, meadow reaches, and riffle-and-run reaches. It also flows outside the park. With the exception of Calf and Cascade Creeks, all its tributaries hosting salmonids drain the Pitchstone Plateau. The main trunk of the Fall River begins above Beula Lake. It cascades out of the lake into a meadow, where it collects more tributaries and hosts solely cutthroat trout, with individuals going to 20 inches or more. No trails lead to this meadow, which is reached by bushwhacking about a mile to the west off the Beula Lake Trail.

Below the meadow, Bradley Falls, a mere 12 feet, is of major significance because it is the upstream barrier for cuttbows. Below these falls a high-gradient riffle-and-run reach drops through swift and broken Cascade Acres. Near the top of this section, Grassy Creek enters with a trail from Grassy Lake Dam, paralleling it to the river. Out of it comes releases from Grassy Lake Reservoir, constructed in the late 1920s as compensation for the rejected reservoir on the Bechler River. Near the bottom of Cascade Acres, Cascade Creek enters and is paralleled by a trail from Ashton–Flagg Ranch Road. A small meadow reach of this creek just inside the park hosts some of the most colorful cuttbow trout anywhere.

It is worth taking a look at Grassy Lake Reservoir because of its significant impact on fishing in the river below the Grassy Creek confluence. First, it is the

Second meadow, going downstream, in the Fall River's tier of five meadow reaches in July. July is peak aquatic insect season, with Pale Morning Dun and Green and Brown Drake mayflies emerging and Golden and Giant Stoneflies blowing in from upstream and downstream fast-water reaches. Fish Lake, just outside the park, is at upper right.

source of rainbow trout that have hybridized with cutthroat trout in the Fall River below Bradley Falls. Second is a variable situation that impacts fishing in the river below the Grassy Creek confluence. This is the release of water from the reservoir to help satisfy irrigation demands on the Snake River Plain below, which can happen any time during the agricultural growing season, June through August. When an increase in flow out of the reservoir into the river occurs, trout feeding on the surface slows significantly for a few days because of the abundance of food scoured from river bottoms and banks. The only way to determine if such a release of water has taken place is to observe the changes of flow monitored by United States Geological Survey flow gauges.

Terraced Falls, the tallest on the river, is just below the Cascade Creek confluence, and after a run of swift, broken water comes Rainbow Falls. Not far below Rainbow Falls, superb fly fishing begins with a series of meadows punctuated by short sections of riffle-and-run water. All of these meadow reaches can be accessed from Loon Lake Road after parking at the Winegar Hole Wilderness Area barricade and then walking the connector trail to the South Boundary Trail just inside the Yellowstone Park boundary. Here you will find cuttbow trout, an occasional cutthroat, and a growing number of brook trout, a few of which reach trophy size.

A few hundred yards up the trail is the bottom of the first of these meadows. Here the river picks up first the intermittent outlet from Fish Lake and Calf Creek. The cover is superb and getting to the river in some places for a proper presentation can be challenging, but the cuttbow here range upward to nearly 30 inches.

Cascade Creek, a Fall River tributary, hosts small but colorful cuttbow trout. It is paralleled by the Terraced Falls Trail and features a small meadow reach just inside the park boundary. Bring small attractor flies and the lightest weight fly rod you own.

Back at the junction of the South Boundary Trail and its connector from outside the park, heading downstream past a brief riffle-and-run stretch takes you to another meadow where willows provide overhead cover and present another challenge for casting flies in the best manner. As in the meadow above, abundant trophy-size trout are present. Next comes another small stretch of swifter water down to the Mountain Ash Creek confluence in a thick pine forest. Here begins a beautiful reach of river flowing into a narrow meadow and having huge holes, side channels, islands, and logjams. The river is larger here and therefore hosts more trophy trout than the upstream meadows. It ends in another riffle-and-run stretch of about a half mile to the smallest yet perhaps most picturesque meadow of all, which also hosts trout ranging to well over 20 inches.

At the bottom of this meadow you hear the Fall River before seeing it, as the river rushes nearly 3 miles over a combination of cascades, freestone riffles and runs, and two waterfalls until reaching the park boundary. The Bechler River enters within a quarter mile upstream of majestic Cave Falls. As it exits Yellowstone National Park, the Fall River's nearly 100-yard width paralleled by Cave Falls Road will attract the fly fisher that prefers riffle-and-run water similar to that on the Henry's Fork as it enters Cardiac Canyon about 30 miles to the west. But here the only enduring sound is that of the Fall River as it enters its canyon to join the Henry's Fork in the Snake River Plain below.

HERING LAKE

This lake, about two-thirds the size of Beula Lake, holds fewer trout but they run considerably larger. The late-summer flying ant swarms bring trout to the surface in a reliable manner.

Access: Ashton–Flagg Ranch Road off US Highway 20 or John D. Rockefeller Jr.
  Memorial Parkway to Beula Lake trailhead
GPS Coordinates: 44.125604, -110.786322
Equipment: 5- or 6-weight system with floating and intermediate lines; caddisfly,
  damselfly, and Speckled Dun patterns, and leech, streamer, terrestrial insect, and
  traditional attractor patterns
Nearest facilities and services: Ashton (Idaho), Bechler and South Entrance Ranger
  Stations, Flagg Ranch Resort
Information resources: Yellowstone National Park; Grassy Lake Reservoir USGS
  topographic map
Salmonids present: Cutthroat trout

Named for Rudolph Hering, topographer and chief meteorologist of the 1878 Third Hayden Expedition to explore Yellowstone National Park, this is the large lake just south of Beula Lake. It was without salmonids until the early 20th century when Yellowstone Park or U.S. Fish Commission personnel released Yellowstone cutthroat trout in nearby Beula Lake. Access to Hering Lake is through the quarter-mile-long narrow meadow separating it from Beula Lake. It's an easy walk to the south after the 2.75-mile trek on the Beula Lake Trail, but once there, wading is limited because of the impinging jack pine forest. The west side and some of the south side of the lake are formed from a steep slope that offers no room for a backcast due to dense timber and a precipitous drop-off into the lake. However, an abundance of downed timber projecting into the lake from this slope makes ideal overhead cover for cruising trout.

Hering, at 60 acres, offers the most habitable section for trout in its deeper west half. Walk around the north shore to the east side of the lake, and one finds shallows that during low-water years reveal mud of a depth that makes wading uncomfortable and water warmed enough for trout to be absent. Thus the best method for successful fishing at Hering Lake is by packing in and using a floatation device, with fins and waders, to fish the entire lake.

Not every year offers good fishing in Hering, for the following reason: After heavy snowfall winters, springtime melting connects Beula and Hering through submerging the meadow between the two in water. Yellowstone cutthroat trout, the sole salmonid resident of the lakes, can thus move freely through the connecting shallows. When receding water later separates the two lakes, cutthroat venturing into Hering from Beula become trapped there until the two lakes reconnect the following spring. Thus Hering's repopulation of trout depends almost entirely on those becoming trapped from Beula. But because of the smaller trout population, the reasonable abundance of food, favorable water conditions, and good overhead cover, the trapped trout grow to a larger size than their brethren in nearby Beula. In fact, only three of the park's lakes hold larger cutthroat than Hering: Heart, Trout, and now Yellowstone Lake.

Fishing on Hering Lake arrives each year when Ashton–Flagg Ranch Road opens for traffic and when the Beula Lake Trail becomes passable. Normally this occurs near the end of June, when the progression of available life-forms in stillwater begins. My favorite time to fish dry patterns here is late in the summer when a flying ant swarm sometimes takes place. When these cinnamon-colored ants pepper the surface, it seems every trout in the lake rises to feed on them.

A several-day stay to fish both Beula and Hering Lakes can be rewarding. One of the three primitive campsites on Beula's west side is a good base for a visit. Fires are not allowed at these sites, and all garbage must be carried out. Permits can be obtained most conveniently at the park's South Entrance Ranger Station or online through the park website. From June into July, mosquitoes can be a major nuisance on the hike into and out of Hering, making a reliable repellent necessary. Potable water is not available, so carrying a purifier is a must. This is also bear country, so all precautions for such should be taken (see the Yellowstone Park website for details). Being close to 7,500 feet in elevation, high-country precautions are prudent when visiting Hering Lake. These mostly concern weather: Intense thunderstorms are possible at any time, and intense sunshine also calls for protection. I have experienced snowfall when visiting in September, but during my visits I can usually rely on having the lake to myself.

MOUNTAIN ASH CREEK

Mountain Ash Creek has the smallest meadow reach of any major Fall River Basin stream. It also is the most isolated and least visited of these, and therefore offers the best chance for tranquil fly fishing.

Access: Ashton–Flagg Ranch Road off US Highway 20 to Loon Lake Road to the Winegar Hole Wilderness Area boundary trailhead
GPS Coordinates: 44.123379, -110.944490
Equipment: 5- or 6-weight system with floating and sink-tip lines; caddisfly, PMD, Brown Drake, Giant Stone, Golden Stone, Gray Drake, Green Drake, Trico, and Yellow Sally patterns, and streamer, terrestrial insect, and traditional attractor patterns
Nearest facilities and services: Ashton (Idaho), Bechler Ranger Station, USFS Cave Falls Campground, Three Rivers Ranch
Information resources: Yellowstone National Park; Cave Falls USGS topographic map
Salmonids present: Brook, cutthroat, and rainbow trout

Mountain Ash Creek is a 8.5-mile walk from Bechler Ranger Station. After turning off the Ashton-Flagg Ranch Road on to the Loon Lake Road and bearing right at all intersections, a barricade prevents further motorized travel at the Winegar Hole Wilderness Area boundary. From the barricade, Mountain Ash Creek is a 3-mile walk. Walking east from the barricade along the closed road brings you to Fish Lake, just outside the Yellowstone National Park south boundary. Here the signed connector trail described for accessing the Fall River takes you to the South Boundary Trail.

At this point it is worth discussing Fish Lake because of the impact its hosted brook trout have on the Fall River and Mountain Ash and Proposition Creeks.

Mountain Ash Creek is in total isolation. Few streams offer the combination of tranquility, unaltered beauty, and large trout found here. Reaching it requires a walk of about 3 miles.

At first glance this lake appears like any other glacial remnant lake in Fall River Basin. Without a perennial inlet and outlet, these lakes do not support a sustaining salmonid population. Fish Lake, however, hosts a population of brook trout that attain trophy size, as well as cutthroat trout. Difficult to catch, and with individuals ranging to over 20 inches, they are protected by being in the nonmotorized Winegar Hole Wilderness Area. They can be caught by anglers willing to pack a lightweight floatation device the mile or so along the closed road to the lake. Getting out in the lake past the lily pads just after ice-out and presenting any fly resembling a dragonfly nymph is likely to attract these large brook trout. However, as the lake warms with the advancing season, algae and weed growth hamper fishing to the point that only rarely will resident brook trout come to the surface to take any floating offering.

During years of higher-than-normal snowfall, enough meltwater is held in Fish Lake to permit brook trout to escape down to a large beaver pond just outside the park boundary. The overflow from this pond allows the brook trout to escape down to the Fall River, and they now populate the river and Mountain Ash Creek below barrier waterfalls in considerable numbers. Nonetheless, Yellowstone cutthroat and cuttbow trout, with individuals exceeding 20 inches, dominate Mountain Ash Creek.

From Fish Lake where the connector meets the park's South Boundary Trail, the junction with the signed Fall River Cutoff Trail is but a few tenths of a mile to the west. On taking it, the Fall River crossing takes place almost immediately. Mountain Ash Creek is less than 2 miles away. It is worth pointing out here that when high with runoff, the Fall and Bechler Rivers isolate Mountain Ash Creek from visits until the water recedes enough to make crossings safe, around the first of July. Only horse and infrequent foot traffic is normal to the creek. The trail fords the creek to a primitive campground, a ranger patrol camp, and the junction with the trail coming from the Bechler Ranger Station.

After gathering nearly all its tributaries, the Fall River begins its drop into an isolated canyon. Boating through this canyon is perilous and not recommended. The canyon can be accessed by foot in a few places, but trophy-size trout are not abundant.

Proposition Creek hosts the most beaver ponds of all Fall River Basin streams. Beaver ponds with enough depth to provide resident trout year-round are numerous in the lower-gradient reaches of Greater Yellowstone streams. In these ponds, the most reliable fly patterns are those that simulate leeches.

At the crossing, the visiting fly fisher has a choice of directions to fish. Downstream, where there is no maintained trail, the possibility exists of fishing down to the Fall River confluence. In this sector the creek flows through the jack pine forest as a riffle-and-run stream punctuated by deep pockets. The gradient eases as it approaches the Fall River, and only a few anglers visit each season to enjoy this isolation. If one chooses to go upstream from the aforementioned crossing, more water can be fished compared to going downstream, and the trail to Union Falls parallels the creek. The only real meadow section is about a quarter mile above the crossing and campground, and the best concentration of large trout can be found here.

The Proposition Creek confluence is the next feature above the meadow reach. This creek, with stair-step beaver ponds in its lower reach, is also becoming a brook trout fishery, but large cutthroat and cuttbow trout inhabit the beaver ponds. Above this confluence, the Mountain Ash Creek gradient steepens noticeably, and downed timber thickens enough in places to hinder fishing. Two miles above, the trail ends at 260-foot Union Falls, the second-highest major waterfall in Yellowstone National Park. Mountain Ash Creek is a fine example of an isolated quality fishery, and if it were located near human habitation, it would be the subject of media attention equivalent to that given to such waters as the Gibbon River above its falls.

Gallatin River Drainage

UPPER GALLATIN RIVER AND FAN CREEK
By Buck Goodrich

In contrast to the seasonal crowded conditions and vehicle noise on the Gallatin River along US Highway 191, both of these streams bask in quietude.

Access: US Highway 191 north of West Yellowstone, Montana, to Bighorn Pass (Upper Gallatin River) trailhead

GPS Coordinates: Bighorn Pass (Upper Gallatin River) trailhead, 44.928154, -110.049322; Fan Creek (Fawn Pass) Trailhead, 44.950684, -111.058485

Equipment: 4- or 5-weight system with floating line, caddisfly, PMD, Golden Stone, and Yellow Sally patterns, and streamer, terrestrial insect, and traditional attractor patterns

Nearest facilities and services: West Yellowstone, USFS Baker's Hole Campground, Parade Rest Ranch

Information resources: Yellowstone National Park, West Yellowstone Visitor Center; Divide Lake and Joseph Peak USGS topographic maps

Salmonids present: Brown, cutthroat, and rainbow trout

The Gallatin River is a hugely popular fly fishing destination in Yellowstone National Park. At times every pullout along US Highway 191 in the park is occupied, and for good reason. This easily approached freestone stream is one of the best the park offers. As it flows with some gradient through broken willows, its sinuous bends contain deep holes offering overhead cover and cooler water for

The Gallatin River has at least moderate gradient throughout its flow in Yellowstone Park. It offers tranquility and fast action upstream of its reach along US Highway 191.

resident salmonids. Brown and rainbow trout populate this river, and from the end of runoff, usually late in June, to well into October, before winter comes knocking on the door, these fish have a reputation for being active feeders. Thus crowds of fly fishers converge on the river to enjoy these trout. This begins from the early-season Giant and Golden Stonefly emergences through the season-long caddisfly activity, the lengthy terrestrial insect season, and on to the Trico emergence. Despite the crowds, with a little walking, you can find solitude on the upper river.

The northwesterly flowing river turns southeasterly from the highway while proceeding upstream. The Bighorn Pass trailhead on the highway offers a chance to find some solitude. It follows

The upper Gallatin River, as with most backcountry waters within the park, is approached by a well-maintained trail. Expect to encounter few visitors while walking to the meadow reach, but be aware that this is bear country, even though fast action from resident trout awaits.

the upper Gallatin River for miles and offers a huge chance for fast fishing action in season. My favorite place on the river is a beautiful meadow about 3 miles up the trail. I think of it as a small Bechler Meadows. Elevation here is 1,000 feet higher at around 7,500 feet, so the season is shorter. It is also prime grizzly bear country, so act accordingly. Here rainbow trout predominate and provide season-long action. Being mostly a dry fly fisher in the midseason, I enjoy presenting terrestrial insect patterns when August rolls around. Dry caddisfly patterns and traditional dry patterns are also extremely effective. However, my all-time favorite to present here is the Humpy. If this meadow were in the Montana part of park, as is the trailhead, I'd be politically correct to call this favorite a Goofus Bug! Here I use it to simulate an ant, horsefly, or when tied blond, a spruce fly.

Back on the highway, the next trailhead downstream is for the Fawn Pass Trail. Follow it up lower Fan Creek and then up Fawn Creek to the Fan Creek confluence, then go up Fan Creek and bushwhack about a mile to another meadow. The creek here is like a much smaller version of the Bechler River or Slough Creek in their respective meadows. Though smaller than the upper Gallatin, it offers the same fast fishing in season, and a 4-weight system applies as well. Rainbow and cuttbow trout appear to occupy the lower creek, but upstream in the meadow, cutthroat trout are present. If this meadow is fished more than a few times in a season, I would be surprised.

Madison River Drainage

COUGAR CREEK

Numerous small but aggressive brook trout and large resident rainbows in the beaver ponds provide all-day, early-season action on lightweight tackle.

Access: USFS Road 178 off US Highway 191 north of West Yellowstone, Montana
GPS Coordinates: 44.766110, -111.113243
Equipment: 4- or 5-weight system with floating line; caddisfly, BWO, PMD, and Yellow
 Sally patterns, and streamer, terrestrial insect, and traditional attractor patterns
Nearest facilities and services: West Yellowstone, USFS Baker's Hole Campground,
 Madison Arm Resort, Parade Rest Ranch
Information resources: Yellowstone National Park, West Yellowstone Visitor Center;
 Richards Creek USGS topographic map
Salmonids present: Brook and rainbow trout

Less than a mile from US Highway 191, the national forest road ends just inside the park boundary where Cougar Creek flows through a long, dense willow thicket. This thicket holds beaver ponds subject to the uncertainties of runoff. Fishing these ponds for their large resident rainbow trout can be an unnerving experience because of the densely vegetated surroundings in this prime grizzly bear habitat, which includes a migration route to and from winter dens in the Gallatin Range to the east. The willow thickets also shelter moose, so there are two major reasons for using a claxon horn. The other residents of this section of Cougar Creek are numerous small brook trout.

DUCK CREEK

A classic meadow stream with challenging yet rewarding fishing.

Access: Duck Creek Road off US Highway 191 north of West Yellowstone, Montana
GPS Coordinates: 44.766125, -111.113223
Equipment: 5- or 6-weight system with floating line; Brown Drake, damselfly, and
dragonfly patterns, and leech, streamer, terrestrial insect, and traditional attractor
patterns
Nearest facilities and services: West Yellowstone, USFS Baker's Hole Campground,
Parade Rest Ranch
Information resources: Yellowstone National Park, West Yellowstone Visitor Center;
Richards Creek USGS topographic map
Salmonids present: Brook, brown, and rainbow trout

Charlie Brooks, in his classic work on the Madison River drainage, *The Living River*, wrote of Duck Creek: "All the anglers I have known, myself included, have misjudged it terribly. It is a fine trout stream but one that takes some knowing." If Duck Creek were outside the Greater Yellowstone Area, it would be a celebrity, but being located between the Gallatin and Madison Rivers, it is bypassed like so many excellent waters located near media giants. It appears as a small riffle-and-run stream barely worth attention at the US Highway 191 crossing. Below the crossing it combines with Cougar Creek, and in Yellowstone National Park it has a much different character. Here it slows and widens as it flows into Koelzer's Pond, an aged private impoundment.

A passing shower on Duck Creek. Early-season weather here can be almost as interesting as encountering the three resident salmonids, so dress accordingly.

Duck Creek in early June. The high-country atmosphere can be chaotic this time of year, and the creek's waters are cold and likely high with runoff. Wet fly presentations are the name of the game.

Park at the turnaround at the end of Duck Creek Road, cross the park boundary, and follow the trace of an old access road to reach this perfect meadow stream. As far as the eye can see in the meadow, Duck Creek meanders west through willow patches and grasses to swing north almost at one's feet. Evidence of beaver activity can also be seen. More often than not, buffalo graze in the meadow, and moose inhabit the willow thickets. The chance of encountering a grizzly bear increases. To the east in the distance, the Gallatin Range towers. To the north, sagebrush slopes spangled here and there with quaking aspen groves end at the meadow. To the south, the Burnt Hole pine forest stands in gray-green contrast to the meadow.

Koelzer's Pond is younger than Hebgen Dam, so after brook, brown, and rainbow trout were introduced into Hebgen Lake, it was not long before they moved into Duck Creek and replaced resident native westslope cutthroat and Montana grayling. During spring, usually in time for the opening of the park's fishing season, runoff is leaving the creek but the meadow remains marshy. At this time rainbow trout migrate to spawn in the stream where it bends back to the forest at the top of the meadow. Brown and brook trout follow them to pick off eggs and to forage on minnows doing the same. I avoid the spawning areas but seek the brown and brook trout as well as the large, ravenous post-spawning rainbows by presenting streamer patterns.

Above the spawning area, a few large beaver ponds are present up to where Gneiss and Richards Creeks combine to form Duck Creek. From this point upstream, the Duck Creek drainage becomes a grizzly bear management area and is closed to human entry. In decades gone by, Richards Pond, at the head of Richards Creek, was famed for hosting enormous brook trout, at the time the largest in Yellowstone National Park. The pond is now closed to human traffic. However, some descendants of these large brook trout inhabit the beaver ponds near the Campanula Creek–Richards Creek confluence.

Toward the end of June, Duck Creek offers dry fly fishing when damselflies from sloughs in the meadows and from the creek itself emerge, mate, and then fly to drop eggs. Evenings feature a variable Brown Drake emergence, and a minor Green Drake hatch occurs in the afternoon. As the meadows dry, presenting terrestrial insects becomes the order of the day. Now utmost stealth is required for fly fishing success. Anglers must stay away from the edge of the creek, tread lightly, and assume the famed "Henry's Fork hunchback" posture for any chance at fooling the wary salmonid residents. Stealth is required through September and into October as brown trout migrate to upper meadow spawning areas, with rainbow and brook trout following to pick off eggs. During this event, it is possible to see individual brown trout rivaling in size those in the nearby Madison River, but the slightest unusual movement or vibration detected sends them swimming away to the nearest overhead cover.

GRAYLING CREEK

The stage is set for a truly native fishery for grayling and westslope cutthroat trout. Let's allow time for the park's native species reestablishment plan to work.

Access: Off US Highway 191 north of West Yellowstone, Montana
GPS Coordinates: 44.830853, -111.077941
Equipment: 4-weight system with floating line; BWO, PMD, and Yellow Sally patterns, and traditional attractor, terrestrial, and streamer patterns
Nearest facilities and services: West Yellowstone, USFS Baker's Hole Campground, Parade Rest Ranch
Information resources: Yellowstone National Park, West Yellowstone Visitor Center; Mount Hebgen USGS topographic map
Salmonids present: Cutthroat trout and Montana grayling

Let us hope for success in the Yellowstone Park efforts to re-establish fluvial grayling in streams determined to be suitable for such action. JOHN JURACEK PHOTO

As with other major streams in the upper Madison River drainage, Grayling Creek historically hosted Montana grayling, westslope cutthroat trout, and Rocky Mountain whitefish, but these fish ceased to exist due to their inability to compete with introduced brown and rainbow trout. By the middle of the 20th century, Grayling Creek became an excellent fishery for the introduced trout. Where it parallels US Highway 191 north of West Yellowstone, it was for decades an alternative for anglers who wanted to escape the crowds on the nearby Madison River but still have a chance at trophy-size trout. Many of these anglers could be encountered just yards from the numerous pullouts placed along the highway within the park, but a wilderness fly fishing experience awaited visitors to the upper reaches of the creek where it turns east away from the highway.

Early in the 21st century, park fisheries biologists determined that Grayling Creek was a top candidate for reintroducing the native species. Water quality remained high, and riparian habitat alteration was minimal. A waterfall downstream from the reach in the park guaranteed that exotic salmonids from below could not migrate upward to the reconditioned stretch. In 2013 and 2014 fisheries crews chemically treated the creek to eliminate the exotic salmonids in preparation for reintroduction. Of course, this action met with mixed responses from the fly fishing community. In 2015 park fisheries personnel hatched 100,000 grayling eggs in the upper reaches of the creek and also began the reintroduction of westslope cutthroat trout. These actions were scheduled to continue for three years. True, an excellent brown and rainbow trout fishery has been lost, but the Madison River drainage abounds in these. If the reintroduction succeeds, the two original native species will move further away from being endangered, and for the fly fisher, the reestablishment will enrich the variety of salmonids the Greater Yellowstone Area offers.

THE GRAYLING LAKES

Superb fishing for introduced grayling. When aquatic insects emerge, mainly Speckled Dun mayflies and damselflies, grayling become active and provide excellent dry fly fishing.

Access: Norris–Canyon Village Road to Grebe Lake or Cascade Lake trailheads

GPS Coordinates: Grebe Lake trailhead, 44.717559, -110.549624; Cascade Lake trailhead, 44.735349, -110.503479

Equipment: 4- or 5-weight system with floating and intermediate lines; caddisfly, damselfly, and Speckled Dun patterns, and leech, streamer, terrestrial insect, and traditional attractor patterns

Nearest facilities and services: West Yellowstone (Montana), Canyon Village, Norris and Canyon Campgrounds, Canyon Lodge and Cabins

Information resources: Yellowstone National Park, Canyon Visitor Education Center and Norris Junction Visitor Center; Cook Peak and Crystal Falls USGS topographic maps

Salmonids present: Grebe and Wolf Lakes, rainbow trout and Montana grayling; Cascade Lake, cutthroat trout and Montana grayling

Wolf is the smallest of the so-called Grayling Lakes, and it is the most remote. Consider it Grebe Lake's little brother—the fish will be smaller, but visits are fewer.

Cascade, Grebe, and Wolf Lakes are known as the Grayling Lakes. All lie around 8,000 feet in elevation. Wolf and Grebe are on the Pacific side of the Continental Divide at the top of the Gibbon River drainage. Cascade Lake is on the opposite side of the divide and therefore in the Yellowstone River drainage.

Each lake was without salmonids until the early 20th century. Grebe Lake received its first stocking of Montana grayling from the State of Montana's Anaconda hatchery in 1921. Rainbow trout had been introduced into Grebe in 1908, and from there both moved down to populate Wolf Lake. So well did grayling do in Grebe Lake that an egg collection station operated there up to the mid-20th century. Grebe and Wolf Lakes would become refuges for the species. Likewise, adjacent Cascade Lake, also originally devoid of salmonids, became a refuge for introduced Montana grayling and Yellowstone cutthroat trout. But not all introductions were successful: Grayling planted in nearby Ice Lake disappeared after a few years, and Grebe Lake's 1912 Yellowstone cutthroat planting failed. The first catch-and-release fishing regulation was applied to park waters in 1969, requiring the release of grayling caught from Grebe Lake.

The headwaters of the Gibbon River lie above 8,000 feet on the Solfatara Plateau, where winter snowfalls can accumulate to tens of feet, thus the source waters remain exceptionally cold until moderated by geothermal inflows below. They combine at Grebe Lake, where the drainage first hosts salmonids introduced by man. At this elevation growing seasons are short.

The trailhead to Grebe Lake is about 3.5 miles east of Norris Junction on the road to Canyon Junction. It is an easy 3.5-mile hike, mostly along an old service road over nearly flat terrain that arrives near the southeast corner of the lake then proceeds to connect with the Howard Eaton pack trail just to the north. Four primitive campsites are nearby. Going west on the Howard Eaton Trail takes one to nearby Wolf Lake.

These trails are not always open when the park's fly fishing season opens, thus it is wise to check to determine their condition before planning an early-season trip. Likewise, ice-out sometimes occurs later on these lakes than the fishing season opening date.

Carrying a floatation device to Grebe Lake allows access to the best fishing it offers, especially near submerged weed beds. Fishing from shore is also productive, and much of the Grebe Lake shoreline is open and firm. Early in the season nymph fishing with small patterns over weed beds is most productive for grayling, but as midsummer approaches Speckled Dun patterns are more effective. By late July dry damselfly patterns are effective. The resident fish seem to respond best when skies are clear and wind is at a minimum. The Gibbon River, holding a few grayling and rainbow trout, leaves the west side of the lake, picks up a few tributaries, and then enters Wolf Lake. This lake is smaller than Grebe Lake, and its resident grayling and rainbow trout also run smaller.

As with Grayling Creek, the Gibbon River drainage above Virginia Cascades is being chemically treated in a three-year action by fisheries biologists of the Yellowstone Center for Resources for inclusion into the controversial Native Fish Conservation Plan. In this plan actions are made to remove non-native fish from certain waters and restore native fish. In the case of the upper Gibbon River drainage including Grebe, Ice, and Wolf Lakes, the plan considers removal of both rainbow trout and adfluvial grayling by chemical and physical means and then introduction of westslope cutthroat trout and fluvial Montana grayling.

The best route to Cascade Lake is to use the segment of the Howard Eaton pack trail that leaves going north from about a half mile west of Canyon Junction. It is an easy 2-mile walk to the lake, and parallels Cascade Creek for most of its length.

Grebe Lake hosts the largest grayling in the park. As with the other Grayling Lakes, it was devoid of salmonids until the early 20th century.

Cascade Lake is the only Grayling Lake that lies on the Atlantic side of the Continental Divide. It's also the easiest to approach. The fly fishing strategies that apply to Grebe and Wolf Lakes apply here as well.

This creek hosts small Yellowstone cutthroat trout and is ideal for using the lightest of tackle. The trail eventually crosses the creek, skirts the east side of the lake, and connects with the trail coming in from Canyon–Tower Junction Road. The entire north shore of Cascade Lake is a meadow sloping gently to the lake and of good footing. Resident Yellowstone cutthroat trout and grayling cruise this shoreline within easy casting distance, hunting for terrestrial insects and life-forms in weed beds, making a floatation device unnecessary. In season, Speckled Dun and damselfly patterns are also effective.

Snake River Drainage

CRAWFISH CREEK

Charlie Brooks described the country through which this stream flows as "jackstraw hell." Blown-down timber extends into the stream, providing overhead cover for small resident cutthroat trout.

Access: South Entrance Road to Crawfish Creek parking area
GPS Coordinates: 44.152039, -110.673683
Equipment: 3- or 4-weight system with floating line; caddisfly, PMD, and Yellow Sally patterns, and terrestrial insect and traditional attractor patterns
Nearest facilities and services: Jackson (Wyoming), South Entrance Ranger Station, Flagg Ranch Resort
Information resources: Yellowstone National Park; Lewis Canyon USGS topographic map
Salmonids present: Cutthroat trout

The Crawfish Creek drainage was once barren of salmonids, with Moose Falls near its Lewis River confluence the upstream barrier to salmonids from the Lewis River and the falls on adjacent Polecat Creek the barrier to fish from the Snake River. Yellowstone cutthroat were introduced to the drainage above Moose Falls in the early 20th century and now thrive. Crawfish Creek would be an even larger stream, but Polecat Creek has cut off some of its upper drainage in a classic example of stream capture.

Access to the creek and to major tributary Spirea Creek above the falls is easy from the small parking area at Moose Falls just 1.5 miles inside the park on the South Entrance Road. Downed timber hinders movement in places but also provides abundant overhead cover along the stream. Hot springs near the top of its drainage and above a short meadow reach provide some warming water. Lightweight equipment to present small dry and nymph patterns is the name of the game here, as it is rare to encounter a cutthroat exceeding much more than a foot in length.

LEWIS RIVER

Fishless until around the turn of the 20th century, this river now holds one of the best trophy brown trout populations in Yellowstone National Park. Some juvenile lake trout also inhabit the river between Shoshone and Lewis Lakes.

Access: Boating across Lewis Lake and up Lewis River Channel; South Entrance Road to Lewis River Channel Loop trailhead

GPS Coordinates: 44.332065, -110613725

Equipment: 6-weight system with floating and sink-tip lines; Giant Stone, Golden Stone, Gray Drake, Green Drake, and PMD patterns, and leech, streamer, and terrestrial insect patterns

Nearest facilities and services: Jackson (Wyoming), Old Faithful and Grant Villages, Lewis Lake Campground, South Entrance Ranger Station, Flagg Ranch Resort

Information resources: Yellowstone National Park; Craig Pass, Lewis Falls, and Lewis Canyon USGS topographic maps

Salmonids present: Brook, brown and lake trout

"The Channel" is the name locals give to the Lewis River between Lewis and Shoshone Lakes, and this piece of the river has an autumn brown trout concentration with few peers in the Greater Yellowstone Area. Not only is it a rearing ground for these trout, many of which move to the two lakes, but the autumn spawning run hosts a legendary number of fish. It's the closest thing the area has to a salmon run, and since the early 1960s, when it was first publicized, it has attracted lots of anglers vying for fish that run up to trophy sizes. At such times some anglers leave Lewis Lake Campground by boat to motor across the lake, then walk the river to present streamer and large nymph patterns to migrating fish, while others walk the Lewis River Channel Loop to the river.

Come October, the run brings much midday fishing competition, and it does not take long to put the fish down. But if the enthusiast decides to camp overnight at the outlet campground at Shoshone Lake to arrive on the river at first light before the

Lewis River Channel is the water trail to Shoshone Lake. It is in high country, nearly 8,000 feet in elevation, thus seasons are shorter, the weather is less predictable, and the waters are cooler. Nevertheless, trophy brown trout and juvenile lake trout respond well to aquatic and terrestrial fly patterns during the summer.

crowds show up, some unusual fishing can be experienced. Weather can interfere, however. One of my late October visits began with an incoming storm. We arrived at the outlet campground, dropped our overnight equipment, and geared up. Dozens of anglers were already on the river, but once it began to snow, they left with abandon. That afternoon about a foot of snow fell, but after dark the storm moved on, the sky cleared, and the air temperature plummeted. We woke up the next morning to 10 below but scrambled into our gear and headed to the river. No one had come to the river that frigid morning, and the result was some of the best brown trout fishing I've ever experienced. We broke camp and left by mid-afternoon, hiked out the 4-mile trail covered with a foot of fresh snow, and drove to Jackson for the biggest steaks in town. This is another example why, particularly in the late season, observing weather forecasts and taking proper equipment is prudent anywhere in the Greater Yellowstone Area.

The river between the lakes sees a lot fewer anglers in the summer, but fishing can be interrupted by the numerous boaters originating from campgrounds along Shoshone Lake. This traffic usually begins in the late morning, but by late afternoon the traffic passes and productive fishing results soon after. In late June Green Drakes hatch in the meadow section of the river. At this time a few Giant Stoneflies also emerge from the upper river and can bring topwater action from trout there and in Shoshone Lake's outlet bay. During July and August terrestrial insects are plentiful along the meadow section, and fish will respond to their imitations. However, presenting streamer patterns is always the best way to encounter the large brown trout living here.

Lewis Lake, because of its proximity to the South Entrance Road and its full-service boat dock at Lewis Lake Campground, can become crowded throughout the season with anglers launching boats. A good alternative to these crowds is to wade the shoreline to present streamer patterns, especially during autumn when both brown and lake trout migrate to spawning areas. By late June fish in the roadside meadow reach below the lake respond to a Green Drake emergence and adult stoneflies blown in from the canyon, and then later to midsummer terrestrial insects. I prefer presenting a hair mouse pattern when I visit the meadow reach in the evening—the resulting takes from the large resident brown trout can be explosive!

In October mature brown trout residing in Lewis Lake also migrate to the outlet to spawn as well to the top end of the meadow below Lewis Falls. Numerous anglers seeking trophy browns also arrive at the river to present streamer patterns to these aggressive fish. From the meadow below Lewis Falls to the park's South Entrance, the Lewis River flows through a dangerous and nearly inaccessible canyon, emerging from the canyon near the South Entrance to join the Snake River. Significant seasonable fishing pressure takes place on both rivers here because they are within easy walking distance of the South Entrance Road. Local fly fishers return in late October, however, to encounter the brown trout run from the Snake River above Jackson Lake.

HEART LAKE

The fourth-largest lake in the park can be temperamental when fished from the shore, but an angler visiting as early as possible in the season can experience some unforgettable fly fishing.

Access: South Entrance Road to Heart Lake trailhead
GPS Coordinates: 44.317436, -110.598184
Equipment: 6-weight system with floating and intermediate lines; damselfly and
    Speckled Dun patterns, and leech, scud, and streamer patterns
Nearest facilities and services: Jackson (Wyoming), Grant Village, Lewis Lake
    Campground, South Entrance Ranger Station, Grant Village Lodge
Information resources: Yellowstone National Park; Heart Lake USGS topographic map
Salmonids present: Cutthroat and lake trout and Rocky Mountain whitefish

Heart Lake Basin lies just south of the Continental Divide, and this location holds some of the most remote large lakes in the park, including Shoshone. The trailhead sign across the South Entrance Road from the northeast corner of Lewis Lake marks the 8.5-mile walk to Heart Lake. It's a long enough distance to discourage most fly fishers, but for those willing to put forth the effort, some of the best early-season fishing in the park awaits, but only after a winter of heavy snowfall. The first 5 miles of trail is a monotonous, gentle ascent through a jack pine forest with plenty of accompanying mosquitoes, but on reaching Paycheck Pass, a beautiful panoramic view of Heart Lake Basin below entices a stop for photographs. There is no potable

Heart Lake looking south toward Jackson Hole. Summertime haze obscures the distant Grand Teton Range. Mt. Sheridan towers on the right.

water up to now along the trail nor is there any in the descent off the pass, where the trail courses through Witch Creek Geyser Basin down to the lake.

Up until the mid-20th century, a primitive road began at the trailhead and ended on Paycheck Pass. Anglers would drive the road, park their vehicle, then portage their boat and gear 3.5 miles down to the lake. Misuse and offal accumulation resulted in closure of the road by the Park Service and placement of the present trail. The result of this closure is that Heart Lake Basin is in near-pristine condition, with only horse and foot passage allowed.

Fishing in Heart Lake Basin now opens on July 1 each year to protect its critical grizzly bear habitat. Lake trout were introduced early in the 20th century and now thrive in the depths of 100 feet and more, coexisting with native cutthroat trout and Rocky Mountain whitefish. In appearance, the cutthroat here are more like the Snake River fine-spotted species than any other, and they fight with noteworthy vigor.

Up until the mid-1980s, the opening of Heart Lake's fishing season coincided with the park's Memorial Day weekend general season opening, and during the month of June I enjoyed the best inland salmonid fly fishing in my 40-year experience through presenting leech, soft-hackle, streamer, and occasional dry patterns. We packed float tubes into the lake for multiday stays when Snake River fine-spotted cutthroat and lake trout cruised shorelines following spawning suckers and responded to streamer and egg patterns. Yes, we endured snow squalls, downed timber, and snow-clogged and flooded trails, but with lake trout caught up to double-figure poundage and cutthroat to several pounds, those days are hard to forget. So is the memory of grizzly bear scat and tracks. But fishing the lake was only part of the attraction in those days. Beaver Creek, 2 miles east on the Heart

Heart Lake Ranger Station is on the National Register of Historic Places. At times it is occupied by on-duty rangers. No services are available at the cabin except friendly conversations with and information from any ranger present.

A large Heart Lake cutthroat trout before being released. The long walk to and from the lake is justified when cutthroat ranging to several pounds forage on adult aquatic insects sitting on the lake surface.

Lake Trail, and Witch Creek had ample populations of large cutthroat, and in Beaver Creek some juvenile lake trout were present, all feasting on eggs released from spawning suckers. In the quarter-mile meadow reach of the Heart River between the lake and the canyon, ravenous post-spawning cutthroat hit streamer patterns with gusto.

Now with the July 1 opening, Heart Lake Basin can still be a fly fishing paradise. Here is how to realize it for a day trip: First, choose to visit as early as possible in a July following a winter of abundant snowfall. Inform park rangers of your intent, and arrive at the trailhead during first light. Be equipped with lightweight waders, rain gear, DEET, bear spray, claxon horn, water purifier, some high-carb food, 6-weight fly gear with intermediate and floating lines, and streamer, Speckled Dun, and adult damselfly patterns. Head down the trail, putting out a blast from that claxon horn once in a while.

On arrival at the lake, 8.5 miles distant, you will pass the Heart Lake Ranger Station, which is sometimes occupied. Forget about fishing adjacent Witch Creek because cutthroat left it weeks ago when the water became too warm, especially for large trout. Go directly to the half-mile-long beach just past the cabin to observe the lake surface. Watch for cutthroat rising to Speckled Duns and adult damselflies. Rig up the floating line and a pattern for either of the two, get into your waders, and wade the shallows ready for action. You will not have to cast far, as the insects will emerge from shallow water warmed to the optimum temperature. When the usual wind comes up by late morning, switch to that intermediate line and present streamer patterns. Either way, your reward will be cutthroat trout ranging to several pounds and juvenile lake trout. If you do not mind walking 2 miles farther down the Heart Lake Trail, those same cutthroat will still be in lower Beaver Creek and will take Pale Morning Dun, Yellow Sally, and traditional dry patterns.

Overnight visits are practical for fishing Heart Lake Basin. Multiday trips are needed to fish Heart River (12 miles from the trailhead), Beaver Creek (10 miles from the trailhead), and the lake in one visit. Any visit to Heart Lake Basin is subject to park backcountry regulations, including a strong suggestion of being in a party of at least four for overnight and longer visits. Several primitive campsites are on the lake or nearby, and their use requires a park backcountry permit. Plan on fishing any of these waters no later than the first week and a half of July because with warming waters the largest trout move to depth and become available only through boating. After mid-July the best shoreline fishing will be where streams descending from Mount Sheridan enter the west side of the lake. Here juvenile cutthroat congregate from the depths to pick off drifting food washed into the lake.

Boating during the summer, usually performed using horses to carry inflatable watercraft, can get the fly fisher equipped with large streamer patterns and a lead-core line out to depths where huge lake trout reside. These fish will move into rocky shallows around the lake by mid-September to spawn and will be available to wading fly fishers equipped with full-sink lines and large streamer patterns. Fishing this time of the year may be enticing because the largest lake trout on record taken from Yellowstone Park waters, a 42-pound behemoth, came from the depths of Heart Lake in the 1930s.

HEART RIVER

Getting here requires a long walk and at least one overnight stay. In the early season, rewards include large cutthroat trout responding to wind-blown stoneflies lighting on the surface of the river just below the lake.

Access: South Entrance Road to Heart Lake trailhead
GPS Coordinates: 44.317436, -110.598184
Equipment: 6-weight system with floating and sink-tip lines; caddisfly, Giant Stone, Golden Stone, and PMD patterns, and streamer, terrestrial, and traditional patterns
Nearest facilities and services: Jackson (Wyoming), Grant Village, Lewis Lake Campground, South Entrance Ranger Station, Flagg Ranch Resort
Information resources: Yellowstone National Park; Heart Lake and Mount Hancock USGS topographic maps
Salmonids present: Cutthroat trout and Rocky Mountain whitefish

Like the Bechler River, the entire Heart River is in total isolation. No roads reach either and no other rivers in the park, except the Yellowstone River above the lake and in its canyon reaches and the upper Lamar River, can boast such a blessing. It's a long haul to reach the Heart River, a bit over 12 miles. Even an overnight pack trip by foot or horseback leaves little time to enjoy fishing the river, thus a trip spanning

Nearly all the Heart Lake drainage is shown in this photo. The Heart River leaves the lake just below the photo's center then falls through its short, steep canyon to enter the sloping meadow reach ending at the Snake River confluence to the left, but not shown in the photo.

at least three days is recommended to do it justice. Without a doubt, the best time to do so is as soon as Heart Lake Basin opens to fishing on July 1, especially after a winter of heavy snowfall, when the abundant snowmelt keeps the water in Heart Lake higher and cooler, thus supplying more water to the river. During early July under such water conditions, adult stoneflies are blown up from the canyon into the quarter-mile reach of the meadow stream at the outlet from the lake.

This part of the river is among the most beautiful streams in the park. Ravenous post-spawning cutthroat in this stretch and in the outlet bay will readily respond to floating stonefly patterns. After a winter of meager snowfall, less water flows into the river, raising its temperature enough to slow fishing to a crawl and move larger fish into the lake. The canyon begins just below the Outlet Creek confluence at the downstream end of the meadow reach. The roaring water can be heard at this point, giving a hint that the river within is steep, difficult to wade, and not really worthy of a fishing visit, as it hosts mostly smaller fish in its length of tumbling water.

Below the canyon the river courses through a gradually sloping meadow similar to the Gibbon River just above Madison Junction, but larger. It runs for a little more than a mile and hosts a good number of cutthroat trout and Rocky Mountain whitefish, some large, until it meets the Snake River below. Here it is clearly not as high a quality fishery as the quarter-mile meadow reach just below the lake.

POLECAT CREEK

A quality small stream that sees few fly fishing visitors. Three species of salmonids respond to dry attractor and terrestrial patterns with gusto.

Access: West from South Entrance Ranger Station at South Boundary trailhead
GPS Coordinates: 44.132222, -110.668578
Equipment: 4-weight system with floating and sink-tip lines; caddisfly, BWO, PMD, and Yellow Sally patterns, and streamer, terrestrial insect, and traditional attractor patterns
Nearest facilities and services: Jackson (Wyoming), South Entrance Ranger Station, USFS Sheffield Campground, Flagg Ranch Resort
Information resources: Yellowstone National Park; Lewis Canyon USGS topographic map
Salmonids present: Brook, brown, and cutthroat trout

Because most of Polecat Creek's reach is in Yellowstone National Park, I cover it here rather than outside the park in Wyoming. From the South Entrance Ranger Station, the creek is a 2-mile walk west on the trail. It can also be reached from the small parking area just west of its crossing on Ashton–Flagg Ranch Road just below the park's south boundary. Fishing it here requires a Wyoming fishing license, and the best waters are above the former Huckleberry Hot Springs resort and below the crossing.

What makes this creek so interesting is that it hosts brook, brown, and cutthroat trout. I have also observed a few Rocky Mountain whitefish in its lower reach.

Once in a while resident fish can be surprisingly large, particularly the brown trout. Nevertheless, a lightweight system is best for this creek, except when targeting the fall run of large browns.

Polecat Creek is another runoff stream, draining the southeast corner of the Pitchstone Plateau. The start of its best fishing depends on the rate of snowmelt in the plateau, which receives some of the heaviest snowfall in the park. The usual progression of aquatic insects emerging from this riffle-and-run part of the creek begins with terrestrial insect populations that build to a late summer peak, becoming more important in the trout's diet. Smaller but eager trout inhabit the creek above the trail crossing, and about a half mile above the crossing a barrier waterfall, almost 50 feet tall, prevents fish passage. Above the falls the stream, once barren, now hosts only small cutthroat trout.

Going downstream from the trail crossing and below the park boundary, another fly fisher is rarely seen. In fact, during my late summer trips when fishing this creek in Wyoming, I have encountered more elk hunters than anglers. As the creek approaches the abandoned resort, its gradient eases but thermal water flows in, warming it to the point of reducing the number of fish present. Approaching the Ashton–Flagg Ranch Road crossing, the creek begins to cool to the point of being more hospitable to salmonids. Weed beds and other aquatic vegetation become widespread and host an array of food forms.

In the autumn months, large brown trout move through to spawn upstream and a medium-weight system is best. Some of these fish appear to remain in the creek above the abandoned resort. A convenient way to enjoy fishing Polecat Creek, and nearby waters, is to camp or lodge at the nearby full-service Flagg Ranch Resort.

SHOSHONE LAKE

Originally devoid of salmonids, Shoshone Lake now rewards boating anglers presenting streamer patterns with trophy-size brown and lake trout ranging to around 20 pounds.

Access: Boating across Lewis Lake from Lewis Lake Campground and up Lewis River Channel; South Entrance Road to Shoshone Lake (Dog's Head) trailhead Old Faithful–Thumb Junction Road to DeLacy Creek trailhead
GPS Coordinates: Shoshone Lake (Dog's Head) trailhead, 44.318601, -110.599237; DeLacy Creek trailhead, 44.446811, -110701665
Equipment: 6-weight system with full-sink line; leech, scud, and streamer patterns
Nearest facilities and services: Old Faithful and Grant Village, Lewis Lake Campground, Lewis Lake and South Entrance Ranger Stations, Flagg Ranch Resort
Information resources: Yellowstone National Park; Craig Pass, Lewis Falls, and Shoshone Geyser Basin USGS topographic maps
Salmonids present: Brook, brown, and lake trout

Shoshone Lake lies at the top of the Lewis River drainage. At 12 square miles, it is the largest roadless lake in the lower 48 states. Originally devoid of salmonids, stocking here began in the late 19th century, and introduced lake trout and lesser

The Lewis River leaves Shoshone Lake to the left. DeLacey Creek enters through the meadow near the upper right corner.

populations of brown and brook trout now reach trophy size. One has to wonder what fishing would be like if Yellowstone cutthroat had been planted here rather than these exotic species.

Two practical land routes reach this lake: the Shoshone Lake (also known as Dog's Head) Trail of 4.5 miles beginning off the South Entrance Road just above Lewis Lake, and the DeLacey Creek Trail of 3 miles beginning off the highway about midway between Old Faithful and West Thumb Junction. For the adventurous, it is possible to leave from the Bechler Ranger Station, travel through the meadows, up the fishable Bechler River Canyon, and across the Pitchstone Plateau, then descend to Shoshone Geyser Basin at the west end of Shoshone Lake. It's a 29-mile hike, which ultimately allows only shoreline wading to catch fish, but above the basin Shoshone Creek offers brook and brown trout to moderate sizes. One can also reach the west end of Shoshone Lake via trail from Old Faithful. It's a little less distance than leaving from the Bechler Ranger Station, but a lot less interesting from a fishing standpoint.

The popular water trail is motorized across Lewis Lake, then up the nonmotorized Lewis River to the also nonmotorized Shoshone Lake. It's a nearly 3-mile trip ideal for canoes, but also possible for drift boats and kayaks, with the last three-quarters of a mile requiring a portage to the lake. Numerous primitive campsites along the shoreline provide bases for float fishing the lake. Some, especially those near the DeLacey Creek and Shoshone Lake Trails and at the outlet, are practical for walk-in camping trips. Because boat trips with overnight stays have become so popular, it is wise to select and reserve any of these campsites early in the year through the Yellowstone National Park website.

Shoreline fishing on Shoshone Lake in the early season results in limited success, and is best just at ice-out or during low-light conditions when juvenile lake and brown trout cruise shallows. Moose and DeLacey Creeks offer fast fishing with lightweight gear for small, colorful brook trout. Through June into the first two weeks of July, fishing from a boat rowed and portaged up the river or from floatation devices packed in on either of the two trails is the best strategy for success, but after mid-July fishing on the lake slows noticeably until fall arrives. Topwater fishing is possible early in the day before winds arrive and late in the day after they subside. During these times midge emergences can be widespread and a sparse Speckled Dun emergence takes place. However, fishing deep around the weed beds is by far the best way to find action. The best approach is to present leech, scud, and streamer patterns around submerged weed beds or by trolling streamer patterns from June into July, and then coming back to do the same in mid-September. By October large lake trout come into rocky shorelines to spawn. Wading to present large streamer patterns on sinking lines can be effective, but be sure to insulate against the lake waters that remain in the 40-degree range. The most practical locations for encountering these lake trout, which range up to 20 pounds, is along the east shoreline, which is paralleled by the Shoshone Lake Trail.

As with Yellowstone Lake, windy conditions prevail on Shoshone. Early mornings and evenings may be wind-free, but midday prevailing westerly winds can whip the lake surface into 5-foot waves, and these have caused fatalities. At just under 8,000 feet in elevation, thunderstorms here can be violent and accompanying winds increase the waves perilously. During these storms air temperatures can plummet, and snow, even in July, is not unheard of. I recall a July Fourth weekend trip in the

Tubing Shoshone Lake's DeLacey Bay requires a 3-mile walk. The reward is the excitement of watching juvenile lake trout and trophy brown trout chasing leech and streamer patterns through the crystal-clear water.

1980s when for three out of four days snow and wind made getting out on the lake uncomfortable. Early autumn snowstorms are always possible, thus extreme-weather precautions should be observed when visiting this lake.

SNAKE RIVER

Easily accessed where it leaves the park at the South Entrance, it offers a wilderness experience to fly fishers willing to travel at least a mile upstream. Cutthroat trout, the dominant salmonids, offer good dry fly fishing, but keep an eye on the sky for incoming thunderstorms that can muddy the river.

Access: East from South Entrance Ranger Station at South Boundary trailhead
GPS Coordinates: 44.136712, -110.665954
Equipment: 5-weight system with floating and sink-tip lines: BWO and caddisfly patterns, and soft-hackle, streamer, terrestrial insect, and traditional attractor patterns
Nearest facilities and services: Jackson (Wyoming), South Entrance Ranger Station, USFS Sheffield Campground, Flagg Ranch Resort
Information resources: Yellowstone National Park; Lewis Canyon and Snake Hot Springs USGS topographic maps
Salmonids present: Brown, cutthroat, and lake (seasonally) trout and Rocky Mountain whitefish

Where it is most easily accessed, this river is subject to lengthy and periodically copious runoff. This condition not only impacts safe access but also affects fishing success, moving the best time to fish well into summer. In addition, storms in the upstream drainage can discolor the Snake in a manner similar to that on the Lamar River. However, under stable conditions this river can offer excellent fishing, the best of which is easily approached near the park's South Entrance. Parking areas are spacious here, and a nearby picnic area offers an excellent location for gearing up. These conveniences can result in crowds, but particularly during times when terrestrial insects are abundant, fishing can be worth tolerating the company.

By walking east on the South Boundary Trail, which follows the river upstream for several miles, you can easily escape most other anglers. Upstream the number of brown trout diminishes, and cutthroat trout and Rocky Mountain whitefish become the only resident salmonids. Nevertheless, by August presenting terrestrial and traditional attractor patterns and caddis patterns will elicit interest from trout into the beginning of October.

Toward the end of October, brown trout run into the river from outside the park. The run does not hold many individuals, and few of them pass the Lewis River confluence about a half mile above the South Entrance. In addition, wading and crossing the river is much safer this time of the year, with numerous locations to do so available. Also at this time, juvenile lake trout, likely from Jackson Lake, follow the migrating brown trout and, of course, resident cutthroat trout are also attracted by the migration. Streamer patterns can be most effective at this time. Thus, for a number of reasons, the Snake River within the park offers its best and safest fishing from August to the end of the park fishing season. However, as the end of the season approaches, winter conditions can prevail, so it is wise to check the weather before heading out for a late-season visit.

Yellowstone River Drainage

BLACK CANYON OF THE YELLOWSTONE RIVER

After runoff leaves the river, this isolated canyon reach can offer great fishing. This begins with a heavy Giant and Golden Stonefly emergence and extends through late summer, when terrestrial insects provide abundant food for resident trout.

Access: Mammoth–Tower Junction Road to Blacktail Deer Creek trailhead or Hellroaring trailhead

GPS Coordinates: Blacktail Deer Creek trailhead 44.955749, -110.593811; Hellroaring trailhead, 44.949066, -110.450544

Equipment: 6-weight system with floating and intermediate lines; caddisfly, Giant Stone, Golden Stone, PMD, and Yellow Sally patterns, and streamer, terrestrial insect, and traditional attractor patterns

Nearest facilities and services: Mammoth (Wyoming), Mammoth Campground, Mammoth Hot Springs Hotel, Roosevelt Lodge

Information resources: Yellowstone National Park, Albright Visitor Center; USGS Flow Station Gage 06191500; Blacktail Deer Creek, Mammoth, and Tower Junction USGS topographic maps

Salmonids present: Brown, cutthroat, and rainbow trout

Ospreys are common Black Canyon inhabitants. They deserve meals of trout. Certainly, they were catching them before man did the same. DAVE LETENDRE PHOTO

Other than the Yellowstone River above the lake, the Black Canyon of the Yellowstone River is the most practical remote part of the Yellowstone River to fish. Forget about fishing in the Grand Canyon of the Yellowstone River. It is too dangerous and expensive in the event a rescue must be performed. The much more approachable Black Canyon holds the river flowing in a near northwesterly direction for about 20 miles. It begins north of Tower Junction just below the Lamar River confluence and exits the park just east of Gardiner, Montana. In this distance the river drops about 1,000 feet in elevation. It is out of sight from park roads, but its track through the country to the north from Mammoth–Tower Junction Road can be frequently viewed.

There are two practical routes for fishing in the canyon. Near the upper canyon the Hellroaring Trail leaves about 3 miles west of Tower Junction (turn left at the gravel pit on the north side of the road). After a short, steep hike, the trail crosses the river using the Yellowstone River Suspension Bridge. The river here has a high gradient with dangerous currents. Some scrambling must be undertaken to find the best fishing spots. Nearby Hellroaring Creek hosts a good Yellowstone cutthroat trout population. Farther downstream off Tower–Mammoth Junction Road, the Lower Blacktail Trail goes a bit more than 4 miles to the Blacktail Suspension Bridge, crosses the river, and proceeds down the north side to exit the park just east of Gardiner. On descending into the canyon, nearby Blacktail Deer Creek offers fishing for small brook trout. This is the most popular route into Black Canyon, with more suitable fishing locations than the upstream Hellroaring access. Plan at least an overnight visit for fishing the river in Black Canyon. Primitive campsites requiring permits are near the river. The trail going to town from the park boundary becomes a scramble in order to avoid private land.

The river is powerful and dangerous, so be cautious when wading. Fast water with rocky runs, rapids, and cascades are the norm. Once committing to either side to fish, it is nearly impossible to cross the river safely, so think about where you want to fish ahead of time. Pools with bedrock bottoms appear placid but hold strong subsurface currents. The river is also challenging for illegal boaters that from time to time embark at Tower Junction or from the bridge over the river on the Tower Junction–Northeast Entrance Road to disembark outside the park at Gardiner. Doing so requires portaging Knowles Falls.

Runoff governs the beginning of practical fishing in the canyon, and this can vary year to year. Upon its conclusion, presentation of annelid patterns can be effective, but as Charlie Brooks said, "This is stonefly water," and my experience agrees. Even in late July when adult Giant Stoneflies provide excellent dry fly fishing, I find that stonefly nymph patterns remain effective. However, these should be in sizes matching the nymph stages of the species present. Of course, this also is major caddisfly water, with many species present, and if stonefly patterns fail to attract trout, consider caddis patterns.

My other experiences in the canyon were in late August, when terrestrials are abundant. Fishing dry patterns for these insects was as effective as presenting dry stonefly patterns about a month earlier. During these warm midsummer days, I found that waders are excess weight when backpacking and that wet wading with reliable felt-sole shoes is safe and entirely comfortable. There is a reason for wearing

The Black Canyon of the Yellowstone River offers fishing in isolation. Here it is the park's largest river, offering trophy cuttbows that respond to dry attractor and streamer patterns.

waders, however, and that is the biggest population of rattlesnakes in the park. The canyon is the lowest elevation in the park, and during summer it can heat to uncomfortable daytime temperatures. There is no potable water in the canyon, so bring water purification items.

Cuttbow trout dominate the population here, and Yellowstone cutthroat are present in respectable numbers. Individuals up to two pounds are common, with an occasional fish going larger. The nearly 40-foot-high Knowles Falls forms an upstream barrier for brown trout in the river below, though every year a brown trout or two are reportedly caught above the falls.

Finally, the Yellowstone River through the Black Canyon is a unique wilderness setting. It is 4 or 5 miles from a major park highway for most of its course, and the two suspension bridges are the only major man-made structures. Unlike the Lewis River channel between Shoshone and Lewis Lakes, which has a major highway about the same distance away, no boats are present, at least legally. But unlike the Lewis River channel, the river in the canyon can temporarily become discolored when inflow from the Lamar River drainage carries silt released from unstable banks due to strong summertime thundershowers. That's another reason for checking weather conditions before venturing into the canyon. Nevertheless, the river in Black Canyon is a wonderful location to visit, and it has a small group of dedicated enthusiasts. It offers vigorous trout in fast water, a beautiful setting, and an excellent chance for solitude.

BLACKTAIL POND

Legends abound of trophy-size brook trout here, but recently there's been little to substantiate such stories.

Access: Mammoth–Tower Junction Road to Blacktail Ponds parking area
GPS Coordinates: 44.933088, -110.602760
Equipment: 4-weight system with floating and intermediate lines; midge, Speckled Dun, and damselfly patterns, and leech, scud, and streamer patterns
Nearest facilities and services: Mammoth (Wyoming), Mammoth Campground, Mammoth Hot Springs Hotel
Information resources: Yellowstone National Park, Albright Visitor Center; Blacktail Deer Creek USGS topographic map
Salmonids present: Brook and cutthroat trout

"Shaky Lake" is the common name for this pond that lies in a meadow about 7 miles east of Mammoth and a few hundred yards north of Mammoth–Tower Junction Road. It is not open to human visitation until around the first of July to protect nesting birds and immature vegetation. Yellowstone cutthroat trout have been reintroduced here to accompany introduced brook trout.

Once the area opens, walk close to the shoreline of the pond, and you will feel tremors beneath your feet. If you remain for a while at most locations along the shoreline, you will gradually submerge with the sphagnum moss as it bends downward due to your weight. A distinct benefit is that the moss harbors a good amount of aquatic insects, scuds, and leeches. Mud greets you if you try to wade other locations along the shoreline.

Midges make up most of the food for trout in Blacktail Pond, as well as in most stillwaters. Always bring a good assortment of patterns that imitate midge larvae, pupae, and adults.

GARDNER'S HOLE WATERS

The park's most extensive brook trout population resides here. They are typically aggressive when seeking food, so almost any fly pattern attracts their attention.

Access: Norris-Mammoth Road to Glen Creek trailhead or Bighorn Pass trailhead
GPS Coordinates: Glen Creek trailhead, 44.933235, -110.727792; Bighorn Pass trailhead, 44.887340, -110.735819
Equipment: 3-weight system with floating line; caddisfly, damselfly, BWO, PMD, and Yellow Sally patterns, and leech, soft-hackle, streamer, terrestrial, and traditional attractor patterns
Nearest facilities and services: Mammoth (Wyoming), Indian Creek Campground, North Entrance Ranger Station, Mammoth Hot Springs Hotel
Information resources: Yellowstone National Park, Albright Visitor Center; USGS Flow Station Gage 06191000; Mount Holmes and Quadrant Mountain USGS topographic maps
Salmonids present: Brook trout

Gardner's Hole hosts the Gardner River drainage above Rustic Falls and Sheepeater Canyon. It hosts the Gardner River itself and Fawn, Glen, Indian, Obsidian, Panther, Straight, and Winter Creeks, all formerly barren but now brook trout waters because of U.S. Fish Commission plantings over a hundred years ago. Such an exotic release seems odd by today's fisheries philosophies, but around the end of the 19th century, eastern states anglers had the commission's ear, and they held cutthroat trout in contempt. Brook trout were the favored salmonid, and they now thrive here to near overpopulation. None of these stream-dwelling brook trout are big, but all are aggressive feeders. The same goes for those in Grizzly Lake on Straight Creek and Beaver Lake on Obsidian Creek. In all, Gardner's Hole waters host the highest population of brook trout in Yellowstone National Park.

Small fish being the case here, most fly fishers move on to the Yellowstone River or the lower Gardner River to the north or go south to the Madison River drainage. Nevertheless, Gardner's Hole waters have something to offer. The small streams here are superb for entry-level fly fishers of all ages and heaven for light-tackle enthusiasts.

Exiting difficult-to-wade Beaver Lake, Obsidian Creek picks up Straight Creek, to which Winter Creek is a tributary, and flows for a few miles along Norris-Mammoth Road, where pullouts are numerous. Obsidian and Indian Creeks join the Gardner River at Indian Creek Campground, Panther Creek comes in just upstream, and Fawn Creek enters a ways above. The Bighorn Pass trailhead in the campground provides a point from which the Gardner River upstream can be accessed. Glen Creek comes into the river just above Rustic Falls, about 4 miles to the north, where a trailhead offers access to the northwest corner of Gardner's Hole. Indian Creek Campground, just off Norris-Mammoth Road, is an ideal base for fishing Gardner's Hole waters, with trails going to each nearby stream.

When the trout are on a feeding spree, almost any small pattern, dry or wet, will produce. Low-light conditions, particularly evenings, are the best times to encounter feeding trout here. It is the fast paced that can be realized on Gardner's

Brook trout offer lightweight tackle challenges in the upper Gardner River drainage. This part of the drainage was originally devoid of salmonids, but introduced brook trout, mostly small in size, make for fast fishing.

Hole streams that brings entry-level fly fishers into the sport in a quick, enjoyable, and memorable manner.

There is one exception to the small brook trout found in the meadow streams of Gardner's Hole. That is Fawn Lake, where brook trout range to nearly 2 pounds. Depending on weather, late June through September is the best time to fish this remote lake, which is a 5-mile hike from the Glen Creek trailhead on Norris-Mammoth Road. It is best fished by packing a floatation device and gear, as its shoreline is mostly marshy. Leech and damselfly nymph patterns seem to work best in this small pond. Gardner's Hole fishing enthusiast Mike Miller says the trail to the lake is "uphill both ways," especially when packing a floatation device.

LAMAR RIVER

The roadside reach of this river is one of the most visited streams in Yellowstone Park. However, a walk of about 3 miles upstream offers solitude and a better chance to view wildlife.

Access: Northeast Entrance Road to Lamar River trailhead
GPS Coordinates: 44.869218, -110.166238
Equipment: 4-weight system with floating and sink-tip lines; caddisfly, BWO, Golden Stone, PMD, and Yellow Sally patterns, and streamer, terrestrial insect, and traditional attractor patterns
Nearest facilities and services: Cooke City (Montana), Slough Creek Campground, Northeast Entrance Ranger Station, Roosevelt Lodge
Information resources: Yellowstone National Park, USGS Flow Station Gage 06188000; Opal Creek USGS topographic map
Salmonids present: Cutthroat and cuttbow trout

This is the major stream in the park's northeast corner, and its drainage features some of the most scenic streams in the Greater Yellowstone Area. Some of the best waters in this part of the park—the Lamar River, Slough Creek, and Soda Butte Creek—are essentially roadside and therefore have been major media subjects for decades. It's a situation similar to the Madison River drainage upstream of the park's west entrance, and the same crowding through much of the season can be expected because of nearby roads.

It is possible to escape the crowds by venturing up the river through its beautiful meadow, but a quicker way is to use the Lamar River Trail. On ascending the trail, company will be reduced to mostly hikers, photographers, and wildlife viewers. A roadside parking lot on the Northeast Entrance Road at the bridge over Soda Butte Creek, about a half mile above the confluence with the river, gives access to the trailhead. It is also possible to use the horse trail ford across the river below the confluence, but as with so many places in the Greater Yellowstone Area, early-season runoff determines whether fording streams is perilous or not. Normally runoff abates here soon after the first of July, thus from this time of year into the autumn months (when the crowds recede), venturing upstream in the Lamar River Valley is safest.

A good day-trip candidate for fishing this area is to walk the trail a little more than 3 miles to the Cache Creek crossing, then follow the creek to its confluence with the river about a half mile below. Cache Creek also offers fishing for Yellowstone cut-throat trout and the occasional cuttbow. Lightweight tackle is the name of the game

The roadside sections of the Lamar are some of the most popular fly fishing destinations in the park. Upper reaches offer much more tranquility. JOHN JURACEK PHOTO

here. Two primitive campsites near the Cache Creek crossing offer a base of operations for overnight stays to explore the river and creek above. The creek itself makes a good alternative to fish if the river becomes discolored from the effects of heavy upstream thunderstorms. The upper Lamar River is another small-stream paradise.

PELICAN CREEK

Pelican Creek is on the rebound as cutthroat trout populations in Yellowstone Lake improve. Plan to fish here at the mid-July opening for fast action from ravenous post-spawning trout.

Access: East Entrance Road to Pelican Creek trailhead
GPS Coordinates: 44.559840, -110.318346
Equipment: 4-weight system with floating line; caddisfly, PMD, and Yellow Sally patterns, and soft-hackle, streamer, terrestrial insect, and traditional attractor patterns
Nearest facilities and services: West Yellowstone (Montana), Bridge Bay and Fishing Bridge Campgrounds, Lake Lodge
Information resources: Yellowstone National Park, Lake Village Ranger Station and Fishing Bridge Visitor Center; Lake Butte and Mount Chittenden USGS topographic maps
Salmonids present: Cutthroat trout

Prior to its closure because of the whirling disease and lake trout crises that devastated Yellowstone Lake's cutthroat trout population, this creek held a spawning run second only to the Yellowstone River above the lake. On its annual July 15 opening and for a few weeks after, it was also a leading candidate for introducing entry-level fly fishers to the joys of finding, hooking, playing, and releasing trout. Post-spawning cutthroats in the creek numbered in the many thousands while heading back to Yellowstone Lake, and they were ravenous enough to take any wet fly offered along with many dry patterns. Certainly their energy levels were low after the rigors of spawning, and upon being hooked the resulting fight was not up to the best of their ability. But with dozens of fish responding to passing flies in a day, the neophyte fly fisher learned quickly from the concentrated experience. For the experienced fly fisher, just being there to view the surroundings and the fish and to offer a variety of patterns was a wonderful experience.

Yellowstone Park's efforts to restore cutthroat populations in Yellowstone Lake and related waters appear to be successful, and springtime spawning runs into its tributaries are improving. While its spawning run remains a shadow of that in the mid-20th century, Pelican Creek is again open for fishing. The season begins on July 15, as in the past, and the country surrounding it is as beautiful as it's ever been. But perhaps more than anywhere else in the Greater Yellowstone Area, the chance for encountering a grizzly bear is good, and even better for buffalo. Though not as good as it once was, the creek is still worth a visit.

Pelican Creek is mostly a meadow stream. Its first mile above the lake remains closed to fishing to protect migratory waterfowl. Above the closure, the meadow through which it flows is large enough to host many visiting fly fishers without crowding. So before the end of July, walk the approximately 2-mile trail into the meadow, where the creek will appear as a smaller version of Slough Creek in its upper meadows. Higher up in the meadow, tributary Raven Creek also hosts post-spawning cutthroat. Take a variety of patterns in small and medium sizes. Trout ranging upward to a bit more than 20 inches will greet you in response to your flies. Play them quickly and revive them thoroughly, for they deserve another chance to help reestablish the once-famed population in the lake.

SLOUGH CREEK AND MCBRIDE LAKE

Slough Creek is one of the most visited streams in the park, but anglers can find solitude and easier trout in the wooded sections. McBride Lake, nearby, offers a true wilderness fly fishing experience.

Access: Northeast Entrance Road to Slough Creek Campground Road trailhead
GPS Coordinates: 44.943578, -110.308021
Equipment: 5- or 6-weight system with floating and sink-tip lines; caddisfly, BWO, Golden Stone, Brown Drake, Gray Drake, Green Drake, Mahogany Dun, PMD, Trico, and Yellow Sally patterns, and streamer, terrestrial insect, and traditional attractor patterns for Slough Creek; damselfly, midge, and Speckled Dun patterns, and leech, scud, and streamer patterns for McBride Lake
Nearest facilities and services: Cooke City (Montana), Slough Creek Campground, Northeast Entrance Ranger Station, Roosevelt Lodge
Information resources: Yellowstone National Park; Lamar Canyon USGS topographic map
Salmonids present: Cutthroat and cuttbow trout

The meadow reaches of Slough Creek are equaled in beauty and expanse only by the meadow reaches of Fall River Basin streams, Idaho's upper Blackfoot River, and the Henry's Fork coursing through Harriman State Park. The large trout—whether the cuttbows in the lowest meadow or the Yellowstone cutthroat of the first and second meadows above the campground—combine with the breathtaking scenery to lure large numbers of fly fishers. In season, I have counted nearly 50 vehicles parked at the Slough Creek trailhead just below the Slough Creek Camp-ground. True, some of these represent hikers and photographers, while others are clients of the Silver Tip Ranch located outside the park (ranch reservations featuring superb backcountry fishing on Slough Creek can be made through the Yellowstone Park Foundation). I have also counted dozens of vehicles parked in the pullouts on benches above the creek in the meadow reach below the campground. While gearing up, walking to the water, casting, and playing then releasing fish, or even while imbibing a favored beverage at the end of a day of fishing, I have heard languages from all corners of this planet. Thus the popularity of the creek in these meadows rivals that of the Firehole and Madison Rivers, and for good reason. Slough Creek is in magnificent surroundings, is easily approached, and hosts strikingly beautiful large trout.

I am not going to add to the expansive available information on fishing Slough Creek; rather, I offer an alternative to fishing the relatively crowded meadow reaches. If you walk up the Slough Creek Trail to the top of the first meadow above the campground, you will observe that the creek upstream flows out of a timbered area. At this point the trail is about a quarter mile southeast of the creek. By midsummer it will be easy to find a trail made by anglers over to the creek. Follow this trail to the creek and proceed to fish upstream where it leaves the timber. The character of the stream in the timbered reach is much the same as that in the meadow: deep holes at bends and deep runs punctuated by short riffle stretches.

This character continues, with a small waterfall included, for about a mile to the second meadow above the campground. One significant difference here makes this part of the creek more forgiving than that in the meadow: the timber that provides an overhead background, which helps hide a person from view of trout in the water below. Yes, the timber means that backcasts must be performed more carefully, but my experience is more hits from trout, as large as those in the meadow reaches. Present the same patterns used in the meadow reaches. Certainly you will encounter fewer anglers in this section than you will out in the beautiful meadow reaches.

Back at the downstream end of the timbered reach, the creek can be crossed safely only after runoff, usually sometime in early July. After crossing the creek and then proceeding in a slightly northwest direction for about half a mile, the exploring fly fisher will arrive at another of the park's lakes hosting solely cutthroat trout. This is McBride Lake: long, narrow, partly bordered by timber, and not very deep, but hosting Yellowstone cutthroat growing to around 15 or 16 inches. In season they

By the 1980s Slough Creek, a classic meadow stream, was "discovered" by the fly fishing media. Now it is a destination in demand. JOHN JURACEK PHOTO

McBride Lake is a short walk from Slough Creek's first meadow above the campground. Consider a visit to encounter cutthroat trout ranging to moderate size, but eager to take any fly pattern resembling a leech.

will take with gusto almost any wet offering. Such activity goes on into the summer until an algae bloom takes over, making the lake appear to be made of pea soup, and slowing down the fishing action.

TROUT LAKE

A former hatchery site, Trout Lake hosts some of the largest cuttbows in the park, rivaled in size only by the cuttbows of Fall River Basin streams and lower Slough Creek.

Access: Northeast Entrance Road to Trout Lake trailhead
GPS Coordinates: 44.892152, -110.123169
Equipment: 5- or 6-weight system with floating and intermediate lines; damselfly, midge, and Speckled Dun patterns, and leech, scud, and streamer patterns
Nearest facilities and services: Cooke City (Montana), Northeast Entrance Ranger Station, Pebble Creek Campground, Roosevelt Lodge
Information resources: Yellowstone National Park; Mount Hornaday USGS topographic map
Salmonids present: Cutthroat and cuttbow trout

Fishing season on the lake opens on June 15 each year to protect migrating waterfowl and resident cutthroat trout that concentrate in the small north-side inlet creek to spawn. Few park waters offer fish watching of the quality this creek offers,

Trout Lake was a park fish hatchery. Now it offers an excellent chance to encounter very large cutthroat and cutthroat rainbow hybrid trout seasonally.

and at times fish-watching enthusiasts and photographers nearly equal the number of anglers plying the lake. Visits by park rangers are frequent during spawning times in order to minimize abuse of the fish present. Only river otters and other wildlife are not denied fish in the creek at this time!

Trout Lake, formed by damming the inlet creek in the early 20th century, is a mere six-tenths of a mile from the Northeast Entrance Road and therefore can be heavily fished, particularly just after its opening. Up to the mid-20th century, Trout Lake was a park fish hatchery. Formerly named "Fish Lake" by locals, its past includes fame as a source of table fare for miners residing just outside the park. Rumors of large trout in nearby Buck and Shrimp Lakes are groundless, though over the years "Johnny Appleseed" (clandestine) attempts have been made to introduce Trout Lake fish into these lakes.

There is a definite strategy for fishing this lake so rich in aquatic insects, scuds, and leeches. Shoreline fishing can be productive because much of the west and north sides are bordered by sloping meadows. Carrying a lightweight floatation device up the short, steep trail, however, gives access to the entire lake. For a few weeks after opening, fishing either way can be superb, with large cutthroat and cuttbow being caught on a fairly regular basis. Presenting subsurface patterns is the surest way to successful fishing. However, as summer moves into July, an algae bloom and warming waters slow fishing enough that visiting nearby Soda Butte and Slough Creeks and the Lamar River can be more enjoyable. By autumn, atmospheric cooling and decreasing sunlight begin cooling the lake and clearing its algae bloom. Thus by the last weeks of October, excellent fishing can be experienced through presenting leech and scud patterns in the lake. During this time the number of anglers in this part of the park decreases rapidly, so solitude, not only on the lake but on nearby streams, is quite possible.

UPPER YELLOWSTONE RIVER

This is the most isolated region in the park. A visit here to fish the river and its tributaries takes planning, preparation, and timing.

Access: East Entrance Road to Thorofare trailhead
GPS Coordinates: 44.505710, -110.275437
Equipment: 4-weight system with floating line: caddisfly life cycle, soft-hackle, streamer, terrestrial insect, and traditional attractor patterns
Nearest facilities and services: West Yellowstone (Montana), Bridge Bay and Fishing Bridge Campgrounds, Lake Lodge
Information resources: Yellowstone National Park, Lake Village Ranger Station and Fishing Bridge Visitor Center; Badger Peak, The Trident, and Trail Lake USGS topographic maps
Salmonids present: Cutthroat trout

The upper Yellowstone River's distance from any human population center provides protection for trout. Most of this part of the river is in Wyoming's Bridger-Teton National Forest, with the downstream portion within the park. Time also protects trout during the spawn, much of which takes place when runoff and remaining snow make human travel to this part of the river difficult, if not dangerous. Here the river is relatively inhospitable. It offers little in the way of food items compared to the lake, limited overhead cover, and a short growing season, but offers good spawning habitat. Now that the cutthroat population of Yellowstone Lake is improving due to

The upper Yellowstone River is the most remote large water in the Greater Yellowstone Area. Fish here from when runoff is waning to around the end of July. Resident cutthroat will take nearly any fly pattern presented.

Jackson Hole outfitters offer pack trains to visit the upper Yellowstone River. Reaching remote country through the services of such outfitters surely provides more physical comforts than backpacking.

ongoing and effective lake trout eradication efforts, more cutthroat trout are entering the river for springtime spawning, then returning to the lake relatively quickly.

Timing a visit here is therefore of major importance. That visit should take place during the peak of the trout's return to Yellowstone Lake, and the river within the park provides the best chances for improved fishing. Runoff can greatly interfere with June fishing, making early to mid July the most practical time to plan a visit.

All the above comments also apply to Thorofare Creek, the major tributary to the river above the lake. I made a trip there in early July back in the late 1970s when I was strong as an ox and just as smart. (I am not that strong anymore, but I am just as smart!) I left the Heart Lake trailhead and packed over to the southeast arm of Yellowstone Lake into Thorofare country. The trip was an odyssey, but luckily I had good weather. Mosquito repellent was a major necessity, and I grew to dislike vacuum-dried meals. My only human contact was horsebound rangers on two occasions. I hit the nail on the head and caught dozens of ravenous cutthroat trout, jaded somewhat by spawning efforts. They took any fly pattern offered, whether presented deep or just below the surface. They were exact copies of the Pelican Creek post-spawners that I would soon come to know. I fished there a day and a half before returning to the trailhead. I've never repeated this 60-odd-mile round-trip, and have found that a pack trip using the same route, from the south entrance or from the Turpin Meadows trailhead south of the park, is a much easier way to experience this country.

By the end of July, most adult fish, along with many juveniles, will have returned from the inhospitable river to the lake, and an August visit might end up being a sight-seeing trip. So even though spawning run numbers are improving, think hard about scheduling a fishing trip to this remote fishery, even in early July. If you do, be sure to consider the alternative of using one of the numerous outfitters that provide pack trips to the Thorofare country. If you choose a pack trip, I know from experience that your feet will surely thank you!

PART 2

EASTERN IDAHO

Nearly all the attention here goes to the hallowed fisheries of the Henry's Fork, Henry's Lake, and Island Park Reservoir, making these waters major players in the regional economy. Famed fly shops and guide services are located along US Highway 20, recently honored in the media as "The Fly Fishing Highway." The highway continues on to West Yellowstone, Montana, and its similar array of famed fly shops and guide services.

Sunset in Teton Basin features alpenglow on the Teton Range. Scenery can be distracting in Teton Basin. Concentrate on that drifting dry fly, and enjoy the scenery when fishing for the day is done.

As with West Yellowstone, numerous iconic personalities are part of the local fly fishing lore of Island Park. Here the Henry's Fork is famed for trout responding to its early-season progression of stonefly emergences, a season-long progression of mayfly emergences, and mid- and late-season terrestrial insects. Also present is easy and abundant access to some of the best and most scenic waters inhabited by salmonids. Fly fishers from around the world assemble to enjoy these waters, and numerous works have been published on fly fishing here. Of course, the array of fly patterns developed for all fly fishing situations on the Henry's Fork by such tiers as the House of Harrop, Mike and Sheralee Lawson, Bing Lempke, and Andy Puyans has no equal.

Henry's Lake is famed for producing large brook, Yellowstone cutthroat, and cuttbow trout. In the early season, it competes little with the Henry's Fork as a fly fishing destination, and its once-famed damselfly emergence has diminished. Nevertheless, it has numerous enthusiasts. Most regional fly shops offer guide services for it, and the number of fly patterns developed for Henry's Lake by such tiers as Bill Schiess exceeds those of most stillwaters. In the late season, it is likely the most visited fishery in Island Park, as most of its resident trout move to shorelines. During this time, wading shorelines can be just as productive as fishing from a boat, and thus autumn visits to the lake can exceed those to the Henry's Fork.

Island Park Reservoir is best fished by boating, and its northwestern shoreline is a major destination. Here submerged springs act, as in Henry's Lake, as refuges for trout from warming waters. Thus when reservoir waters drop and therefore warm through irrigation demands, boat-borne anglers flock to these springs to present an array of wet patterns, although not as extensive as those developed for Henry's Lake, to entice the trophy-size trout finding refuge there.

As of late, the South Fork reach (from Palisades Dam to the Henry's Fork confluence) has surpassed the Henry's Fork with respect to fly fishing visitation. More than the Henry's Fork below Island Park Dam, this reach is a major tailwater fishery and cutthroat trout stronghold. The same is true for its lesser-known tributaries, which we will discuss, some for the first time in print. Regional shops offer guide services to these locations. So beyond the two storied eastern Idaho rivers within the Greater Yellowstone Area, are waters available that offer a combination of tranquility and quality not found on the Henry's Fork or the South Fork reach? The answer is yes, and in some cases these are easily accessed, while others require more time and effort to enjoy.

Island Park Area and the Henry's Fork Drainage

ALDOUS LAKE

Large cutthroat and a great Callibaetis hatch are the draw on this small upland lake.

Access: Interstate 15 and Clark County Road A-2 to Ching Creek Road to trailhead
GPS Coordinates: 44.508324, -111.841993
Equipment: 5-weight system with floating and intermediate lines; damselfly, dragonfly, midge, and Speckled Dun patterns, and leech, scud, snail, and streamer patterns
Nearest facilities and services: Dubois (Idaho), USFS Stoddard Creek Campground, Al Taylor rental cabin, Eagle Ridge Ranch
Information resources: Caribou-Targhee National Forest, Dubois Ranger District Office; Antelope Valley USGS topographic map
Salmonids present: Cutthroat trout

Though no more than a tarn, Aldous Lake is a place of legend for some local anglers. It sits on a Centennial Mountains bench on the Pacific side of the Continental Divide about 20 miles north and a bit east of Kilgore, a tiny ranching community offering no services other than a convenience store and small RV park. Roads beyond here are mostly improved gravel at best, including the route to the lake that begins just west of Kilgore and winds through beautiful meadows and timbered uplands to climb within 1.25 miles of the lake. Melting deep snows dictate that most

Snail shells, such as these along the Aldous Lake shoreline, are an indicator of the dissolved bicarbonate richness of a body of water. This presence speaks not only to the rich mineral content of the water, but also to the size of resident salmonids.

years the upper end of this road cannot be opened until early June. Winters are so severe here that hardy ranchers and their stock move out soon after the first hint of the oncoming season. As soon as roads permit, local fly fishers in the know (few in number) make preparations to hike the 1.25 miles up to Aldous Lake to encounter Yellowstone cutthroat ranging to around 2 feet in length. Within the lake major springs create a continuous inflow of quality water, which results in trout being able to hold over for a lifetime.

Natural spawning is extremely limited in the outlet creek, so the Idaho Department of Fish and Game occasionally supplements the population through releasing fingerlings. The consistent inflow from springs also permits Aldous to host an excellent array of aquatic life-forms because of abundant weed beds and the high bicarbonate content. Imitating these and presenting them on intermediate lines makes for good early-season fishing as soon as the lake can be reached. As the end of June approaches, the most interesting fishing begins as aquatic insects start to mature. Now a floating line is just the ticket for the most fun. This insect activity also provides good indicator fishing because of emerging insects. An advantage of Aldous's small size and surrounding timber is that wind barely ruffles most of its surface, thus the dry fly fishing lasts longer into the day than on larger lakes where wave action hinders the vision of both fly fisher and fish near the surface. Add to these the terrestrial insects falling from downed timber projecting into the lake, and surface fishing here can be excellent.

The lake is almost totally bordered by timber, with a shoreline either muddy, steep, or backed up by a slope. Thus the visitor must possess superb roll-casting skills if equipped only to wade, or be willing to pack a portable floatation device up the trail to the lake. Packing one is the most practical choice because it easily allows access to the entire lake.

About 25 years ago my wife, Carol, and I spent a late July weekend camping and fishing here. A single sedan bearing a Utah license plate and rental car identity was parked at the trailhead when we arrived. We geared up, then hiked to the lake. On arrival we observed a single fly fisher float-tubing out in the lake. Speckled Duns were emerging, and he was doing well catching responsive cutthroat trout. We set up camp, and I launched the float tube with fly fishing equipment on board then paddled out into the lake, making sure not to crowd the visitor. He greeted me with a decidedly Bronx accent. "This is the best trout fishing I have experienced anywhere!" he exclaimed while playing a nice cutthroat.

"Glad to hear that, but how did you find this place?"

"I was fishing the Henry's Fork in Harriman State Park and from Wood Road 16." He continued, "I did not come from New York to be among as many fly fishers as I see in the Catskills. So yesterday I stopped at Mike Lawson's Henry's Fork Anglers to relate this situation. A shop employee recommended Aldous Lake, so I got directions, rented a float tube and fins, strapped them to my pack, and here I am at this great place." He left after an hour or so, complaining about having to return the float tube and fins then drive back to Salt Lake City to catch a morning flight to LaGuardia.

BUFFALO RIVER

A beautiful lightweight tackle stream with prolific mayfly emergences, upstream tranquility, and small, eager trout.

Access: US Highway 20 at Buffalo River Campground
GPS Coordinates: 44.427016, -110.370207
Equipment: 3- or 4-weight system with floating line; caddisfly, BWO, PMD, Golden Stone, and Yellow Sally patterns, and terrestrial insect and traditional attractor patterns
Nearest facilities and services: Ashton (Idaho), USFS Buffalo River Campground, Pond's Lodge
Information resources: Caribou-Targhee National Forest, Island Park Ranger Station; Island Park and Island Park Dam USGS topographic maps
Salmonids present: Brook and rainbow trout

The Buffalo River is that beautiful stream one passes over on US Highway 20 between Pond's Lodge and the Island Park Ranger Station. The Buffalo River Bridge is the dividing line between private downstream shoreline and public land upstream. The only practical access downstream is by launching a boat, so we will discuss fishing the river upstream. Here the river is wide with a low gradient and optimal temperature, but shallow enough to lack overhead cover for large fish.

In 1937 a power dam was constructed at the Buffalo River's confluence with the Henry's Fork near the top of Box Canyon to provide the prime contractor with the electrical power needed for building the nearby Island Park Dam. At this time Yellowstone cutthroat trout were the major salmonid in the Henry's Fork, and large numbers of them moved into the Buffalo River to spawn in upstream and tributary gravels. The fish ladder constructed with this dam proved ineffective in allowing this run to continue, so for decades the Idaho Department of Fish and Game released hatchery-reared rainbow trout into the river to provide a put-and-take fishery. However, near the end of the 20th century, efforts spearheaded by the Henry's Fork Foundation resulted in an effective fish ladder over the dam, and now an early spring run of cuttbow trout passes to once again spawn in upper reaches of the river and some tributaries. After spawning, these fish soon return to the Henry's Fork, and the Buffalo River functions as a nursery for their progeny.

Small brook trout also populate the river, and along with the juvenile hybrids provide sport for fly fishers equipped with lightweight gear. Small patterns for midges and mayflies and terrestrial insect patterns bring responses from these. The full-service Buffalo River Campground, on the north bank just above the bridge, provides a base for fishing here and for joining the crowds fishing the Henry's Fork. Tributary Elk Creek forms the east boundary of the campground and also hosts small brook trout. Not far above and on the opposite side, Tom's Creek, hosting beautiful spawning gravel, enters. It can be fished in isolation by taking Chick Creek Road east off US Highway 20 to the old railroad grade, then walking about a half mile up the grade to the creek. Small brook trout rule the roost here, and they are excellent eating. Staying on the road eventually takes one to Chick Creek and its hosted small brook trout, also good in the frying pan.

HARRIMAN FISH POND

Great damselfly fishing on a piece of water overshadowed by the adjacent Harriman State Park reach of the Henry's Fork.

Access: Mesa Falls Scenic Byway to Fish Pond access road
GPS Coordinates: 44.319415, -110.426624
Equipment: 5- or 6-weight system with floating and intermediate lines; damselfly, dragonfly, midge, and Speckled Dun patterns, and leech, scud, snail, and streamer patterns
Nearest facilities and services: Ashton (Idaho), USFS Buffalo River Campground, Pond's Lodge
Information resources: Caribou-Targhee National Forest, Island Park Ranger Station; Last Chance USGS topographic map
Salmonids present: Brook and rainbow trout

"Many of those big fish pictures you see credited to the Henry's Fork actually came from the Fish Pond!" Mike Lawson offered with a smile.

Most folks travel unknowingly by it on the upper end of the Mesa Falls Scenic Byway, where you get a glimpse of the pond through the jack pine forest as you pass by. You can also see it looking north from the famed Wood Road 16 access to the lower Harriman East property. That small meadow stream that parallels the lower road is the Fish Pond's outlet.

Pontoon boating is an excellent way to fish many Greater Yellowstone waters having road access. When fishing with friends, a good strategy is for everyone to try something different until the taking pattern is found.

Harriman Fish Pond visits are miniscule compared to those at the nearby Henry's Fork. However, the pond hosts rainbow trout growing to sizes just as large. Fishing from a boat is the best way to encounter them.

The Harriman family dammed Osborne Spring's outlet decades ago and released rainbow trout to create a place for Railroad Ranch guests to fish. The resulting pond also served as a supply for watering stock. It is about 10 feet at its deepest and surrounded by forest, except for the southeast corner and at the dam. The well-signed access road on the Mesa Falls Scenic Byway leads to the north end of the pond, where a parking area and primitive boat launch are located for nonmotorized boats. Deep mud greets anyone trying to wade most of the shoreline. This makes the dam about the only practical place to fish from land.

The Harrimans' rainbow trout grew to legendary size, and brook trout entered from the inlet creek. Stories abound of rainbows exceeding 10 pounds being taken from the pond, which hosts a rich number and variety of food forms. Some ancient, grainy photos of these fish exist in private collections and in Dean H. Green's *History of Island Park*. Now the rainbow trout released by the Idaho Department of Fish and Game that become holdovers grow nearly as large as those in the Harriman days, but other than local anglers, few fly fishers know of their existence.

Significant constraints stand in the way of encountering these unusually large Harriman Fish Pond rainbow trout. Beginning in the early season, there has to be holdovers that survived through the winter. They can be counted on being present as long as the pond is kept at or near full pool through the winter. Plenty of food is available to these fish, which can gorge on pupae forming early-season midge swarms. If you arrive at the pond and experience midges filling your eyes, ears, and nose but see no rise forms, fish are full of midge pupa, so depart to another fishing location. If there are rise forms, present midge pupa patterns under an indicator or small leech, dragonfly nymph, or snail patterns using a floating line. You may encounter rainbow trout in sizes equivalent to the largest in the nearby Henry's Fork. Fishing these patterns will be an effective strategy for most of the spring months, but on doing so you will notice the advancing submerged vegetation. This will dictate channels for fishing all your patterns under an indicator until Speckled Duns and damselflies emerge to mate and lay eggs on the surface.

As spring turns into summer, another constraint arrives in the form of hatchery catchables released by the Idaho Department of Fish and Game. Getting a fly pattern past these 12- to 15-inch-long fish to the large holdovers becomes nearly impossible. It is true these fish grow quickly, but by autumn they are mostly reduced to the dinner table through family fishing. Those remaining will become holdovers on surviving the winter.

Returning to fish the pond in autumn, these survivors, ranging up to a few pounds, can be encountered as well as those holding over from previous years. Autumn is surely the best time to fish this pond, now that most angler visits are past and fish of larger size make up a good portion of the population. Weed beds are decreasing and most fly fishers are traveling north to Henry's Lake or to intercept Hebgen Lake brown trout in the upper Madison River. Little do most of them know that the Harriman Fish Pond holds trout as large as they will encounter in either of those iconic locations.

HENRY'S LAKE OUTLET IN THE FLAT RANCH PRESERVE

Stellar fishing can be had after big springtime water releases from Henry's Lake. The outlet offers solitude and fishing to many of the same hatches as on the Henry's Fork.

Access: US Highway 20 to Flat Ranch Preserve
GPS Coordinates: 44.569625, -110.366236
Equipment: 5- or 6-weight system with floating and sink-tip lines; damselfly, flav, Gray Drake, Green Drake, PMD, and Speckled Dun patterns, and leech, streamer, and terrestrial insect patterns
Nearest facilities and services: Ashton (Idaho), USFS Upper Coffee Pot Campground, Mack's Inn Resort
Information resources: The Nature Conservancy, Flat Ranch Preserve Visitor Center; USGS Flow Station Gage 13039500; Big Springs USGS topographic map
Salmonids present: Brook, cuttbow, cutthroat, and rainbow trout

Does the Henry's Fork begin at the outlet of Henry's Lake or at Big Springs? It's a subject of friendly debate that has been going on over pitchers of beer for decades. United States Geological Survey maps indicate the origin at the outlet of Henry's Lake, but most fishing maps produced in the Greater Yellowstone Area show the beginning at Big Springs and name the reach from the lake down to the springs Henry's Lake Outlet. It's a situation similar to that of the Snake River in Idaho, where the local community, anglers included, refers to the river between Palisades Dam and the Henry's Fork as "the South Fork." Above and below this reach, it is

Fly fishing quality in the Flat Ranch section of Henry's Lake Outlet depends on water management in the lake above. Regardless of this management, the early season offers the best time for a visit. JOHN JURACEK PHOTO

known as the Snake River. To angling visitors not "in the know," this causes some confusion because in Idaho alone there are several South Forks. For our purposes, I'll adopt the Henry's Lake Outlet version because this part of the Henry's Fork is generally overlooked, but can offer some excellent fishing on a conditional basis.

In August 1995 the Nature Conservancy obtained property along Henry's Lake Outlet just east of US Highway 20 and converted it into a working cattle ranch to be managed in a manner that minimizes environmental impact. This became the Flat Ranch Preserve. Over the years the stream and its riparian zone has recovered to a near-natural condition, though work remains to bring it totally back. When viewed from the ranch visitor center just off the highway, the trace of the stream at its upper end appears as a line of willows about half a mile to the east. Because of this abundant overhead cover, the best fishing the stream offers is along these well-willowed reaches. The surroundings in the spacious meadow are pastoral and beautiful, particularly when early-season wildflowers are in bloom. Waterfowl, shorebirds, hawks, ospreys, and sandhill cranes flourish. Antelope, deer, and moose frequent the willow patches and meadows, and mink, muskrat, and beaver populate the riparian zone. The stream itself almost begs to be fished, and the ranch property now stands in contrast to the riparian zones immediately above and below it, where overgrazing has ruined stream banks and silted in runs and holes.

Angling on the stream within the ranch is restricted to artificial flies and lures. Catch-and-release fishing and barbless hooks are suggested. On occasion, anglers and recreationists in rafts or canoes float through to the Henry's Fork below. To monitor usage and impact on its property, the Nature Conservancy asks that all

The Nature Conservancy's Flat Ranch Preserve visitor center is the jump-off point for fishing the Henry's Lake Outlet section of the Henry's Fork. Chat with the attendant to obtain fishing information, and at the end of fishing, fill out the preserve log at the center to help conservancy staff evaluate their management of the river and its salmonid population.

visitors, anglers included, check in at the visitor center and on leaving relate their experience in the center's log book. Superb fishing can be enjoyed here, but only conditionally as it, like many Greater Yellowstone Area streams, is subject to irrigation diversion.

As a storage reservoir, Henry's Lake is the highest water source in the Henry's Fork drainage. Normally water is kept there as long as possible, and the flow into Henry's Lake Outlet rarely exceeds much more than 100 cubic feet per second, which flushes some trout out of the lake. These releases are enough to sustain good fishing through much of the season. Flows are usually reduced after midsummer, when agricultural demands for water decrease. Because of these reduced flows, many fish move downstream through the outlet to its confluence with the Henry's Fork, slowing fishing success in the outlet.

When dry winters force water managers to use more Henry's Lake water for the upcoming growing season, flows out of the lake can exceed 300 cubic feet per second into the late spring. When this happens, many thousands of trout from lake shallows are flushed into the outlet. These are mainly cutthroat ranging up to around 5 pounds, but brook trout and trophy-size cuttbows are also present. After equilibrating in the stream, these displaced trout begin to seek food similar to what was present in the lake, so presenting leech, streamer, and even damselfly nymph patterns bring the most responses. On adjusting to their new environment, they begin to feed on aquatic insects which, with the higher flow at optimal temperatures, become active in huge numbers. Mayflies, midges, caddisflies, crane flies, and even stoneflies blown in from canyon reaches below are available.

As the season progresses, terrestrial insects become available, and these provide excellent dry fly fishing. Later in the summer, flows out of the lake recede, causing water in the outlet to warm. Most trout now move downstream into the Henry's Fork, where cooler water and better overhead cover prevail. The result is that even during years when high water prevails in the early season, fishing slacks off here after midsummer.

So what is the key to encountering the superb fishing that the stream in the Flat Ranch Preserve can offer? The best way is to follow springtime water flow reports, available online, from the United States Geological Survey's stream gauge just below the Henry's Lake Dam. If a large increase in flow, up to at least 150 cubic feet per second, occurs and is sustained for at least a week during springtime, excellent fishing can result in the Flat Ranch portion of the outlet, perhaps extending into midsummer. Thus this recovering meadow stream offers a less-crowded alternative to the nearby Madison River and Henry's Fork.

HORSESHOE LAKE

This is the only eastern Idaho water, still or moving, that hosts Montana grayling. There is a good chance for solitude on this lake just outside Yellowstone National Park's west boundary.

Access: Mesa Falls Scenic Byway to Cave Falls Road to Horseshoe Lake Road
GPS Coordinates: 44.104403, -111.153578
Equipment: 4-weight system with floating line; damselfly, midge, and Speckled Dun patterns, and leech and scud patterns
Nearest facilities and services: Ashton (Idaho), USFS Warm River and Cave Falls Campgrounds, Three Rivers Lodge
Information resources: Caribou-Targhee National Forest, Ashton Ranger Station; Bechler Falls USGS topographic map
Salmonids present: Rainbow trout and Montana grayling

Horseshoe Lake Road leaves Cave Falls Road near the east end of the Church of Jesus Christ of Latter-day Saints Girls Camp to end at the northwest corner of the lake. The Yellowstone National Park west boundary is only a few hundred yards to the east of the lake. There are only primitive campsites here and undeveloped facilities for launching nonmotorized boats. Where the road ends, an unmaintained trail descends into Robinson Creek Canyon at one of its deepest locations. The lake is surrounded by a jack pine forest and has a muddy shoreline, thus it is only practical to fish from a floatation device or a small boat such as a canoe or kayak.

The grayling population in Horseshoe Lake must be supplemented each year from stocks in Montana hatcheries. This is because the lake has no perennial inlet or outlet holding spawning habitat. The same applies to rainbow trout that are also present and replenished from stocks in Idaho hatcheries. The State of Idaho Juvenile Detention Facility maintains a summer camp, not open to the public, on the east arm of the lake; therefore, fishing is mostly confined to the larger west arm of the lake.

Tranquil Horseshoe Lake is eastern Idaho's only water body hosting grayling. They reliably respond to the lake's Speckled Dun emergence, but you will need a nonmotorized watercraft to enjoy them.

Few salmonid species can match the beauty of grayling. Once native to several streams in the upper Missouri River drainage, they now inhabit only a few waters in the Greater Yellowstone Area, where they respond reliably to aquatic insect emergences.

Fishing on Horseshoe Lake begins when the road accessing it becomes passable, usually by the middle of June. With midges emerging, good dry fly fishing results as both grayling and rainbow trout feed on the surface. Surface fishing improves greatly by the middle of July. At this time the best strategy is to present Speckled Dun emerger, dun, and soft-hackle patterns in front of lily pad beds during afternoon hours. Small patterns presented on lightweight tackle work best here, as the grayling seldom reach 14 inches and the rainbow trout 17 inches. Good surface fishing extends well into September, the whole time with a good chance of solitude.

LOWER FALL FIVER

The mid to late June Giant Stonefly emergence on the river downstream of the Kirkham Bridge is fairly crowded; afterwards, solitude can be found with fish rising to dense evening caddisfly emergences.

Access: Mesa Falls Scenic Byway to Cave Falls Road or US Highway 20 to Ashton–Flagg Ranch Road to trailhead for Boone Creek confluence
GPS Coordinates: 44.055704, -111.117300
Equipment: 5-weight system with floating and sink-tip lines; caddisfly, BWO, Giant Stone, Golden Stone, PMD, Trico, and Yellow Sally patterns, and streamer, terrestrial insect, and traditional attractor patterns
Nearest facilities and services: Ashton (Idaho), USFS Cave Falls and Warm River Campgrounds, Three Rivers Lodge
Information resources: Caribou-Targhee National Forest, Ashton Ranger Station; Ashton Visitor Center; USGS Flow Station Gages 13046995 and 13047500; Ashton, Newdale, Warm River, Porcupine Lake, and Sheep Falls USGS topographic maps
Salmonids present: Cutthroat and rainbow trout and Rocky Mountain whitefish

Outside Yellowstone National Park, the Fall River has limited access as well as a somewhat reduced fishing season. It's akin to many Greater Yellowstone rivers that have upper reaches flowing through public land and lower reaches flowing through private land. After the Fall River leaves the park, it flows several miles through Caribou-Targhee National Forest, first in Wyoming, then into Idaho, but always in its remote canyon. Here it is beautiful to behold, but perilous for float fishing. There are no practical sites from which to launch or take out in this canyon, which hosts two major waterfalls and several dangerous rapids. There is limited walk-in access from both Cave Falls Road, paralleling the river on the north, and Ashton–Flagg Ranch Road, paralleling it on the south. From Cave Falls Road, it can be fished at Cave Falls Campground in Wyoming and from Steele Lake Road just inside the Idaho border. Any other access from Cave Falls Road in Idaho requires bushwhacking for a considerable distance.

From Ashton–Flagg Ranch Road, the Fall River can be accessed and fished by walking a gated road to the Boone Creek confluence 3 miles inside Idaho from the Wyoming border. The reward after a 1-mile walk to the river is a series of holes holding cuttbow trout large enough to rival the biggest in the Box Canyon of the Henry's Fork. These waters are above the several irrigation diversions, which

The lower Fall River can be fished by wading throughout the fishing season or by boating before and after the irrigation season. For miles above the US Highway 20 crossing, it has good access for boating and wading and a reliable summer evening caddisfly emergence.

The Idaho side of Ashton–Flagg Ranch Road features spectacular scenery as well as access to the lower Fall River and several quality small streams. Watching alpenglow advance on the Teton Range's west slopes from the road is an end-of-day event worth observing.

compromise the quality of the river farther west. At all these access points, wading can be perilous because of the high gradient and the slippery and rocky nature of the riverbed. During runoff, wading here is downright dangerous; only from late July into autumn can safe wading be done to enjoy large trout taking caddisfly, terrestrial insect, and traditional attractor patterns.

About 2 miles below the Boone Creek confluence, the Fall River leaves national forest land and proceeds through mostly private land to its Henry's Fork confluence. Access along this reach is limited but possible at any bridge and for a short length upstream from the village of Chester. From these access points, the visiting angler may wade legally by remaining within the high-water mark. A few miles after leaving national forest land, the river enters another nearly inaccessible canyon bordered by private land and dangerous enough in places to deny even kayakers safe passage. In addition, several irrigation diversions reduce the flow to a point that by midsummer, warm waters restrict trout activity to early morning spinner falls and late daytime caddisfly activity. The result is that the best fishing on the river below the canyon is when runoff is abating and irrigation diversion has yet to peak. At this time, Giant and Golden Stonefly adults mate and return to the river to lay eggs. Float-fishing to present dry stonefly patterns can be productive at this time, and for this weeklong event the lower Fall River has gained local fame.

ROBINSON CREEK
By Doug Gibson
Diverse hatches of Green Drakes, PMDs, caddisflies, Golden Stoneflies, and midges just after runoff make for interesting fishing to five species of salmonids.

Access: Mesa Falls Scenic Byway to Cave Falls Road to Robinson Creek Road
GPS Coordinates: 44.085394, -111.253989
Equipment: 4-weight system with floating line; caddisfly, PMD, Giant Stone, Golden Stone, Green Drake, and Yellow Sally patterns, and terrestrial insect and traditional attractor patterns
Nearest facilities and services: Ashton (Idaho), USFS Warm River Campground, Three Rivers Lodge
Information resources: Caribou-Targhee National Forest, Ashton Ranger Station; Warm River Butte USGS topographic map
Salmonids present: Brook, brown, cutthroat, and rainbow trout and Rocky Mountain whitefish

Robinson Creek is the most western major stream in Yellowstone National Park's Cascade Corner, and it along with Little Robinson Creek are the only streams in the Idaho portion of the park that host salmonids. It runs through prime bear country, and within the park it flows through a relatively gentle canyon and can be reached from two points. From Idaho, it can be reached in its upper portion by going north on Fish Creek Road, which leaves from the Three Rivers area, to Snow Creek Road and following this road to its end near the Yellowstone National Park west boundary. Not far from the end of this road, one passes Teardrop Lake, which hosts small

Hosting five salmonid species, with some growing to trophy size, Robinson Creek is a small-stream treasure. For most of its length it is a freestone stream offering solitude in addition to an excellent salmonid population and prolific insect hatches in season.

brook trout but is also stocked with catchable rainbow trout. Holdover rainbows can grow to several pounds, and using nonmotorized watercraft in the early season is the best way to encounter them.

From the end of Snow Creek Road, a primitive trail of less than half a mile reaches the creek where it parallels the West Boundary Trail. Here only Yellowstone cutthroat trout inhabit the stream, which flows swiftly in riffles and runs. This seldom-visited location offers near isolation to the visiting fly fisher and is ideal for lightweight tackle. The other route to this upper portion is from the Bechler Ranger Station where the West Boundary Trail begins and after 4 miles accesses Robinson Creek at its junction with Little Robinson Creek. Brook trout coming from Little Robinson Lake (Number 1765 in Yellowstone National Park's designation) at the head of Little Robinson Creek are common in addition to the native cutthroat trout. From this location Robinson Creek drops into a widening and deepening isolated canyon as it flows southwesterly out of the park. This canyon forms the middle reach of Robinson Creek, with the only practical access being the unmaintained trail leaving from Horseshoe Lake.

Farther downstream the canyon becomes less abrupt. Here it parallels Cave Falls Road, from which there are some access points, the best of which is the road going past the LDS Church's girls camp. The creek now hosts not only brook, cutthroat, and brown trout, but also rainbow trout. Its gradient increases again below a small meadow, where decades ago log plunges were placed in the creek to improve the holding water habitat downstream in the Caribou-Targhee National Forest. Access to the stream below the meadow becomes more difficult as the canyon deepens again but is possible at the national forest boundary, where a county road drops into the canyon to connect Fish Creek and Cave Falls Roads.

From here on downstream there is a population of Rocky Mountain whitefish, in addition to the four other salmonids. Private land borders the creek here, but in Idaho it is legal to access a navigable stream, such as Robinson Creek, if one remains within the high-water mark, and access is also allowed at all public road crossings. Thus with respect for private land, the creek can be fished in this location for miles downstream, if one is willing to bushwhack. The Three Rivers Ranch owns the land where Robinson Creek flows to its confluence with the Warm River. Guests of the ranch can fish this excellent water with easy access.

Robinson Creek drains the southwest corner of the Madison Plateau in Yellowstone National Park and therefore is a major runoff stream. There are no irrigation diversions from the creek, so fishing here usually begins by mid-June. By autumn, run-up brown trout from the Henry's Fork enter to spawn in isolated locations, and some of these exceed 20 inches. All of these events make Robinson Creek a most interesting small stream to visit, especially when you take into account the trophy-size trout in its lower reaches.

SAND CREEK PONDS

By Kelly Glissmeyer

Evening and early morning are sure to offer the best fishing for large trout in the 8- to 10-pound range responding to emerging aquatic insects.

Access: US Highway 20/St. Anthony Business Route to Sand Creek Road
GPS Coordinates: 43.972319, -111.652848
Equipment: 5- or 6-weight system with floating, intermediate, and sinking lines; damselfly, dragonfly, midge, and Speckled Dun patterns, and leech, scud, snail, and streamer patterns
Nearest facilities and services: St. Anthony (Idaho), IDF&G Sand Creek Ponds Campground, Riverside Guesthouse Inn
Information resources: Idaho Department of Fish and Game, Upper Snake Region Office; Blue Creek Reservoir USGS topographic map
Salmonids present: Brook and rainbow trout

I heard the whisperings on these ponds, and committed to visit them someday. That day finally came and my eldest son, a few of his friends, and I made a late July drive to Sand Creek Pond #4. The morning would be a learning experience for all of us, with me landing only a small, planted "banana" trout and one smaller brook trout. During lunch a neighbor who had fished the ponds for decades gave us some leech patterns, tips, and tactics. The tips on presentation and those shared flies resulted in a successful afternoon with several good rainbows hooked, landed, and released. Now we frequent the ponds regularly every summer and fall, finding exciting subsurface as well as dry fly fishing opportunities, with many large fish being caught.

Sand Creek Ponds #1 through #4 were originally established in 1947 as part of an expansive wildlife management area by Idaho Fish and Game to protect wintering elk, moose, and deer herds. According to Fish and Game, as of 2015 Ponds #2 and #3 have held no fish. Pond #4 remains closed to fishing until July 1, with nonmotorized boats allowed after July 15.

Although my largest fish landed to date at the Sand Creek Ponds was from Pond #1, we usually limit our fishing to Pond #4. At about 70 acres, it is larger than the other three ponds combined and features parking, restrooms, and a dock for public boat launch. Pontoon boats and float tubes are ideal for fishing these ponds, but a few anglers launch their drift boats or skiffs and row around the ponds in search of their quarry. Though first impressions may lead one to believe this is a bass or bluegill pond, the extensive cattails, bulrushes, and lily pads make exceptional cover for resident trout. Food sources are numerous and rich, and rainbow trout exceeding 20 inches are common.

An added bonus of fly fishing for larger trout at Sand Creek is the opportunity to sight-fish to trout targeting emerging insects in the surface film. It boils down to "gulper" fishing on dry flies, with the early spinner fall lasting until around 9 a.m. The action slows down during midday breezes, but returns around 7 p.m. and lasts until dark. Nymph patterns suspended under an indicator will work well during the midday lull. Small twitches result in massive takes by some large trout. If fishing in shallower water, I prefer to suspend them under a parasol emerger fly as an indicator. During non-hatch times, a good leech pattern does the trick. Many colors work well, with black, brown, and olive producing most often. Try a two-pattern rig, one weighted with the other unweighted.

I use exclusively twisted monofilament leaders of my own design, which turn over like a dream and stretch when setting the hook on fish, in turn protecting fragile tippets. I prefer fluorocarbon tippets in the 3X and 4X range—longer leaders for dry fly presentations and shorter leaders for stripping leeches and such. Remember to take along a floatation device, a good anchor, and potable water to stay hydrated.

SHERIDAN RESERVOIR
By Steve Hyde

Abundant large, vigorous Kamloops rainbow trout reside in this pay-to-fish reservoir that provides a quality fishing experience.

Access: US Highway 20 to Old Shotgun Road to Yale-Kilgore Road
GPS Coordinates: 44.468335, -111.677421
Equipment: 5- or 6-weight system with floating and full-sink lines; damselfly, dragonfly, and Speckled Dun patterns, and terrestrial insect, leech, scud, snail, and traditional attractor patterns
Nearest facilities and services: Ashton (Idaho), Eagle Ridge Ranch
Information resources: Eagle Ridge Ranch (www.eagleridge.com); Sheridan Reservoir USGS topographic map
Salmonids present: Kamloops rainbow trout

Privately owned but accessible Sheridan Reservoir has a long history of hosting large, superbly conditioned rainbow trout. Present leech patterns in the early season and again with streamers during autumn months. In the midseason, present damselfly, Speckled Dun, and grasshopper patterns to the cruising large trout.

This reservoir is a place of legend. Formed in the early 20th century as a water supply for the Woods Livestock Company, it was named Stringer Lake for a later owner. Later in the century, it became known by its present name, but when rainbow trout were first introduced is uncertain. For several decades the Kamloops strain of rainbows has resided here, and some individuals grow to what I label celebrated sizes. My wife, Sue, and I manage Eagle Ridge Ranch, a full-service guest ranch offering year-round outdoor activities to groups and individuals. One of my tasks is to maintain Sheridan Reservoir's reputation as an outstanding fishing destination. A reservation system applies, allowing 10 rods per day on ranch waters. Some local fly fishing shops have guiding agreements for ranch waters.

Sheridan Reservoir comprises around 300 acres, bordered mostly by meadows, at about 6,500 feet in elevation. Ice-out usually occurs in late March or early April, and the north end of the reservoir rarely ices over. With depths up to 20 feet, there is plenty of habitat for fish to hold over. A rich variety of food forms aids in growing the famed resident rainbows. The first time I walked its shoreline, I was impressed by the number of snails just under the surface. Although fishing can begin soon after ice-out, with snail, streamer, dragonfly nymph, and leech patterns being effective, the best fishing takes place from around mid-May through September as the usual sequence of aquatic insects emerge.

Fish can be caught anywhere on the reservoir. The south side is timbered, and good fishing results when ants and other insects fall onto the water from the trees. A good strategy during summer months when terrestrial insects are abundant is to fish the north bay, where cooler water diverted from Sheridan Creek enters the reservoir. Larger fish congregate here to take advantage of increased dissolved oxygen as well as to feed on terrestrial insects blown onto the water. Stealth and accurate casting are required here, but the reward could be the best fish of the year. When wind roughens the reservoir surface, switching to wet flies will bring success. After September aquatic insect hatches slow, it is back to the strategy that works in the early season.

Sheridan Reservoir was formed by diverting some of Sheridan Creek into a hollow and damming the east end. Water returns to the creek through the dam. This practice continues, but the current owner of Eagle Ridge Ranch is applying large-scale restoration efforts to the entire stream on the property. Seven miles of Sheridan Creek flow through the ranch, and decades ago it had a reputation for being an important spawning steam for trout residing in Island Park Reservoir. The top half of the creek has some gradient, while the bottom portion has a lower gradient in the form of a meandering meadow stream. Before the current owner focused reclamation attention on the creek, degradation had slipped in, mainly from overgrazing and removal of willow thickets, both bringing on siltation. Limiting cattle access through electric fencing, creating in-stream structure, improving spawning habitat, and replanting the riparian zone have brought the creek back to the point that fish reside permanently, taking advantage of water cooler than in Island Park Reservoir, overhead cover, and the abundant food supply. Some of these fish rival in size those in Sheridan Reservoir.

Just as encouraging is the return of Golden Stoneflies to the creek, as well as the presence of Brown, Gray, and Green Drakes to supplement caddisflies and smaller mayflies. All these improvements make the creek a destination in itself and demonstrate that a thoughtful owner with foresight and esteem for salmonids can sustain a profitable cattle operation with minimal impact on a quality stream and productive stillwater fishery.

TETON RIVER IN TETON BASIN
By Doug Gibson

The pastoral beauty and legendary population of trout in this classic meadow stream reach is alluring. Plentiful and varied season-long mayfly emergences makes dry fly fishing a must here.

Access: Teton county roads off Idaho Highway 33
GPS Coordinates: 43.723491, -111.187826
Equipment: 5- or 6-weight system with floating and sink-tip lines: caddisfly, BWO, Golden Stone, Gray Drake, PMD, Trico, and Yellow Sally patterns, and soft-hackle, streamer, terrestrial insect, and traditional attractor patterns
Nearest facilities and services: Driggs (Idaho), USFS Teton Canyon Campground, Teton Valley Lodge
Information resources: Driggs Visitor Center; Idaho Department of Fish and Game, Upper Snake Region Office; USGS Flow Station Gage 13052200; Bates, Fourth of July Peak, and Tetonia USGS topographic maps
Salmonids present: Brook, cutthroat, and rainbow trout and Rocky Mountain whitefish

The Teton River is not alone in hosting summertime recreational traffic, and these folks have a right to enjoy the river. If you visit early in the day or from dinnertime to sunset, you will experience a better measure of solitude.

The Teton River here differs enough from the lower reaches to be considered a different stream. Instead of the brawling canyon and placid but somewhat degraded run in the Snake River Plain, here it is the quintessential meadow stream. Runoff is a major event on the river because it drains most of the Teton Range west slope, part of the Snake River Range to the south, and much of the Big Hole Mountains. Teton Basin (also known as Teton Valley) holds views of the Teton Range breathtaking enough to be distracting. That combined with pastoral beauty has attracted many new residents. The Teton Regional Land Trust protects land along tributaries to the river and strives to protect the river itself. Through interacting with agencies, landowners, and municipal governments, the trust and its actions are one of the reasons the salmonid population has flourished. In addition, the attitudes of natives in the valley toward the river have changed from considering it to be an agriculture and ranching tool to recognizing that its natural beauty and salmonid population are also large contributors to the Teton Basin economy.

Yellowstone cutthroat and Rocky Mountain whitefish are native here, as in the river below, with introduced brook and rainbow trout present in fair numbers. The river in the basin is nearly totally bordered by private land, but seven public access locations have boat launches. Here the river is barely large enough for drift boats, so a better strategy is to use personal watercraft such as a pontoon boat, which disturbs the river to a lesser degree, is easier to navigate around the meanders, and is more quickly launched into and removed from the water. Wading is also a good strategy for fishing this section of the river. Remembering that public use is legal within the high-water mark of navigable streams, there is much opportunity for wading from the public access points on the river. As in the canyon below, runoff determines the beginning of fly fishing season. At its beginning, a few windblown adult Golden Stoneflies from the canyon reach the river in the lower basin, so patterns simulating them are effective. And, as in the canyon, streamer patterns are productive.

When the river clears and drops, Yellow Sally stonefly and caddisfly activity brings fish toward the surface. The famed PMD emergence and terrestrial insect bounty begin in July to last into September, and late-season Mahogany Duns and BWOs extend the mayfly activity here. But with the human population boom and appreciation for the river has come increased recreational use. During summer, canoeists, kayakers, paddleboarders, inner-tubers, and even swimmers come to the river. Anglers using flat-bottom boats equipped with small outboard motors also go up and down the river seeking rising trout. Certainly all these folks have a right to enjoy the river, but their daytime presence makes early mornings and evenings the best times to enjoy feeding trout until September rolls around. These are the reasons why I prefer the canyon reach for finding relative solitude and uninterrupted fishing.

TETON RIVER CANYON
By Doug Gibson
The canyon reach of the Teton River is isolated and has limited access but offers unforgettable fly fishing.

Access: Idaho Highway 32 to Spring Hollow Road or North 4350 East to Bitch Creek Slide trailhead
GPS Coordinates: 43.926967, -111.289635
Equipment: 5- or 6-weight system with floating and sink-tip lines; caddisfly, BWO, Golden Stone, Gray Drake, PMD, Trico, and Yellow Sally patterns, and soft-hackle, streamer, terrestrial insect, and traditional attractor patterns
Nearest facilities and services: Driggs (Idaho), USFS Teton Canyon Campground, Three Rivers Lodge
Information resources: Driggs Visitor Center; Idaho Department of Fish and Game, Upper Snake Region Office; USGS Flow Station Gage 13052200; Drummond, Lamont, Linderman Dam, and Newdale USGS topographic maps
Salmonids present: Brook, cutthroat, and rainbow trout and Rocky Mountain whitefish

I've lived most of my life almost within casting distance of the Teton River. I have guided on it for more than 40 years and still slip away to it for an evening of fishing and solitude. Access is limited on the canyon reach because of the June 1976 Teton Dam collapse. This failure changed the physical character of the river for about 35 miles down from where water from the dam backed up near the Badger Creek confluence, and including on the Snake River Plain. Formerly the canyon reach was a series of riffles and runs. Some of this remains, but much of the river in the canyon is a series of stillwaters punctuated by brief, dangerous rapids formed when sodden canyon walls collapsed into the river after the dam failure. Since the failure, however, both the trout and the aquatic insect population have returned to healthy levels, and the Teton has regained its reputation as one of the best trout streams in

The Teton River–Bitch Creek confluence seen from the top of the famed Bitch Creek Slide. "Steep as a cow's face" describes the descent to the river, but once there, unique canyon scenery, solitude, and abundant aquatic insect emergence with fish ranging well into trophy size are the rewards.

the region. It can be fished in relative solitude by boating or, although somewhat limited, by wading. Before discussing fishing by either method, two aspects of danger must be noted.

First, the Teton River Canyon is major rattlesnake habitat. May into June, when the snakes molt and are therefore most aggressive, is the most dangerous time, but they are always present. Be cautious and remain within the high-water mark. In September, which is an excellent time to fish the river, these snakes seek dens for the winter and are a diminishing presence.

Second, no one should float the river in the canyon unless they or a person in their party has a thorough knowledge of portage and dangerous rapids locations. This fact dictates that rafting is not only more practical, but also safer than boating. Consider portaging a several-hundred-pound drift boat over several steep rapids in a day, and enjoyment of the excellent trout population minimizes. A lightweight and flexible raft is so much easier to use, therefore resulting in more fishing time.

The season begins on the canyon reach as runoff ends, usually by the end of June. Access to the highest place in the canyon is at the Felt Dam, reached from Idaho Highway 32. This location does not have a boat launch. It's suitable only for wading with difficulty, but can offer some good fishing. The next public access downstream that is practical for wading and to begin a float trip is reached off Highway 32 a few miles west of Lamont, Idaho. The access road (North 4350 East)

Bringing a four-legged friend is practical in low bear-density areas. A dog provides great company and will likely enjoy the outing as much as you.

goes south a few miles past farms and ends on a bench overlooking the canyon. At the edge of the bench, a steeply pitched slope of about 300 yards runs down to the confluence of Bitch Creek with the river. It's the famed Bitch Creek Slide, down which for decades rafts and boats of all kinds would be roped in then slid uneasily to the river. The Teton Dam failure put an end to using hard-sided boats through the canyon. Nevertheless, this location offers solitude for the wading fly fisher fit enough to negotiate the slide down and the climb back up. There is the choice of also fishing Bitch Creek above the confluence.

The next practical access downstream is off Idaho Highway 33 just west of Clementsville and is private. Here a diplomatic approach allows both waders and rafters to use the Linderman family's private road descending nearly to the river. Farther downstream, and once again off Highway 32, Spring Hollow Road goes southwesterly from Lamont to the north side of the river. As one approaches the river, not yet in sight, a strip of concrete becomes the road. Why the forlorn concrete strip? It was meant to be a boat launch onto the reservoir formed by the Teton Dam. From here, there is good walk-in fishing but the presence of rattlesnakes makes ascending or descending the canyon walls dangerous.

The Teton Dam Road leaves Highway 33 a few miles east of Newdale and goes north a mile or so to the dam site. From here, the visitor goes to the right, then down the concrete boat ramp to the river. The access at the dam site allows enough river for good wading. A primitive boat launch gives access to about 5 miles of river until another primitive public access at the Hog Hollow Bridge north of Newdale. Here good walk-in fishing can be enjoyed.

TETON RIVER IN THE SNAKE RIVER PLAIN
By Doug Gibson

Trophy-size cutthroat trout are abundant, and properly presented terrestrial insect patterns reliably bring them to the surface anywhere there is access.

Access: Teton Dam Road and Hog Hollow Road (at Newdale) from Idaho Highway 33
GPS Coordinates: 43.934418, -111.608507
Equipment: 5- or 6-weight system with floating and sink-tip lines; caddisfly, BWO, Golden Stone, Gray Drake, PMD, Trico, and Yellow Sally patterns, and soft-hackle, streamer, terrestrial insect, and traditional attractor patterns
Nearest facilities and services: St. Anthony and Rexburg (Idaho), Riverside Guesthouse Inn
Information resources: Idaho Department of Fish and Game, Upper Snake Region Office; Rexburg Visitor Center; USGS Flow Station Gage 1305500; Moody, Newdale, Rexburg, and St. Anthony USGS topographic maps
Salmonids present: Brook, cutthroat, and rainbow trout and Rocky Mountain whitefish

The river below the Hog Hollow Bridge essentially begins its run onto the Snake River Plain to meet the Henry's Fork. On the plain, it has recovered from the devastation caused by the Teton Dam failure and has the potential to be a major angling destination, suitable for walk-in fishing as well as float fishing, but nearly all of the river is bordered by private land that limits access. Attempts by the Idaho Department of Fish and Game to establish public access and boat launch facilities have met with staunch opposition by landowners bordering the river.

Where the Teton River breaks out onto the Snake River Plain, float as well as wade fishing can be enjoyed.

Above the town of Teton, the river peculiarly splits into north and south forks. By irrigation season, the north fork is nearly unfit for salmonid habitation, but the south fork hosts cutthroat trout, with some of the largest individuals in the entire river present. Except for a mile or so of water just below where the river splits and above, the south fork is best fished by floating with smaller craft such as a kayak, pontoon boat, or raft. Even so, numerous diversions must be portaged, and fences crossing the river can be encountered. Private land limits the number of takeout points mostly to bridges. Aquatic insect hatches on this section are diminished compared to the river in the canyon and in the basin because of extensive animal husbandry diversion for irrigation and municipal uses. Nevertheless, many species are represented, and terrestrial insects are major food forms for foraging trout and Rocky Mountain whitefish.

I have come to know landowners along the river here. Some, mostly natives like me, are usually hospitable to a polite request and personal introduction, to access the river. Others, usually imported from other parts of the country, can be hostile. On one of my guiding trips on this section of river, a new landowner accosted me to the point of wading into the river to grab my boat in an attempt to turn me and my clients back upstream. Knowing the law, I resisted, stayed composed with difficulty, and continued down the river. Idaho law states that all waters within the high-water mark of any navigable stream are in the public domain. The landowner apparently did consult the law after I challenged him to do so. During succeeding trips down the river past his property, he did not repeat his attempt to turn me away. I include this incident because with the arrival of absentee and unknowing landowners, such occurrences seem to be increasing. If there is potential for you to be challenged on an Idaho navigable stream, such as the Teton River, review the state laws pertaining to use of such waters, and keep calm and use courtesy if such an incident materializes. Your chance for amicable resolution improves greatly by doing so.

NORTH FORK OF THE TETON RIVER
By Doug Gibson

All of the creek above the highway is a beautiful riffle-and-run freestone stream populated by Yellowstone cutthroat, with trophy-size individuals rivaling those in the Teton River.

Access: Jackpine Road and abandoned railroad line, both off Idaho Highway 32
GPS Coordinates: 43.939721, -111.179221
Equipment: 4-weight system with floating line; caddisfly, BWO, Golden Stone, PMD, Trico, and Yellow Sally patterns, and terrestrial insect and traditional attractor patterns
Nearest facilities and services: Driggs (Idaho), USFS Teton Canyon Campground, Teton Valley Lodge
Information resources: Caribou-Targhee National Forest; Drummond, Lamont, and McReynolds Reservoir USGS topographic maps
Salmonids present: Cutthroat trout and Rocky Mountain whitefish

Lower Bitch Creek is most practically reached from the famed Bitch Creek Slide. From here, fish upstream and stalk active trout concentrated in pools. MILLI AND JIMMY GABETTAS PHOTO

In the extreme north of the basin, one can escape not only floating recreationists but all boat-borne anglers by visiting the North Fork of the Teton River, also known as Bitch Creek. It can be accessed above but mostly below where it crosses Highway 32 north of Felt, Idaho. Farther upstream, the old railroad grade can be bicycled or walked from Jack Pine Road to reach public access where a trestle crosses the creek. At the time of this writing, the Gillette family allowed "foot traffic only" access to the creek across their land bordering Jack Pine Road. Visitors are asked to stay within the high-water mark on this property after reaching the creek. The family appreciates it if visitors pick up trash, although little accumulates because of appreciative fly fishers.

Upper reaches are in Wyoming and thus require a Wyoming fishing license. Below the highway the creek drops into a steep and increasingly inaccessible canyon on its way to meet the Teton River at the Bitch Creek Slide. As with the Teton River Canyon, rattlesnakes present a common danger in this canyon. Bitch Creek, like the Teton River, is a major runoff stream, so when it becomes fishable depends on when runoff from the west slope of the Teton Range abates, usually around the first of July.

WARM RIVER
By Mike Lawson

Lower sections of this river hold surprisingly large rainbow trout. Above the cascades tranquility reigns with a good chance for encountering medium-size trout that respond to almost any presented dry fly pattern.

Access: Eccles Road, North Hatchery Butte Road, Warm River Road, and Warm River Spring Road off Mesa Falls Scenic Highway

GPS Coordinates: 44.205582, -111.251885

Equipment: 4- or 5-weight system with floating line; caddisfly, BWO, Golden Stone, PMD, and Yellow Sally patterns, and terrestrial insect and traditional attractor patterns

Nearest facilities and services: Ashton (Idaho), USFS Warm River Campground and Pole Bridge Campground, USFS Warm River rental cabin, Three Rivers Ranch

Information resources: Caribou-Targhee National Forest; Hatchery Butte, Snake River Butte, and Warm River USGS topographic maps

Salmonids present: Brook, brown, and rainbow trout

As a youngster I lived in Sugar City, Idaho. In those days I fished many local waters, including the Warm River. This was back when the Yellowstone Branch Line of the Union Pacific Railroad operated between Ashton, Idaho, and West Yellowstone, Montana. I remember catching a ride on a lineman's handcar to fish between

Historic Warm River Cabin once hosted a state fish hatchery and now can be rented through Caribou-Targhee National Forest. Good fishing is at its doorstep, and isolated sections of the Henry's Fork are only minutes away.

Bear Gulch and Warm River Campground. He'd let me off at a power line where a trail leaves the railroad grade to give access to some good water in the river below. I also walked up the grade from the campground to fish some of the excellent water this mostly overlooked small river offers. Back then rainbow and brook trout and Rocky Mountain whitefish made up the Warm River salmonid residents.

These days I ride my mountain bike on the abandoned grade now labeled "Yellowstone Branch Line Trail" to the excellent water. You can do the same starting either near Warm River Campground or above the cascades from Warm River Spring Road. You can also access some of the lower river in the Three Rivers area from the Mesa Falls Scenic Byway (Idaho Highway 47), but so do many folks. By walking or biking on the railroad grade, you can find solitude as well as great fishing, with some fish of pleasing sizes as well as a few that rival the largest in the Henry's Fork.

Things have changed a bit for the Warm River, much to my appreciation. Here's why: Back in the early 1980s, the Snake River Cutthroats, the Trout Unlimited chapter based in Idaho Falls, partnered with the Idaho Department of Fish and Game to introduce brown trout to lower Henry's Fork tributaries and enhance the few in the river at that time. The club bought the eyed eggs, which the department rose to fingerlings in the now-closed Ashton Fish Hatchery. The Warm River was a principle target for planting these fingerlings, and it has become a major spawning location for Henry's Fork brown trout. Department biologists had researched brown trout strains in an effort to determine a "best fit" for the Henry's Fork. I believe they succeeded because the river from Lower Cardiac Canyon downstream hosts those robust brown trout that everyone enjoys. Now the Warm River boasts brook, brown, and rainbow trout as well as Rocky Mountain whitefish from its Henry's Fork confluence upstream to Warm River Spring. Incidentally, the Idaho state record brown trout coming out of Ashton Reservoir a few years ago was likely a progeny of this introduction.

Speaking of Warm River Spring, what it does to the river physically is similar to what Big Springs does to the nearby Henry's Fork. Both springs, photogenic and unique, enhance their parent river with major infusions of high-quality water. Warm River Cabin, located at the spring, can be rented by contacting Caribou-Targhee National Forest. Below its spring, the Warm River offers riffles and runs, pocketwater, incoming springwater, beautiful gravel substrate, and some holes above and below the cascades. Here caddisfly and stonefly species predominate, as in any stream of similar gradient, but significant BWO and PMD populations offer interesting seasonal variety.

Above Warm River Spring, the river diminishes. Locally we refer to it as the Little Warm River. Its physical character also differs noticeably from the larger river below the spring. There are beaver ponds and swampy areas, as should be expected in this relatively flat area of Island Park, but also some areas featuring riffles and runs and corner holes where the river twists and turns through some hollows. The Little Warm River can be accessed from several roads coming east from the Mesa Falls Scenic Byway.

As with the lower river, I have a history on the Little Warm River. During my college years I worked summers surveying roads for Targhee National Forest. Our camp was at Pineview. Evenings after work I would go to the river with lightweight tackle to enjoy the small but aggressive brook trout. They would, and still do, take almost any small dry or wet pattern offered. Some of them made scrumptious dinners for us. This work also provided me a chance to explore this part of the river, and doing so convinced me that it is a great candidate for family fishing or for the lightweight tackle enthusiast or entry-level fly fisher because of abundant easy access and the aggressive brook trout. To my knowledge, these are the sole salmonid residents of this part of the river, and Pole Bridge Campground is a great base for fishing the river for them.

Yes, my image speaks of the Henry's Fork. But scratch its surface and you will see other waters meaningful to me. The Warm River is one of these. This is not just because of its importance to the Henry's Fork, but also because it is among my most pleasant outdoor memories, and because it remains an excellent fishery.

Snake River Drainage

UPPER BLACKFOOT RIVER

Above the reservoir it is mostly a meadow stream with brief sections of canyon water. Yellowstone cutthroat trout dominate, with a minor population of rainbow trout just above the reservoir and a few brook trout scattered throughout.

Access: Idaho Highway 34 to Blackfoot River Road
GPS Coordinates: 42.814195, -111.350564
Equipment: 5-weight system with floating and sink-tip lines; Brown Drake, BWO, caddisfly, crane fly, PMD, Speckled Dun, and Trico patterns, and streamer, terrestrial insect, and traditional attractor patterns
Nearest facilities and services: Soda Springs (Idaho), USFS Mill Creek Campground, Johnson Guard Station rental cabin, Sheep Creek Guest Ranch
Information resources: Caribou-Targhee National Forest, Soda Springs Ranger District Office; USGS Flow Station Gage 13063000; Upper Valley USGS topographic map
Salmonids present: Cutthroat trout

As with numerous western rivers, natural or man-made structures divide each into specific reaches that should be addressed individually for fishing purposes. The Blackfoot River Reservoir separates the river into two parts, each of distinct character. Thus we will deal with each part separately because significant differences apply in fishing strategy, regulations, geography, and physical approach.

The upper river begins at the confluence of Diamond and Lanes Creeks and ends in the reservoir, all in eastern Idaho's Caribou County. In this reach it hosts Yellowstone cutthroat trout to the near exclusion of other salmonids. The Trout Unlimited Home Rivers Office, the Idaho Department of Fish and Game, and certain landowners are cooperating to return the river and its drainage to a condition that favors native cutthroat trout, which are close to being endangered. Although a good population of these trout are present, much has been lost here. Until about 50 years ago, hundreds of thousands of large cutthroat would leave the reservoir to travel upstream into the river and then into tributaries to spawn during springtime.

The river in the Blackfoot River Wildlife Management Area is a classic meadow stream. Picturesque and tranquil, it hosts a cutthroat trout population with individuals exceeding 20 inches that take terrestrial insect patterns with abandon.

During good water years, they would remain in the river through the summer months, and stories remain from the days up until the early 1970s when the creel limit on the river was seven pounds and one fish! Those days are gone due to natural phenomena, mining, overgrazing, and management of the reservoir in a manner unfavorable to trout.

Today the fishing season on the upper river and its tributaries opens each year on July 1 in order to protect spawning cutthroat. During the season, which extends to the end of November, no bait is allowed, barbless hooks are required, and catch-and-release fishing for cutthroat trout applies. The July 1 opening coincides with good times on the Madison River and South Fork reach, where the stonefly emergences peak on both, and on the middle Henry's Fork, with flavs and Brown Drakes making for great afternoons and evenings, and with the famed damselfly emergence on Henry's Lake and nearby irrigation reservoirs. Because of these events, you will find few fly fishers on the 20-odd miles of river above the reservoir when it opens for fishing. On most of the river, owners grant trespass on inquiry or require a trespass fee, and the Monsanto Industries Purchase Area welcomes anglers to their signed property along miles of the river.

Recently the Monsanto Company purchased land (Fox Hills Ranch) containing 8 miles of the upper Blackfoot River. The company has opened the land to non-motorized access, allowing extensive fishing opportunity. However, the upstream Blackfoot River Wildlife Management Area of 1,800 acres holds the best of the river in the entire upper drainage. Here about 6 miles of the river flows through a nonmotorized, two-tiered meadow reminiscent, although on a smaller scale, of the meadows above the campground on Yellowstone Park's Slough Creek. Pullouts

Sheep moving to and from allotments can be encountered early and late in the season respectively. During the summer grazing season, these herds will be away from most fishable waters. Seeing them is a reminder of the Old West.

provide access to the river and its Yellowstone cutthroat trout population with individuals ranging to well over 20 inches.

My introduction to fishing here began when this property was the Stocking Ranch, owned by Revi Stocking. The Stocking family, Mormon pioneers, began the ranch near the start of the 20th century to establish a base of operations for raising cattle and sheep. Revi once allowed access to the river, but after his ranch house was ransacked one winter, he posted the property with numerous signs along his bordering fences. Woe to anyone he caught trespassing! Legendary were stories of trespassers having shotgun pellets fly over their heads or air released from their tires. So I fished with longing on Forest Service property bordering the lower end of the ranch. Finally after several years of doing so, I stopped at the ranch entrance with the intention of asking permission to fish. On my approach to the ranch house, an elderly lady came to the door. Using utmost diplomacy, including hat in hand, I ask her for permission to fish.

"Well, let me ask the boss," came her reply.

She left the door and my eyes followed. On the other side of the adjoining room an elderly gentleman sat, without glasses, reading a newspaper by sunlight.

"He wants to go fishing!" she loudly repeated to the obviously deaf man. He turned around to see me standing at the doorway, togged out in fishing gear.

"Tell him to bring me my dinner!"

A courteous approach gifted me with what I had dreamed about for years! But more important, I had a new friend. To be sure, Revi got his dinner entrée that evening. It was now my pleasure not only to fish for resident cutthroat trout ranging to well over 20 inches, but to stop by to offer gifts and share stories with Revi and his wife. So here is an example to consider when asking to fish private land. Diplomacy, including the offering of personal and vehicular identification, can open doors to some superb fishing.

Revi Stocking died in 1992, not quite 90 years of age. His wish was that the ranch not be developed, but preserved as he remembered it. Real estate developers slathered over the 1,800 acres of meadowland containing a meandering river surrounded by stately quaking aspen groves and pine forests on higher slopes. But there were major drawbacks. First, winter closed the area to motorized-transportation, and second, no electrical and telecommunication utilities were nearby. These slowed developmental plans to a crawl.

Meanwhile, the Idaho Department of Fish and Game saw the value of this land as a preserve for all forms of native wildlife and approached the Stocking family with an offer to buy the ranch with the promise to retain its near pristine character as Revi wished. The family accepted, and thus was born the Blackfoot River Wildlife Management Area. Within it, fly fishers now have a uniquely beautiful setting to catch and release native Yellowstone cutthroat trout in solitude not experienced in the more famed waters nearby.

LOWER BLACKFOOT RIVER

Canyon water with deep holes, riffles, and runs dominates here. In places access is either difficult or downright dangerous, but with active caddisfly and midge populations, early autumn fishing can be excellent.

Access: US Highway 91 and Wolverine Road to Blackfoot River Road, Trail Creek Road, and Blackfoot Reservoir Road
GPS Coordinates: 43.039298, -111.856056
Equipment: 5-weight system with floating and sink-tip lines; BWO, caddisfly, and crane fly patterns, and streamer, terrestrial insect, and traditional attractor patterns
Nearest facilities and services: Idaho Falls (Idaho); BLM Cutthroat, Graves Creek, and Sage Hen Campgrounds on Blackfoot Reservoir Road and Trail Creek Campground on Trail Creek Road
Information resources: Bureau of Land Management, Idaho Falls Field Office; USGS Flow Station Gage 13066000; Dunn Basin, Meadow Creek Mountain, Miner Creek, and Paradise Valley USGS topographic maps
Salmonids present: Cutthroat and rainbow trout

For the first several miles below the Blackfoot River Reservoir, access is relatively easy along the river. Public land abounds, with some private ranches. There are a number of routes to this part of the river, but the most convenient are from the Blackfoot Reservoir Road. Cattle husbandry is the major industry here, and because of it riverbanks in some locations have been damaged enough to cause silting of streambeds in low-gradient locations. All county roads here are graveled, and primitive roads lead to the river. Four Bureau of Land Management campgrounds sited

Below the Blackfoot River Reservoir the river runs through an increasingly wild and dangerous canyon. But there are several access points where one can enjoy trout responding to attractor, streamer, and caddisfly and midge patterns.

on the river provide bases from which to explore the excellent Yellowstone cutthroat trout population hosting many trophy-size individuals as well as occasional rainbow and brook trout.

The river here is as different from the river above the reservoir as day is to night, but there are physical and man-made limits to enjoying it. After miles of good access, the river gradually drops into a dangerous and isolated canyon. Flowing for miles within, the river finally drops onto the Snake River Plain, where it is not worthy of being a fishing destination. Thus fishing on the lower river concentrates on the several-mile reach from just below the reservoir to around the Trail Creek Campground. Within this reach the fishing season is greatly impacted by the flow of irrigation water out of the reservoir. This flow begins with springtime irrigation demands on the Snake River Plain and ends after those demands cease around the first of October. During that time, variable high flows slow fishing but allow float-fishing to present streamer patterns bringing moderate success.

Where it can be accessed before irrigation flows enter, usually in early May, the river provides good fishing when roads become passable. Presenting small streamer and midge patterns brings success. After irrigation flows subside, the best fishing begins as low water concentrates fish into numerous deeper holes and runs and the ongoing hunting season reduces the number of anglers. Pleasant weather prevails, rattlesnakes have denned up, and terrestrial insects abound along riverbanks. Presenting terrestrial patterns brings responses from resident trout, especially during afternoon hours. Sparse October Caddis, BWO, and Trico emergences also bring trout to the surface. Presenting streamer patterns remains successful but is mainly limited to deeper waters because of extensive aquatic vegetation growth in shallow waters. Wading is the only practical means to fish at this time, as low flows make navigating exposed boulder fields nearly impossible. Fishing pressure is minimal, thus a quality angling experience is a near certainty.

MAIN STEM SNAKE RIVER

Avoid it during runoff and irrigation season. Before and after these times, visitors can experience excellent streamer fishing.

Access: Numerous access points within municipal boundaries, bridge crossings, and bordering state and BLM land
GPS Coordinates: 43.415318, -112.111759
Equipment: 6- or 7-weight system with floating and sink-tip lines; BWO, caddisfly, midge, and PMD patterns, and streamer, terrestrial insect, and traditional attractor patterns
Nearest facilities and services: Idaho Falls (Idaho), Idaho Falls RV Park
Information resources: Idaho Falls Visitor Center; Idaho Department of Fish and Game, Upper Snake Region Office; Bureau of Land Management, Idaho Falls Field Office; USGS Flow Station Gage 13057000; Deer Parks, Firth, Idaho Falls North, Idaho Falls South, and Lewisville USGS topographic maps
Salmonids present: Brown, cutthroat, and rainbow trout and Rocky Mountain whitefish

In eastern Idaho the main stem Snake River begins at the North Fork (Henry's Fork) and South Fork reach confluence. Meandering through the nearly featureless Snake River Plain, the main stem is degraded by irrigation diversion, rendered less scenic by municipal development, and possessed of an unnatural water profile during the regional growing season. A number of small hydropower facilities are established along the river. All this makes the main stem appear as a waterway to avoid, which is wrong because this river possesses a good population of brown and rainbow trout and Rocky Mountain whitefish as well as a remnant cutthroat trout population. Interestingly, the Idaho Department of Fish and Game has released a number of sturgeon in appropriate places along the river.

Numerous walk-in locations spangle the river course because it runs through or by municipal, state, and Bureau of Land Management lands and it is legal in Idaho to access a stream adjacent to any public road. Nevertheless, much of the river is bordered by private land, meaning float fishing can be more fruitful than walk-in fishing. The river features several boat launch facilities, maintained by state or federal agencies or by municipalities. Within the hosted salmonid population are many exceedingly large trout, both brown and rainbow. These number more than those in either the Henry's Fork or the South Fork reach and are the basis for considering the main stem a destination fishery.

The best times of the year for fishing the main stem are before and after the agricultural growing season. Seasonal irrigation demands begin in May and normally extend into late September. During this time river flows vary unpredictably, thus

All of eastern Idaho's Greater Yellowstone Area waters drain through the main stem Snake River, which is a superb seasonal fishery. Although flowing through agricultural and municipal areas, it offers large, robust brown and rainbow trout along with a few cutthroat trout.

impacting behavior of resident salmonids. These variations also impact aquatic insect behavior and have been a major factor, along with siltation, in the elimination of populations of some species.

The early season coincides with rainbow trout spawning runs. Weather this time of year determines if an outing will be physically comfortable, and ice remaining along shorelines can hinder access. Some boat launch facilities may not open until warmer nights prevail. Weather during the autumn is usually pleasant and coincides with brown trout spawning runs. This activity, along with clear water of normal flow, brings out more boating and wading anglers. Professionally guided trips during the late season are nearly as popular here as on the Henry's Fork and the South Fork reach above. During both seasons, streamer fishing under low-light conditions is most effective for encountering larger individuals of each species; however, some dry fly fishing takes place because of BWO, caddis, and midge emergences. Remnant emergences of other mayflies occur in scattered locations, even at times during irrigation season.

Overlooked by more glamorous waters upstream, the main stem Snake River can be considered a diamond in the rough. With the proper approach and reasonable effort, it has the possibility in season of outshining those upstream neighbors because of its excellent population of large trout.

Salt River Tributaries

CROW CREEK

Mostly a meadow stream, the Salt River's major tributary is best accessed in its upper reaches, where attractor and caddisfly patterns reliably bring responses from trout. Access over private land in the lower section is difficult to obtain.

Access: Crow Creek Road off Wyoming Highway 236 from US Highway 89
GPS Coordinates: 42.657011, -111.044421
Equipment: 4-weight system with floating and sink-tip lines; caddisfly, BWO, Golden Stone, PMD, Trico, and Yellow Sally patterns, and soft-hackle, streamer, terrestrial insect, and traditional attractor patterns
Nearest facilities and services: Alpine (Wyoming), USFS Pine Bar Campground, Hansen-Silver Guest Ranch
Information resources: Caribou-Targhee National Forest, Palisades Ranger Office; Idaho Falls, Elk Valley, Sage Valley, and Snowdrift Mountain USGS topographic maps
Salmonids present: Brown and cutthroat trout and Rocky Mountain whitefish

"Ya ain't gonna get no elk with that there fly pole!"

That was the cheerful comment offered by passing hunters years ago while I geared up on Crow Creek Road. I was beginning efforts to pursue early October run-up browns from the Salt River, with no other anglers in sight. It was not the only time I was subjected to good-natured ribbing while fishing during the late season. Crow Creek, southwest of Fairview, Wyoming, is the farthest upstream of the major creeks running east out of Idaho into the Salt River, and at least up to the Sage Creek confluence, is the largest. It is the least likely to be dewatered

Crow Creek is the major Salt River tributary. This creek features a late September brown trout run from the Salt River, when presenting streamer patterns with the utmost stealth becomes particularly effective. JOHN JURACEK PHOTO

in low water years and therefore frequently allows run-up brown trout during late summer and autumn.

Crow Creek Road parallels the creek for several miles. Unfortunately, much of the lower reaches in Idaho belong to absentee landowners, making access difficult. Above, the creek flows through national forest land for a ways soon after the Sage Creek confluence, then through another stretch of private land. Here landowners seem more willing to grant access, and there is no problem with access on the national forest land. As with ascending Jackknife and Stump Creeks, fewer brown trout and Rocky Mountain whitefish and more cutthroat trout inhabit this stream. Finally, as with Jackknife and Stump, Crow Creek enters national forest land to end by branching into tributaries. Are you interested in the Tenkara presentation technique that has proven so effective for small waters? You could not ask for a better location for trying it than on upper Crow Creek or on any of Idaho's Salt River tributaries!

JACKKNIFE CREEK

A great destination if you enjoy fishing beaver ponds and solitude. Expect cutthroat trout ranging to moderate sizes and a few large brown trout, especially near the Idaho-Wyoming border.

Access: Creamery Road off US Highway 89 to Jackknife Creek Road and trailhead
GPS Coordinates: 43.035064, -111.120477
Equipment: 4-weight system with floating and sink-tip lines; caddisfly, BWO, Golden Stone, PMD, Trico, and Yellow Sally patterns, and leech, soft-hackle, streamer, terrestrial insect, and traditional attractor patterns
Nearest facilities and services: Alpine (Wyoming), USFS McCoy Creek Campground, Hansen-Silver Guest Ranch
Information resources: Caribou-Targhee National Forest, Palisades Ranger Office, Idaho Falls; Etna and Tincup Mountain USGS topographic maps
Salmonids present: Brown and cutthroat trout and Rocky Mountain whitefish

Jackknife Creek, west of Etna, Wyoming, is the first, going upstream, of these excellent small waters. Paralleled by the graveled Jackknife Creek Road for a few miles, it enters national forest land just west of the Idaho-Wyoming state line. Here it flows through a meadow of sporadic willows and deep holes, and hosts a few large brown trout and some trophy cutthroat. The middle reach of this creek has undergone a recent reclamation project where the closely adjacent road and a bridge have been eliminated and replaced by a trail. In this reach, beaver ponds are numerous and the surroundings are beautiful. During low-water years trout residing in these beaver ponds tend to become sluggish during midsummer and move toward the top of the ponds, where an inflow of water allows a better virtual concentration of dissolved oxygen. Thus these locations as well as deeper runs are the best places to try during these times, and under such conditions playing fish swiftly and releasing them without leaving the water helps their survival.

STUMP CREEK

The Idaho portion of this stream has a lengthy meadow reach with some beaver ponds and flows through alternating public and private land.

Access: Smoky Canyon Mine Road off Wyoming Highway 238 and US Highway 89
GPS Coordinates: 42.784611, -111.064347
Equipment: 4-weight system with floating and sink-tip lines; caddisfly, BWO, Golden Stone, PMD, Trico, and Yellow Sally patterns, and leech, soft-hackle, streamer, terrestrial insect, and traditional attractor patterns
Nearest facilities and services: Alpine (Wyoming), USFS Pine Bar Campground, Stump Creek Guard Station rental cabin, Hansen-Silver Guest Ranch
Information resources: Caribou-Targhee National Forest, Palisades Ranger Office; Etna, and Tincup Mountain USGS topographic maps
Salmonids present: Brown and cutthroat trout and Rocky Mountain whitefish

Heading west off Highway 238 at the south end of Auburn, Wyoming, Smoky Canyon Mine Road provides access to Stump Creek. Beaver ponds begin just above the Smoky Canyon Mine Road crossing, and they spangle this creek for miles upstream. Below the crossing in Idaho, access is possible on some Bureau of Land Management land. There is much private land around the crossing, including the Tyghee Creek confluence, but with a courteous approach, some landowners will grant trespass. Fly shops in Star Valley and in Alpine, Wyoming, can supply contact information for these landowners. So good is the water quality and flow on Webster

A stay in Caribou-Targhee National Forest's Stump Creek Guard Station offers a tranquility not present in commercial accommodations. The number of quality small streams nearby is almost unmatched in the Greater Yellowstone Area.

Creek, a Stump Creek tributary, that the State of Wyoming has established their Auburn Fish Hatchery there, one purpose of which is to raise Snake River fine-spotted cutthroat trout.

At the Smoky Canyon Mine Road Bridge, Stump Creek Road turns right and follows the creek upstream. This is the route of the original Lander Cutoff, a former emigration route to California and Oregon. Not far upstream of this location, a fly fishing friend of mine caught a 27-inch brown trout a few years back. He sent me a picture of it with recognizable surroundings, so I have to believe him, assuming this was the true location. Snake River fine-spotted cutthroat trout here range to trophy size. Not far above on USFS Road 109, the Stump Creek Guard Station can be rented from Caribou-Targhee National Forest. The farther upstream one travels, the fewer brown trout and the more cutthroat inhabit the creek. Near the national forest boundary, the road becomes passable to only four-wheel-drive vehicles, but fishing remains good.

TINCUP CREEK

Even with easy access and a fair amount of fishing traffic, Tincup hosts a good cutthroat trout population, especially upstream of the paralleling highway.

Access: Idaho Highway 34 from Wyoming Highway 239 and US Highway 89 to Tincup Trail
GPS Coordinates: 42.978599, -111.167706
Equipment: 4-weight system with floating line; caddisfly, BWO, Golden Stone, PMD, Trico, and Yellow Sally patterns, and leech, soft-hackle, streamer, terrestrial insect, and traditional attractor patterns
Nearest facilities and services: Alpine (Wyoming), USFS Pine Bar and Tincup Campgrounds, Hansen-Silver Guest Ranch
Information resources: Caribou-Targhee National Forest, Palisades Ranger Office; Idaho Falls; Stump Peak, Thayne West, and Tincup Mountain USGS topographic maps
Salmonids present: Cutthroat trout and Rocky Mountain whitefish

"My dad, Jim Gabettas, Senior, cut his fly fishing teeth in the Tincup Creek drainage while tending sheep on my grandfather's allotment. That was about seventy years ago. The grazing allotments, tranquility, and near pristine conditions still reign in the drainage. So the two of us frequently visit this stream and its tributaries, which remain cutthroat trout strongholds. They are in my personal heritage," relates Jimmy Gabettas.

Tincup Creek is mainly a riffle-and-run stream with a few beaver ponds where paralleled on the north side by Idaho Highway 34. It is also the site of two developed campgrounds, one a few miles west of the Idaho-Wyoming border and the other just above the South Fork of Tincup Creek confluence. Local Trout Unlimited chapters and Caribou-Targhee National Forest are performing a restoration project here in which willows are being replaced and, in a few reaches, the stream is being restored to its natural channel. This action is certain to improve the habitat for the currently

The South Fork of Tincup Creek has beaver ponds hosting Snake River fine-spotted cutthroat up to near trophy sizes. This stream may experience only a few visits during the season.

Family visits to remote waters such as upper Tincup Creek provide pleasant fly fishing learning platforms. Lightweight gear and dry flies are most appropriate.

good population of cutthroat trout. Being close to the highway, it is likely the most heavily fished of the Salt River tributaries, but that isn't saying much compared to pressure on the nearby South Fork reach, Salt River, and Palisades Reservoir tributaries and the fact that most travelers are heading to and from Grand Teton and Yellowstone National Parks by this route.

The confluence with the South Fork of Tincup Creek is between the two campgrounds and is marked by a parking lot off Highway 34 and a stock bridge across the creek. Cross this bridge and follow the well-maintained Tincup Trail onto its tributaries, and you are in for a real treat if you enjoy fishing beaver ponds in isolation. A small leech pattern is sure to gain interest from resident cutthroat trout ranging to moderate sizes. What is more enjoyable is to drift traditional dry patterns with the slow current in these ponds and watch their measured, deliberate rises to take your offering.

A few miles above the upstream campground, Tincup Creek leaves the highway and parallels Tincup Road for a few miles. Along this road the creek may be smaller, holds only small cutthroat trout, and is much more isolated than on its lower reach.

South Fork Reach Tributaries

BEAR CREEK

Picturesque Bear Creek drains country southwest of Palisades Reservoir. Its motorized trail is narrow enough to restrict anything larger than small trail bikes.

Access: US Highway 26 below Palisades Dam to River Road to Bear Creek Road and Bear Creek trailhead
GPS Coordinates: 43.283090, -111.222311
Equipment: 4-weight system with floating line; caddisfly, Golden Stone, PMD, Trico, and Yellow Sally patterns, and soft-hackle, streamer, terrestrial insect, and traditional attractor patterns
Nearest facilities and services: Alpine (Wyoming), USFS Calamity Campground, The Lodge at Palisades Creek
Information resources: Caribou-Targhee National Forest, Palisades Ranger Office; Idaho Falls Visitor Center; Palisades Dam and Red Ridge USGS topographic maps
Salmonids present: Cutthroat trout

Bear Creek is the most remote of the South Fork reach tributaries we will discuss, and it is the only one not adjacent to a fully developed Forest Service campground. Bear Creek Road runs about 10 miles to the trailhead just above the confluence with the reservoir and offers striking views of the reservoir and surrounding country. From here the well-maintained motorized trail follows Bear Creek for several miles. It is suitable only for trail bikes and used mostly for foot travel and by horse parties. About 2 miles in on the trail, the picturesque Caribou-Targhee National Forest's Current Creek Guard Station, with potable springwater nearby, offers an enticing location for a lunch break in beautiful surroundings.

As with all major South Fork reach tributaries, Bear Creek can be high and discolored with springtime runoff, but well-placed streamers presented in deeper holes

Bear Creek hosts a springtime Yellowstone cutthroat trout run with individuals exceeding 20 inches, many of which remain in the creek well into summer. A few beaver ponds are present where leech patterns are most effective, but elsewhere Bear Creek beckons to be fished with dry fly patterns.

during this time can bring strikes from fish ranging to over 20 inches. After spawning, many of these trout soon descend back to the reservoir, but with good water conditions some stay until late summer, when the creek warms and drops to base level. The most enjoyable time to fish Bear Creek is during the summer terrestrial insect season. Much of the lower part of the creek flows through a sloping sagebrush and grass meadow that becomes rich with ants, beetles, crane flies, and hoppers. Undercut banks, a few deep holes, and abundant overhead cover from willows provide shelter for trout and therefore signal where to concentrate fishing efforts. In lower-gradient reaches, beaver ponds add variety and offer a chance to present leech and damselfly patterns. As with the other South Fork reach tributaries, it's difficult to leave this beautiful stream at the end of a visit.

BIG ELK CREEK

Big Elk Creek is a fly fishing treasure. Walk up its excellent trail about 1.5 miles. If scenery does not distract you, present terrestrial insect and dry attractor patterns and watch cutthroat trout ranging to 20 inches rise in their deliberate manner to take your offering.

Access: US Highway 26 to Big Elk Creek Road to Big Elk Creek trailhead
GPS Coordinates: 43.283090, -111.110337
Equipment: 4-weight system with floating line; caddisfly, flav, Golden Stone, PMD, Trico, and Yellow Sally patterns, and soft-hackle, streamer, terrestrial insect, and traditional attractor patterns
Nearest facilities and services: Alpine (Wyoming), USFS Big Elk Creek Campground, The Lodge at Palisades Creek
Information resources: Caribou-Targhee National Forest, Palisades Ranger Office; Idaho Falls Visitor Center; Mount Baird USGS topographic map
Salmonids present: Cutthroat trout and kokanee salmon

Big Elk Creek should be a media star, with resident cutthroat trout ranging to over 20 inches as well as a late-summer kokanee salmon run. Famed for its August afternoon western green drake emergence, this creek is an aquatic treasure.

Big Elk Creek Road proceeds through a large Forest Service campground, and after about 3 miles ends at a trailhead with a toilet and stock corral. It's a popular jump-off point for backpackers, hikers, tour groups, photographers, horse parties, and to a lesser extent, anglers. While walking up this nonmotorized trail, you can hear Big Elk Creek roar in the hollow below in its descent to Palisades Reservoir. Numerous springs on either side of the hollow contribute cold quality water to the flow.

Around 1.5 miles up the trail, the visitor breaks out of the pine forest into an open hollow through which the creek courses with lesser gradient. Here begins some of the best fishing these four South Fork reach tributaries offer. The reason becomes obvious on viewing the creek flowing through a series of deep holes below. Shaded by broken willow patches, this series of holes host Snake River fine-spotted and Yellowstone cutthroat trout ranging to over 20 inches, which rivals the largest in the South Fork reach. These holes continue upstream, where the trail descends to the creek.

With sources in the Wyoming high country, Big Elk Creek carries more runoff than the other tributaries, as can be realized by observing the surrounding mountains that climb to 10,000 feet and provide breathtaking scenery. Thus the best time to fish it begins soon after the first of July, when terrestrial insect populations begin to expand. Big Elk Creek is a great example of how heat radiating from a stream can dictate when hosted aquatic insects emerge. Applying this to Big Elk's celebrated August Western Green Drake emergence dictates fishing strategy. Because of the numerous springs that feed it and the high-elevation sources, Big Elk begins a midsummer day with water temperatures in the low 40s. Hours of warming are required to reach water temperatures at which these insects emerge.

Emergence usually begins in mid-afternoon and extends until early evening hours, with cutthroat trout, the sole salmonid inhabitant of the creek, responding to duns and emergers with gusto. To encounter this event, begin with a leisurely walk up the trail around midday after lunch, enjoy the trout fishing during afternoon hours, then descend the trail with the goal of a hearty dinner.

McCOY CREEK

Easily accessible, uncrowded, and hosting eager cutthroat trout, McCoy Creek's meadow reach is a standout destination for the entry-level or young fly fisher. It's a creek for all seasons.

Access: US Highway 89 to McCoy Creek Road
GPS Coordinates: 42.182265, -111.109291
Equipment: 4-weight system with floating line; caddisfly, Golden Stone, PMD, Trico, and Yellow Sally patterns, and soft-hackle, streamer, terrestrial insect, and traditional attractor patterns
Nearest facilities and services: Alpine (Wyoming), USFS McCoy Creek Campground, USFS Caribou Mountain Guard Station rental cabin, Hansen Silver Ranch
Information resources: Caribou-Targhee National Forest, Palisades Ranger Office; Idaho Falls Visitor Center; Alpine and Poker Peak USGS topographic maps
Salmonids present: Cutthroat trout and Rocky Mountain whitefish

McCoy Creek hosts an early-season run of Snake River fine-spotted cutthroat trout, with some trophy-size individuals. After most runoff has left the creek, it can be a destination.

Of the South Fork reach tributaries we discuss, McCoy Creek is the only one paralleled by a road. This well-maintained road leaves US Highway 89 3 miles south of Alpine, Wyoming, skirts the southeast end of Palisades Reservoir then parallels the creek for miles. A fully developed Forest Service campground near the confluence of the creek with the reservoir provides a convenient base from which to not only visit McCoy Creek, but also explore the Salt River drainage.

McCoy Creek is a major spawning tributary and, as with adjacent Bear Creek, a runoff stream of mainly freestone character. Certain reaches are of some gradient, but about 2 miles above its confluence with Palisades Reservoir, the gradient eases in a sloping meadow featuring pockets of gravel suitable for spawning, open bankside willow thickets, and deep holes in every bend. This part of the creek is ideal for spawning, considering the presence of quality gravel, overhead cover, and deep holes for protection. It is also ideal for walk-in wade fishing. Numerous pullouts provide excellent access and minimize walking.

During the spring after a winter of abundant snowfall, streamer fishing for post-spawning cutthroat trout can be effective as runoff recedes. This is one my favorite times for a visit, and has resulted in encountering many trophy-size cutthroat trout that have temporarily taken up residence in deeper pools. Several miles upstream, beaver ponds offer a different approach. Their bounty of leeches discourage wet wading, while offering a sure way to encounter the numerous but small cutthroat trout. Another time I find this creek enjoyable is during midsummer, when grasshoppers populate these meadows. A lightweight system is ideal for encountering cutthroat trout to moderate sizes looking for these as well as other terrestrial insects.

PALISADES CREEK

This is the most popular of the South Fork reach tributaries. It hosts an excellent population of cutthroat trout.

Access: US Highway 26 to Palisades Creek Road to Palisades Creek trailhead
GPS Coordinates: 43.397178, -111.214781
Equipment: 4-weight system with floating line; caddisfly, flav, Golden Stone, PMD, Trico, and Yellow Sally patterns, and soft-hackle, streamer, terrestrial insect, and traditional attractor patterns
Nearest facilities and services: Idaho Falls (Idaho), USFS Palisades Creek Campground, The Lodge at Palisades Creek
Information resources: Caribou-Targhee National Forest, Palisades Ranger Office; Idaho Falls Visitor Center; Palisades Peak and Thompson Peak USGS topographic maps
Salmonids present: Cutthroat and cuttbow trout

In addition to being below Palisades Dam, Palisades Creek is unique among these tributaries in that there are two lakes in its drainage. Both Upper and Lower Palisades Lakes were formed by ancient landslides, and both have subterranean outflows. This flow ensures that the creek below is well supplied with water throughout the season. The lower creek flows through private land; however, where the access

Lower Rainey Creek hosts large trout that respond to the same insect emergences taking place on the nearby South Fork reach. It's only a few yards off US Highway 26 in Idaho's Swan Valley, yet is bypassed because of the adjacent South Fork reach.

road enters the full-service campground and trailhead, it flows completely through national forest land.

Four miles of freestone stream with varying gradient parallel a well-maintained nonmotorized trail to Lower Palisades Lake, although in places diverging onto a ridge above the creek. It is practical to fish the lower lake through packing in a lightweight floatation device; insulated waders are a must for floating. Leech and damselfly patterns are appropriate for fishing the lake. The creek can be accessed through scattered openings in willow thickets along the way. Trout, mostly Yellowstone cutthroat but also a few cuttbows, all ranging to near trophy size, lie within the deepest holes or forage underneath the abundant overhead cover. The same applies to nearby Rainey Creek, where a deep portion flows along the highway holds large brown and cutthroat trout and is seldom visited because of the fly fishing excitement generated by the adjacent South Fork reach.

More than the other South Fork reach tributaries, Palisades Creek is a caddisfly and stonefly stream with a lesser mayfly population, although lower-gradient reaches host some mayflies in significant numbers. Downstream of the lake, the best fishing occurs from mid to late summer when terrestrial insects are plentiful. For about a half mile above the lower lake, the creek meanders at an easy gradient through a marshy area holding an occasional beaver pond. However, because Palisades Creek, as with its neighbor Big Elk Creek, has a major runoff component, these ponds are not always present. Nevertheless, the best fishing on the creek is here just above the lower lake.

Lower Palisades Lake is best fished by wading where the creek enters. Here fish concentrate to feed on items drifting in, whether terrestrial insects, aquatic insects, or leeches from beaver ponds and marshes above. Above the marshy area the creek returns to a higher gradient, but diminishes noticeably after the flow from Upper Palisades Lake enters. Situated in Dry Canyon at an elevation above the creek, this lake offers fishing along the shoreline for smaller trout.

Palisades Creek is a freestone stream of high-enough quality to be a destination for fly fishers seeking solitude. It also offers cutthroat trout ranging to trophy size that respond well to dry attractor, caddis, and terrestrial patterns.

PART 3

SOUTHWESTERN MONTANA

All Greater Yellowstone Area waters in Montana are on the Atlantic side of the Continental Divide, and ultimately they all are part of the Missouri River drainage. Included in what we will discuss are much of Gallatin, Madison, and Yellowstone watersheds as well as part of the Beaverhead watershed. The Gallatin, Madison, and Yellowstone Rivers also have significant portions in Yellowstone

Upper Red Rock Lake and lower Red Rock Creek are in a superbly scenic setting. The lake hosts one of the best grayling populations in the Lower 48. The creek provides their spawning and rearing habitat.

123

Montana grayling are nearly in the endangered species category; therefore, future sportfishing restrictions are possible. When in a feeding mode, small dry fly patterns that imitate drifting terrestrial and adult aquatic insects interest them. Use lightweight gear to enjoy their deliberate rise and take.

National Park. Fly fishers from around the world assemble to enjoy these rivers, and a nearly uncountable number of works have been published on fishing each of them.

For the entire 20th century, nearly all the fly fishing attention went to the Gallatin, Madison, and Yellowstone Rivers, with little thought given to their tributaries within the Greater Yellowstone Area. The original native salmonid species, except for Rocky Mountain whitefish, have been reduced to remnants here. Realizing the economic value of these great destinations for fly fishers, Montana has efforts under way to protect the remnants and, where deemed practical, reestablish them. Many of these actions are taking place in the state's share of Greater Yellowstone Area waters.

We discussed the reasons for this attention earlier and how these famed rivers brought visitation to not only Yellowstone National Park waters, but also those waters conveniently reached from Montana towns including Bozeman, Gardiner, Livingston, and West Yellowstone. It began with visits and resulting literature from Dan Bailey, Joe Brooks, and Ray Bergman. Later Pat Barnes, Charlie Brooks, Bud Lilly, Don Martinez, Merton Parks, and Ernie Schwiebert extolled the virtues of these waters. In the second half of the 20th century, Charlie Brooks's spellbinding books, most based on the quality fisheries within the Madison River drainage, brought even more attention to Montana's famed rivers. More recently, John Bailey, Bob Jacklin, John Juracek, Craig Mathews, and Richard Parks are champions of these rivers. Most of their attention has been on the famed larger rivers and not so much on other waters, the big exception being Yellowstone Lake and the gulper phenomena on Hebgen and Quake Lakes as soon as individual floatation devices became popular. In total, it is likely that more attention has been given to and more is known about Montana waters within the Greater Yellowstone Area than those in Idaho, Wyoming, and Yellowstone National Park. However, Montana also hosts some excellent backcountry waters within the Greater Yellowstone Area that haven't received as much attention but offer some superb fishing.

Gallatin River Drainage

GOLDEN TROUT LAKES
By Bob Jacklin

Golden trout in an alpine setting; reaching them requires some strenuous physical effort.

Access: US Highway 191 to end of Portal Creek Road and Golden Trout Lakes trailhead
GPS Coordinates: 45.258321, -111.127716
Equipment: 3- or 4-weight system with floating and full-sink lines; damselfly, dragonfly, midge, and Speckled Dun patterns, and leech and scud patterns
Nearest facilities and services: Big Sky (Montana), USFS Red Cliff Campground, Windy Pass Rental Cabin, The Lodge at Big Sky
Information resources: West Yellowstone (Montana) Visitor Center; Custer-Gallatin National Forest, Supervisor's Office; Bozeman; Hidden Lake and The Sentinal USGS topographic maps
Salmonids present: Golden trout

Golden Trout Lakes is a series of three small lakes high up the Portal Creek Drainage just below Eagle Head Mountain in the eastern section of the Gallatin National Forest. The lakes are just to the north of the Big Sky area and on the east side of the Gallatin River. At about 9,000 feet in elevation, ice usually leaves these lakes around the first of July. July and August are the best times to fish here. These lakes were stocked via horseback, like many others in Montana, with California golden trout fingerlings in 1938.

Take the Portal Creek Forest Service road east, past the right-hand fork going to Hidden Lakes, all the way to the end, about 8 miles. Drive carefully; a

Nonnative golden trout are present in some Greater Yellowstone Area alpine lakes, but not in great numbers. They provide lightweight tackle action and are sought in many cases for their beauty alone. LOOP FLY USA PHOTO

four-wheel-drive vehicle is advised. There is a parking area at the trailhead with a marker. From there on, it is uphill through timber and some switchbacks for about 3 miles to the first lake. It can be fished from nearly its entire shoreline. Just across the lake from where the trail meets the water is a small feeder stream. If you follow this stream up, you come to a small lake that also hosts some golden trout. To survive, golden trout need an outlet stream and/or an outlet feeder where spawning can take place. To the right of this little spawning stream is another small lake, which seems to be fishless.

There are a few tips to remember when fishing a high alpine lake, especially for golden trout. Most of the food found in alpine lakes occurs along the shallow areas. The fish there are feeding and thus will take your fly. Small flies like midge larvae and dries in sizes 16-20 are most effective. A lightweight rod, floating line, and long, finely tapered 5X leader are ideal for fishing this lake.

I consider the golden trout here to be a real treasure. They give the angler visiting or living in the Greater Yellowstone Area a chance to catch a real California golden trout. The lake is easy to get to with reasonable hiking but requires good health. The fish are small, up to about 8 or 10 inches, but beautifully colored. A good-quality camera should be taken along to capture this coloration, along with the beautiful alpine scenery. As with the nearby Hidden Lakes, high-country precautions for weather should be observed.

HIDDEN LAKES
By Charles Barnes

Striking alpine scenery and usually reliably feeding golden trout make these lakes worth the physical effort required to get to them.

Access: US Highway 191 to Portal Creek Road, USFS Road 2686, and Hidden Lakes trailhead
GPS Coordinates: 45.258211, -111.127531
Equipment: 3- or 4-weight system (5-weight system for lakes hosting larger fish) with floating and full-sink lines; damselfly, dragonfly, midge, and Speckled Dun patterns, and leech and scud patterns
Nearest facilities and services: Big Sky (Montana), USFS Red Cliff Campground, The Lodge at Big Sky
Information resources: West Yellowstone (Montana) Visitor Center; Custer-Gallatin National Forest, Supervisor's Office; Bozeman; Hidden Lake USGS topographic map
Salmonids present: Golden trout

Mountain lakes in the Gallatin and Madison Ranges of Montana offer fishing opportunities that take a lifetime to fully explore. Two of my favorites in the Gallatin Range are the Hidden Lakes and the nearby Golden Trout Lakes. I like these for two reasons: They are among the few lakes in southwest Montana where golden trout can be found and caught fairly easily, and they are surrounded by majestic scenery. At certain times during the summer, huckleberries along the way are another plus. One of my sons caught his first trout, a golden, in one of these lakes. Golden trout

The Hidden Lakes in the Gallatin River drainage offer good chances to encounter golden trout. Presenting small dry flies with lightweight gear is the most satisfying way to fish for these beautiful trout. Have that camera ready to record their beauty. CHARLES BARNES PHOTO

were first planted in two of the Hidden Lakes in 1932, and Montana Fish, Wildlife & Parks continued planting them through 1991.

I've seen passenger cars at the trailhead, but I recommend a four-wheel-drive vehicle because of the rocky and steep road. After winding nearly 4 miles and climbing from an elevation at the highway turnoff of 5,850 feet to about 7,300 feet, the road forks. The left-hand fork is a continuation of USFS Road 984 and goes to the Golden Lakes trailhead; the right-hand fork is USFS Road 2686 and goes about 2.25 miles to the Hidden Lakes trailhead and parking area. The trail goes south for the first mile or so and then swings west, with a total climb of about 500 feet to the first lakes.

The very first lake, which you might not even notice, is several hundred feet north of the trail and is fishless. Much closer to the trail are the adjacent Delta and Epsilon Lakes, around 5 acres each. Both hold small golden trout that, during summer months, will often be rising. Wearing waders not only keeps you dry but can give you an advantage when casting, both to get out to deeper water and to have room to backcast. Wading wet is practical if the weather is good. Epsilon Lake has a pretty good drop-off on the southwest side. There are several primitive campsites in the trees around these lakes; I like the one between the two lakes.

Going farther up the winding trail about four-tenths of a mile, climbing another 300 feet, takes you to Beta Lake. It's a deeper lake than Delta and Epsilon, and although the fishing is relatively slow, I've heard that it holds some golden trout up to 16 inches. One hundred yards to the south and about 30 feet higher is Alpha Lake, about 20 acres and around 100 feet deep. Alpha has produced the largest golden trout of the lakes, at 4 to 5 pounds. Below Beta and not far to the north is Gamma Lake, about 5 acres, which offers good fishing for small trout. The two remaining lakes in the group are barren.

A lightweight rod would be delightful for fishing the lakes holding small fish, but for lakes hosting larger fish, a 5- or 6-weight rod is more appropriate. I've found that small dries (#16) and nymphs (#12-14) with a floating line work well for the small golden trout in Delta and Epsilon Lakes. For the deeper lakes, use a sinking line and larger nymphs. Fishing from shore or wading out from the bank are the primary methods of fishing these lakes; switchbacks on the trail make packing in a float tube and fins difficult unless you're in excellent physical condition. Rain gear is another necessity for fishing these or any high-altitude lakes because thundershowers are frequent and can not only develop any time of day, but remain for days at a time.

HYALITE CREEK AND HYALITE RESERVOIR
By William Liebegott

This system offers catch-and-release fishing for cutthroat in the creek and grayling in the reservoir just outside of Bozeman. The creek is a candidate for a convenient get-away from town for a few hours.

Access: US Highway 191 to South Cottonwood Road to South 19th Avenue to Hyalite Canyon Road

GPS Coordinates: 45.501696, -110.986259 (creek); 45.482457, -110.964279 (reservoir)

Equipment: Hyalite Creek: 3- or 4-weight system with floating line; caddisfly, PMD, Golden Stone, Trico, and Yellow Sally patterns, and soft-hackle, terrestrial insect, traditional attractor, and nymph patterns. Hyalite Reservoir: 3- or 4-weight system with intermediate and sinking lines; damselfly, dragonfly, and Speckled Dun patterns, and leech, scud, and streamer patterns

Nearest facilities and services: Bozeman (Montana), USFS Langhor Campground for Hyalite Creek, USFS Chisholm Campground for Hyalite Reservoir, Maxey rental cabin, Bozeman Inn

Information resources: Custer-Gallatin National Forest, Supervisor's Office; USGS Flow Station Gage 06050000; Fridley Peak, Mount Ellis, and Wheeler Mountain USGS topographic maps

Salmonids present: Brook, brown, cutthroat, and rainbow trout in Hyalite Creek; brook and cutthroat trout and Montana grayling in Hyalite Reservoir

Hyalite Creek is a little south of Bozeman and is a wonderful, idyllic waterway. The area is wild, with black bear and elk. It's small water compared to the Gallatin and Madison Rivers but filled with many feisty trout. A catch-and-release regulation applies to cutthroat. Most of the trout are in the 8-inch range, but I have caught fish longer than 12 inches. It's a lightweight rod stream, but between its beauty and the willingness of the fish, one can have a wonderful time fishing this water. I find the creek to be ideal for Tenkara fishing. I consider the Gallatin River my home water but, during runoff, Hyalite Creek is a handy and more-than-suitable alternative.

Hyalite Creek offers a quality lightweight-tackle alternative for Bozeman-area fly fishers. Having four hosted salmonid species adds to the fun of fishing this creek, and each will take dry flies with abandon. BILL LIEBEGOTT PHOTO

I am a nymph fisherman and almost always use the same fly on Hyalite Creek, a Twist Nymph, but I don't think fly choice on the creek is important. I once took someone's challenge and caught fish, lots of fish, on a bead head tied with blue yarn. Anglers of all terminal gear persuasion fish Hyalite Creek.

Hyalite Canyon was named for a rare translucent opal discovered here well over a hundred years ago. Much of the fishing is adjacent to Hyalite Canyon Road, with frequent pullouts; however, for the adventuresome, remote fishing can be enjoyed in the canyon, especially above the reservoir. It just requires some walking and effort, but deadfalls can make some hikes arduous. Above Hyalite Reservoir the stream is closed until the third Saturday in July to lessen the disturbance to spawning cutthroat. Both the lower and upper reaches close on November 30. The Forest Service has provided a pair of wheelchair-accessible fishing spots in Langhor Canyon Campground below the reservoir. These are on the west side of the creek, but a bridge in the campground and paved paths provide an opportunity for those in need.

Scenic Hyalite Reservoir, approximately 200 to 250 acres, is the water source for the city of Bozeman. Fishing the reservoir is enjoyed by lots of people, mostly for meat. Boats are permitted, as are floatation devices. The lake has a no-wake rule, which adds to the serenity if you are in a float tube. Sitting in a float tube on the reservoir during the spring can be a breathtaking experience because of the nearby snowcapped 10,000-foot peaks. A catch-and-release regulation applies to grayling.

A trip up the canyon to Hyalite Reservoir also provides lots of opportunities for hiking and other outdoor activities. Some of the shorter, easier hikes are to Palisades Falls and History Rock. Fall colors in Hyalite Canyon are spectacular!

TAYLOR FORK
By William Liebegott

A mostly overlooked stream that has some surprisingly sizable trout and excellent hopper fishing.

Access: Taylor Fork Road off US Highway 191
GPS Coordinates: 45.072256, -111.198870
Equipment: 4- or 5-weight system with floating line: caddisfly, BWO, PMD, Golden Stone, and Yellow Sally patterns, and terrestrial insect, traditional attractor, and streamer patterns
Nearest facilities and services: West Yellowstone (Montana), Swan Creek Campground, Wapiti rental cabin, Nine Quarter Circle Ranch
Information resources: West Yellowstone Visitor Center; Custer-Gallatin National Forest, Bozeman Ranger District Office; Lincoln Mountain and Sunshine Point USGS topographic maps
Salmonids present: Brown, cutthroat, and rainbow trout

Bald eagles are revered, and viewing them adds quality to the experience of visiting Greater Yellowstone waters. They are on the increase in the Greater Yellowstone Area, as well they should, being our national symbol. DAVE LETENDRE PHOTO

The Taylor Fork is one of the many tributaries of the Gallatin River, and perhaps the most significant. It certainly is one of the largest. Unfortunately, this stream runs dirty in the spring or during a heavy summer rain, and its discharge colors the Gallatin. The Taylor Fork is about 2.5 miles north of the Yellowstone Park boundary on US Highway 191. Or, if you are in the Bozeman area, it is just less than 48 miles south of Four Corners. It flows under the highway at the 34 mile marker. You can drive the full length of the stream, which is more than 8 miles. Signs on the highway silently trumpet the Taylor Fork.

Several areas are designated for primitive camping along the dirt road. Wapiti Cabin on tributary Wapiti Creek can be rented from Custer-Gallatin National Forest. Whether you are camping or just fishing, it is important to remember that this area is bear country. About 5 miles from the highway, you will come upon the Nine Quarter Circle Ranch. Some restrictions apply there, but they are minimal. On ranch property, no parking is allowed on the road or off it. This minor inconvenience, clearly

As with many streams between the Gallatin and Madison Rivers, the Taylor Fork is mostly bypassed by visiting fly fishers.

marked with signs, runs for less than a mile. As you exit the no-parking area, a large sign on the right announcing the Albino Lake trailhead can easily be seen. From here on, the restrictions end.

The Gallatin River almost doubles in size on combining with the Taylor Fork. It is well worth fishing, but it is best in the summer and fall when the water runs clear. I have caught many rainbows in the 10- to 14-inch range and also a few small cutthroats. Browns in excess of 18 inches might even test you. I have had the pleasure of hooking several 20-inch browns in the Taylor Fork.

The Taylor Fork can be an exciting stream to fish because of its hopper fishing, but I am a nymph fisherman and have had great success on this water with my Twist Nymphs. I've even caught two rainbows at the same time while fishing two Twist Nymphs. The water is deep enough in many areas for nymphing. At the 6- to 7-mile point, the Taylor Fork appears to become a meadow stream because of the terrain; however, careful observation reveals a brisk flow rate due largely to the gradient. This area seems to be an excellent hopper fishing spot. It is in this stretch that the Taylor Peaks loom above you as if they were giant snow cones. Whether you are interested in wildlife, majestic mountains, or good fishing, the Taylor Fork has something for you.

Jefferson River Drainage

LOWER RUBY RIVER
By Tim Tollett

The best time to try for large resident brown and scattered rainbow trout is when runoff recedes until irrigation season drawdowns lower and warm the river.

Access: Montana Highway 41 to Ruby River Road and Montana Highway 357
GPS Coordinates: 45.319814, -112.117731
Equipment: 5-weight system with floating and sink-tip lines; caddisfly, BWO, PMD, Golden Stone, Mahogany Dun, Trico, and Yellow Sally patterns, and soft-hackle, terrestrial insect, and traditional attractor patterns
Nearest facilities and services: Sheridan (Montana), Ruby Valley Lodge
Information resources: USGS Flow Station Gage 06020600; Alder, Beaverhead Rock NE, Laurin Canyon, Ruby Dam, and Sheridan USGS topographic maps
Salmonids present: Brown and rainbow trout

Below Ruby Reservoir the Ruby River meanders past Alder and Laurin to complete its flow in an agricultural valley and join the Beaverhead River near Twin Bridges, Montana. Before the days of large-scale private land buy-ups, access to the river was mostly a matter of courteous inquiry, and on doing so trespass was usually granted. These days, new owners of land bordering the river tend to deny trespass in an absolute manner. Lock-up seems to be the current norm along the

It is legal in Montana to access navigable streams through private lands by use of public bridges and road right-of-ways. In doing so, stay within the high-water mark and respect private land boundaries.

Ruby River Reservoir offers good early-season fishing, which diminishes as irrigation demands deplete its water during the agricultural growing season. Come back in the late autumn when waters cool and impoundment of inflow begins.

river, meaning that access for walk-in fishing below the reservoir has become the basis for controversy. It is true that boating in order to fish is possible, but most of the river is decidedly tight for drift boat use, though not so much for smaller craft. Montana law allows the public to access navigable rivers such as this at any bridge or road right-of-way and, as in Idaho, public presence is legal within the ordinary high-water mark. Well-heeled landowners have contested this access in the courts, and have gone so far as attempting to fence accesses at bridges and obstruct high-water mark access. Where these attempts have failed to prevent the angling public from exercising their lawful access, intimidation by landowners has occurred, but this activity is also illegal and is grounds for prosecution for harassment in the state of Montana.

Controversy benefits no one, public or private. Thus organizations are forming to bring landowners and the public, anglers included, together to gain mutual respect and understanding. The Ruby Habitat Foundation is one such organization, working to raise awareness of the value of the Ruby River and its surroundings. Through its parent Montana Land Reliance, the foundation is obtaining and managing conservation easements, having made both landowners and the public aware that the river and its drainage are a treasure meant to be enjoyed by all but also protected. Some landowners and ranchers along the lower Ruby River are now working with those who want to enjoy the river to establish a dialogue to move away from controversy and establish reciprocal respect for the benefit of the watershed. Cooperation between the Ruby Habitat Foundation and the Woodson family takes place on the Ruby River below the reservoir. We address this cooperation below because it serves as a model for how a protective organization, a landowner, and the public can come together under an umbrella of mutual respect to preserve a natural treasure. In addition to this limited private-land access, five public access sites exist below the Ruby River Dam.

The lower Ruby River (the reach below the dam) is mainly a brown trout fishery. A few rainbow trout are present, reputedly by accident. According to local legend, a sleepy employee allowed the dam gates to remain open long enough to allow their escape. Some are now found not only in the river for a mile or so below the dam, but also in some of the spring creeks in the Ruby River Valley. BWOs begin emerging in April and bring some reliable activity from trout, but June usually features runoff that slows fishing, and early-season irrigation demands can also interfere. The best fishing therefore takes place from July through September. PMDs, then caddisflies and crane flies, followed by terrestrial insects, and finally Tricos and BWOs bring trout to the surface during this season. With the onset of autumn, streamer patterns become important for encountering large brown trout.

THE WOODSON RANCH AND THE RUBY HABITAT FOUNDATION

The Woodson family's concern for the quality of their land and its proper use, combined with a willingness to allow appreciative fly fishers to enjoy an improved trout population, provides an unequaled story in the Greater Yellowstone Area.

Access: Montana Highway 357
GPS Coordinates: 45.361879, -112.121925
Equipment: 4- or 5-weight system with floating line; caddisfly, BWO, Mahogany Dun, PMD, Golden Stone, Trico, and Yellow Sally patterns, and soft-hackle, terrestrial insect, and traditional attractor patterns
Nearest facilities and services: Sheridan (Montana), Ruby Springs Lodge
Information resources: The Woodson Ranch; USGS Flow Station Gage 06020600; Sheridan USGS topographic map
Salmonids present: Brown and rainbow trout

Craig Woodson believed his ranch could be operated for productive agriculture yet benefit wildlife and fisheries. Through foresight he ensured that his vision of land stewardship on the ranch continued with the establishment of the Ruby Habitat Foundation. When he passed away in 2011, operation of the Woodson Ranch, about 10 miles below Ruby River Reservoir near Laurin, Montana, was gifted to the foundation he had created. Also included are miles of a Ruby River braid called Clear Creek, a mile of Alder Creek, and a mile-long, human-augmented spring creek system with a series of deep, rainbow-trout-fattening ponds that also serves to add clarified water back to the Ruby itself.

The Ruby Habitat Foundation, under its parent, the Montana Land Reliance, both nonprofit organizations, continues management of the Woodson Ranch stewardship programs, many of which have been in operation for several years. These

Fly fishers visiting the Woodson Ranch check-in at this cabin. They are guided to their assigned location on the Ruby River within the ranch, or other ranch waters, and offered fly fishing strategies suitable for their visit.

projects include portions of the ranch that serve as demonstrations for small-scale agriculture, experimental wildlife food plots, tree exclosures, soil health trials, and outdoor classrooms for Madison and Beaverhead County children. All these activities are conducted in a manner that does not negatively impact the river and its fish population. These actions are implemented by a professional, conservation-minded agricultural management company (Ranch Resources, Sheridan, Montana) and promoted by a full-time outreach coordinator. On Woodson property, land practices are ongoing to specifically protect the river. These include capturing natural and irrigation runoff to prevent erosion, removing sediment and nutrients from surface water, and recharging of groundwater. Visitors to the property are welcomed to view the results of these actions, and are encouraged to make donations to help sustain progress.

The Woodson Ranch is a destination in demand by fly fishers with a passion for conservation. The Ruby's channels, deep holes, and long riffles; a reconditioned spring creek; a fishing pond; and Alder Creek offer fly fishing for well-conditioned rainbow and brown trout. The foundation limits access to these waters to no more than four rods per day on a reservation basis. The "beat system" applies, meaning any portion of water fished on a given day is closed the following day to minimize human impact on the fishery. Fishing is best from mid-June to the second week of October, with low water during midsummer slowing fishing on some waters at times. Being 85 percent booked for fly fishing during the June-to-October season is common. Catch-and-release fly fishing with single barbless hooks is required. In total, this translates into fishing allowed but managed in the best interests of the resource.

That this treasure is available to a respectful fly fishing public is a gift originating with Craig Woodson, a generous proprietor with a genuine love for the land he owned, and passed on by his family. That it will continue in its current operation also requires mutual respect for the property by the public. This is an excellent example of how a thoughtful and benevolent landowner can gift the fly fishing public, and how that public can not only be in debt to that landowner, but also have an opportunity to express appreciation by helping sustain this unusual gift.

UPPER RUBY RIVER

An isolated freestone stream in beautiful mountain surroundings, perfect for catching trout up to moderate size on lightweight tackle.

Access: Montana Highway 357 to Upper Ruby River Road
GPS Coordinates: 45.049839, -112.011109
Equipment: 3- or 4-weight system with floating line; caddisfly, PMD, Golden Stone, Trico, and Yellow Sally patterns, and soft-hackle, terrestrial insect, and traditional attractor patterns
Nearest facilities and services: Sheridan (Montana), USFS Cottonwood Campground, Vigilante Middle House rental cabin, Upper Canyon Outfitters and Guest Ranch
Information resources: Sheridan Work Center, Madison Ranger District, Beaverhead-Deerlodge National Forest; USGS Flow Station Gage 06019500; Home Park Ranch, Ruby Dam, and Warm Springs Creek USGS topographic maps
Salmonids present: Cutthroat and rainbow trout and Montana grayling

Ruby River Reservoir, stocked nearly every year, offers some early-season rainbow trout fishing through boating and from wading banks. One of the better locations for action, as with almost any reservoir, is near the inlet at the south end of the reservoir. Only primitive boat-launching facilities exist. Waters warm as irrigation demands lower the water level, slowing fishing success as the agricultural season progresses.

Montana Highway 357 pavement ends 12 miles south of Alder. The gravel portion of the highway is well-maintained at least to the Beaverhead-Deerlodge National Forest boundary. For 18 miles above the reservoir the river flows through private land, including Ted Turner's Snow Crest Ranch, with access only at road crossings. Seeing the river winding through the hay meadows and willow thickets and not being able to obtain access is an anxious situation for visiting fly fishers traveling to public land upstream. Landowners here are at least as inhospitable to allowing trespass as most of those below the reservoir.

Access is not immediate when the road, now Upper Ruby River Road, enters Beaverhead-Deerlodge National Forest, as some private ranches encompass the river for about 5 miles. But on reaching the Vigilante Ranger Station, access becomes plentiful. From here the road can be dusty and a bit rough, with chuckholes and washboards by the end of summer, but is good for any vehicle driven with care. Pullouts are numerous, and those in which camping is allowed are indicated by a Forest Service camping sign. The Ruby here is another scenic high-country small river flowing between the Snowcrest and Gravelly Ranges, and it offers the best of such streams without interruptions from boats, though on occasion from curious

The upper Ruby River flows in a scenic setting through Beaverhead-Deerlodge National Forest. Here the river hosts a healthy cutthroat and rainbow trout population with a Montana grayling population attempting to establish.

cattle. Westslope cutthroat and cuttbows make up the salmonid population. Montana grayling are occasionally stocked here, but have yet to establish a sustaining population. Being mostly riffles and runs, it should be obvious that fishing the pools and heads of runs is the best strategy, and wet wading during summer is comfortable.

BOULDER RIVER
By Gregg Messel

A remote river on the northwest edge of the Greater Yellowstone Area that sees little traffic.

Access: Interstate 90 to Montana Highway 69 and County Road 319
GPS Coordinates: 45.049839. -112.011109
Equipment: 4-weight system with floating line; caddisfly, PMD, Golden Stone, Trico, and Yellow Sally patterns, and soft-hackle, terrestrial insect, and traditional attractor patterns
Nearest facilities and services: Whitehall (Montana), Whitetail Creek Motel and RV Park
Information resources: Montana Fish, Wildlife & Parks; USGS Flow Station Gage 06033000; Doherty Mountain, Dunn Creek, and Willow Springs USGS topographic maps
Salmonids present: Brown and rainbow trout and Rocky Mountain whitefish

Blue heron are commonly seen on many Greater Yellowstone Area waters. Statuesque on land and beautiful in flight, they deserve their share of trout.

DAVE LETENDRE PHOTO

There are more than a few Boulder Rivers in Montana, and most of them live up to their name. My favorite Boulder River is in the Jefferson River drainage and is overshadowed by the nearby and immensely popular Beaverhead, Big Hole, Jefferson, and Madison Rivers. This Boulder River is at the extreme northwest end of the Greater Yellowstone Area near Cardwell, Montana, and starts at the modest elevation of 4,000 feet. There is no exception to its name, other than the boulders are a little smaller than some of the other so-named streams. It starts in the aptly named Boulder Mountains aligned between Boulder and Helena, Montana, and flows in a meandering fashion with limited access through hay fields for most of its length.

The lower section hosts the larger brown trout, and the lower 14 miles closes to fishing after September 30 each year to protect spawning fish. I tend to fish the section just upstream from town at the access provided by the Sunlight Mine. To access the stream here, leave Interstate 90 at the Cardwell exit: Westbound turn right off the interstate, turn right onto Highway 69, then take the first turn right onto Cottonwood Canyon Road; eastbound turn right off the interstate and go under it, turn left onto Highway 69, then turn right onto Cottonwood Canyon Road. Continue to the Sunlight Mine access, where there is a parking lot, a sign, and a map of the area.

This Boulder is an interesting river with a variety of aquatic insects. Runoff leaves it sometime in June, depending on previous winter snowfall and springtime warmth. There is an excellent pre-runoff BWO hatch, but I love fishing it in late July and early August when there are prolific Trico hatches. I wade wet. After putting a bottle of water in my vest and rigging up, it's time to head upstream. One word of caution: Fish here are spooky, so take a look at the head of any pool for rising fish prior to stepping into the river. The air is usually filled with Tricos, and the fish tend to stack up and wait for the spinner fall. I prefer to be on the stream early in the morning, around 7 a.m., when the hatch begins and present soft-hackles and small nymphs.

Around 10 a.m. it is time for spinners and dry flies, so I switch and head upriver. The fish are mostly browns running 10 to 14 inches, some rainbow trout running about the same size, and a few Rocky Mountain whitefish. Larger fish are available, but require stealth and concentration to encounter them. The river is easy to wade, and you rarely get over ankle deep on crossing riffles. The stream meanders and has multiple pools to fish until you come to a diversion dam for irrigation; additional accesses can be found upstream. In the evening this time of year, be sure to have strong mosquito repellant handy.

A couple of summers ago, Bud Lilly asked me if I had ever fished this river. I told him I had and suggested we take a morning to fish it. Bud, then in his late 80s, has macular degeneration and cannot see well, so he fishes vicariously through other anglers. We arrived at the stream and I set a chair in the shade for Bud, rigged a rod with a Griffith's Gnat, and headed for the stream. I caught a few fish then went back to the truck and told Bud about my experience. Bud asked what time it was and I stated it was about noon. He then offered: "I have another section of the river I want you to fish because it's Hopper Time."

We drove upriver and into another hay field. Bud was specific when I pulled out my hopper box, as it was late July and, he stated, the hopper needed to be about an inch long. I showed him my pattern, of which he approved. Bud stood on the bank and on my first cast to the pool, a nice brown took the hopper with gusto, much to Bud's delight. I landed the brown and fished other holes, taking more browns on the hopper pattern. When we fished the stream later in August and he asked what time it was, I now answered "Hopper Time!" On Montana rivers during the summer, "Hopper Time" begins around noon because by that time the hoppers have warmed up and they start hitting the stream. Be sure to observe the size and color of the hoppers in order to "match the hatch."

WILLOW CREEK RESERVOIR

A remote reservoir, enjoyed mainly by local fly fishers, that provides the best action for holdover rainbows before agricultural drawdowns begin.

Access: Harrison Lake Road from US Highway 287
GPS Coordinates: 45.700367, -111.705612
Equipment: 5-weight system with full-sink and intermediate lines; damselfly, dragonfly, midge, and Speckled Dun patterns, and leech, scud, and streamer patterns
Nearest facilities and services: Three Forks (Montana), Harrison Lake Campground, Sacagawea Hotel
Information resources: Three Forks Visitor Center; Willow Creek Reservoir USGS topographic map
Salmonids present: Rainbow trout

Looking for an early-season out-of-the-way place to fish? This reservoir could be it. It is a few miles east of Harrison, Montana, and is called Harrison Lake locally. As with so many small irrigation reservoirs in the Greater Yellowstone Area, it features holdover trout, in this case rainbows that can exceed 20 inches. Its irregular shape indicates the submerged confluences of tributary creeks and results in an extensive shoreline relative to its surface area.

Just above the reservoir, Willow Creek splits into its north and south forks, most of each flowing through private land. Both forks host small trout, mainly rainbow, with some brown trout in the south fork. Bridge locations can provide access to

Trico emergences can leave thick coatings of spinners on anything nearby. Stillwaters such as Willow Creek Reservoir have inlet streams where windblown Trico swarms can entice nearby fish to feed vigorously.

each creek. Below the reservoir, Willow Creek enters an isolated canyon and flows mainly through private land. Landowners just below the dam allow a few rods a day on request, and in the autumn migrating brown trout to large sizes are present in the creek. The canyon is also prime rattlesnake habitat, but realizing that they den up by the end of September, and staying below the high-water mark can result in some good fishing for rainbow and brown trout to moderate sizes. Below the canyon, only a few bridges provide access to the creek between the end of the canyon and its confluence with the Jefferson River.

The best time to fish the reservoir is early spring, when cool waters prevail. Floatation devices are ideal for cruising nearby shorelines, but make for tough paddling when prevailing southwesterly winds come up. Once irrigation takes place, water levels drop and the lake water warms. This slows fishing and brings on recreationists in the form of jet-skiers, water-skiers, and boaters, pretty much putting an end to tranquil stillwater fishing until autumn.

Madison River Drainage

LOWER COUGAR CREEK

Overshadowed by nearby famous waters, this stream in its section outside Yellowstone National Park is widely overlooked. It holds run-up rainbow trout in the early season and run-up brown trout in the autumn.

Access: Cougar Creek Road (USFS Road 1781) off US Highway 191 north of West Yellowstone, Montana

GPS Coordinates: 44.765889, -111.113556

Equipment: 4- or 5-weight system with floating line; caddisfly, BWO, PMD, and Yellow Sally patterns, and streamer, terrestrial insect, and traditional attractor patterns

Nearest facilities and services: West Yellowstone (Montana), USFS Baker's Hole Campground, Madison Arm Resort, Parade Rest Ranch

Information resources: West Yellowstone Visitor Center; Custer-Gallatin National Forest, Hebgen Lake Ranger District Office; Mount Hebgen USGS topographic map

Salmonids present: Brown, brook, and rainbow trout

Almost totally overlooked, lower Cougar Creek hosts large brown and rainbow trout. Dense willow thickets border it in places providing generous overhead cover for trout that may dart from underneath to take a well-placed streamer pattern.

The Cougar Creek bridge is a few miles north on US Highway 191 of the Madison River bridge near Baker's Hole. A stone's throw south, Cougar Creek Road parallels it almost to Hebgen Lake's Grayling Arm. Nearly a half mile below the crossing, Duck Creek enters Cougar Creek to enhance its flow going into the Grayling Arm. Getting from the road to the creek involves passing through a thick downfall jack pine forest for a few hundred yards, then through willow thickets not as thick as those along the creek's Yellowstone National Park flow, but dense enough to make carrying bear spray and a claxon horn prudent. Yes, bears, bison, and moose can be present. So are beavers, whose ponds intermittently spangle the creek based on runoff variations.

Following beaver trails through the willows speeds passage to the meandering creek, along which willows alternate with grassy sandbars. In the early season, its course can be marshy with clouds of mosquitoes, but the reward can be rainbows and a few brown trout eagerly taking post-runoff leech and Woolly Bugger patterns. Usually by mid July, presenting terrestrial insect patterns can be productive until the flow drops to base level, usually by late summer. By the middle of September, a brown trout run out of the lake begins, but it is sparse compared to those in the Madison River and the South Fork of the Madison. Extreme stealth is the name of the game, and the best technique seems to be drifting a streamer pattern in targeted water through the use of a floating line and long tapered leader. It is challenging fishing that lasts well into October, but it offers the satisfaction of fooling migrating brown trout at their wariest.

SOUTH FORK OF THE MADISON RIVER
By Bob Jacklin

Once a fine grayling stream, the South Fork features alternating freestone and meadow reaches. It does not host big numbers of trout, but it holds some large individual browns and rainbows.

Access: US Highway 20 to Madison Arm Road
GPS Coordinates: 44.676995, -111186382
Equipment: 4- or 5-weight system with floating and sink-tip lines: caddisfly, BWO, Golden Stone, Green Drake, PMD, and Yellow Sally patterns, and terrestrial insect and streamer patterns
Nearest facilities and services: West Yellowstone (Montana), USFS Lonesomehurst Campground, Basin Station rental cabin, Madison Arm Resort
Information resources: Custer-Gallatin National Forest, Hebgen Lake Ranger District Office; West Yellowstone Visitor Center; Madison Arm USGS topographic map
Salmonids present: Brook, brown, and rainbow trout and Rocky Mountain whitefish

The most interesting part of the South Fork of the Madison River is mainly a meadow stream that crosses US Highway 20 just 4 miles west of West Yellowstone. At first sight at the highway crossing it is deceptive, appearing to be a small riffle-and-run stream. But not far below the bridge, it changes in character to the beautiful meadow stream that mostly local fly fishers try. From the highway bridge downstream to the South Fork Arm of Hebgen Lake, the river offers about 4 miles of public access as it somewhat parallels the Madison Arm Road just to the east. This road leaves Highway 20 just a few hundred yards east of its crossing and heads in a northerly direction. Pullouts along this road provide ample access to the river, made up of oxbow after oxbow loaded with deep pools, thick willows,

Bob Jacklin nets a brown trout, which are much sought after by fly fishers during autumn months. Most of the Madison River tributaries host this event, and streamer flies presented on sink-tip lines and stout leaders give the best result for encountering them.

The South Fork of the Madison River offers brown and rainbow trout and Rocky Mountain whitefish, all ranging to trophy sizes. A pleasant time to fish its meadow reaches is when PMDs are emerging in late June and then again during midsummer afternoons when terrestrial insects are numerous. JOHN JURACEK PHOTO

and beaver lodges. The water is crystal clear, and its temperature in midsummer can be about 43 degrees in the early morning.

This clear and cold meadow stream is primarily a spawning ground for Hebgen Lake, with a run of rainbow trout in the spring and brown trout in the fall. Before Hebgen Lake was created in 1910, the South Fork was a quality grayling fishery with westslope cutthroat and Rocky Mountain whitefish also present, but competition from introduced brown and rainbow trout doomed them by the mid-20th century. A good population of large Rocky Mountain whitefish remains, and they love to hit a deeply fished nymph pattern. There are some good-size resident trout in the stream; however, fishing for them is generally slow and success requires patience and stealth to the utmost.

As the river flows downstream to Hebgen Lake, the water widens with a smooth and even flow. This section holds several pools and offers some good dry fly hatches and fishing through the season. Western Green Drakes, Blue-Wing Olives, and Pale Morning Duns are some of the hatches, with *Callibaetis* mayflies and grasshopper fishing in the late summer season. Above the Highway 20 bridge, much of the river is closed to fishing as it flows through the historic and private Madison Fork Ranch. Above the ranch property, the South Fork is a small mountain brook, which gets its start well above Mosquito Gulch in the Custer-Gallatin National Forest. Here it has a population of small brook and brown trout. It can be reached by following Mosquito Gulch Road south off Highway 20 a few miles west of West Yellowstone. Solitude here is reliable, and with a lightweight outfit to present small attractor and nymph patterns, you can have a good day of fishing.

The fishing in the lower section of the South Fork is quite good from late June through the summer. This estuary area of the South Fork Arm is skirted by undeveloped roads, making for easy access. Wading is easy here, and float tubes or pontoon boats can also be conveniently launched to fish the estuary. Presenting streamer patterns in the early season can be extremely effective in attracting post-spawning rainbow trout coming back to the reservoir. Some of these attain large sizes. During autumn the use of a floatation device in the estuary for presenting streamer patterns can intercept brown trout moving to the South Fork to spawn. With stealth and good timing, these browns can also be encountered in the stream itself.

WEST FORK OF THE MADISON RIVER AND SMITH LAKE

The West Fork of the Madison River is mostly a small freestone stream ideal for lightweight and Tenkara tackle.

Access: US Highway 287 to West Fork Road to Smith Lake trailhead
GPS Coordinates: 44.849077, -111.582033 (Smith Lake); 44.886573, -111.586058 (West Fork of the Madison River)
Equipment: West Fork of the Madison River: 3- or 4-weight system with floating line; caddisfly, PMD, Golden Stone, Trico, and Yellow Sally patterns, and soft-hackle, terrestrial insect, and traditional attractor patterns. Smith Lake: 4-weight system with floating line; damselfly, dragonfly, and Speckled Dun patterns, and leech, scud, streamer, and terrestrial patterns.
Nearest facilities and services: West Yellowstone (Montana), USFS Madison Campground, Slide Inn
Information resources: Madison Ranger District Office Beaverhead-Deer Lodge National Forest Madison Ranger District Office; Freezeout Mountain and Cliff Lake USGS topographic maps
Salmonids present: Brown trout in Smith Lake; brown, cutthroat, and rainbow trout in West Fork of the Madison River

The Madison River deserves attention from any fly fisher. From time to time, however, too much attention can be given to some of its select locations. There are ways around the crowds if one does not mind getting out the lightweight gear and trying an enchanting small stream and an unusual stillwater body. The Lyon Bridge provides the gateway to these waters: the West Fork of the Madison River and the nearly secretive Smith Lake.

The West Fork enters the Madison River at the Beaverhead-Deer Lodge National Forest's Madison Campground. In this area it meanders through a narrow meadow with intermittent willows. Deep holes at most meanders hold surprisingly large rainbows and the occasional brown trout. Though being adjacent to so many popular campgrounds, nearby lodges, and the Madison River itself, this part of the West Fork is heavily fished. Farther upstream, this is not the case. Beginning just above the Madison Campground, the West Fork Road (USFS Road 209) parallels its namesake creek. For about a mile, the West Fork occupies a small canyon. Here it begins its upstream run as a freestone stream through timbered country punctuated by small meadows. Numerous pullouts and primitive campsites are present.

Smith Lake is a hidden gem in the Madison River drainage offering brown trout to trophy sizes. Try it early in the season with leech and damselfly patterns and late in the season with streamer patterns at its upper end.

Ideal for summertime wet wading, the West Fork continues for over 20 miles, picking up tributaries mainly from the Gravelly Range. Rainbow and brown trout in good numbers occupy most of this length. Some westslope cutthroat are present in upper reaches. In 2014 and 2015 eyed grayling eggs were planted in a Montana Fish, Wildlife & Parks program to reestablish the grayling population. In total, the West Fork can be a pleasing contrast to the nearby Madison River for the experienced fly fisher, but it is a near-perfect candidate for the entry-level angler because of its size, approachability, and the aggressive nature of its resident trout.

About 3 miles south on the West Fork Road from Madison Campground there is a pullout that includes a concrete outhouse. The West Fork is just a stone's throw away. On its far bank the trace of an old ford is present. Cross the stream, ascend the short ford, and follow what remains of a road for a bit over 100 yards to a long, narrow water body situated in a hollow. This is Smith Lake, formed over a hundred years ago by an enterprising fish farmer to raise Rocky Mountain whitefish for markets in the bustling mining communities not far to the north. The stream, dammed to form the lake, begins as the subterranean outlet of Wade Lake just to the south. The trace of the road goes left to the barely discernable dam. Below it the outlet stream, Lake Creek, proceeds north to become a West Fork tributary.

Cross the dam and proceed up the far bank to the submerged gravel bars that provide room suitable for a backcast. The setting is beautiful, but the Rocky Mountain whitefish have long departed to be succeeded by brown trout that grow to trophy sizes. They can be encountered as soon as runoff allows safe passage over the West Fork, and this is one of the better times to enjoy the resident browns. A good reason for this suggestion can be seen below the Smith Lake surface in the form of extensive weed beds. These, of course, host multitudes of damsel and dragonfly nymphs, leeches, scuds, and Speckled Dun mayfly nymphs, but by early July the vegetation begins to mat the lake, making subsurface fishing a considerable challenge. Thus early-season visits allow more presentation options, dry and wet. Almost any time during the season, packing in a lightweight floatation device allows more coverage of the lake than wading the shoreline. Presenting emerger patterns under an indicator or dry terrestrial insect patterns by either option can be productive in the summer, especially early or late in the day. Consider a visit to this unique little lake during any visit to the West Fork of the Madison River.

Graben Lakes

CLIFF LAKE

One of the two graben lakes in the Madison River drainage, Cliff has trophy rainbows that swim the shallows just after ice-out. Graben lakes are formed over a block of rock that has dropped relative to surrounding country rock.

Access: US Highway 287 to Cliff Lake Road
GPS Coordinates: 44.793549, -111.557482
Equipment: 6- or 7-weight system with floating and full-sink lines; damselfly, dragonfly, and Speckled Dun patterns, and leech, scud, and streamer patterns
Nearest facilities and services: West Yellowstone (Montana), USFS Cliff Lake Campground, Wilderness Edge Resort, Slide Inn
Information resources: West Yellowstone Visitor Center; Custer-Gallatin National Forest, Hebgen Lake Ranger District Office; Cliff Lake USGS topographic map
Salmonids present: Rainbow trout

Cliff and Wade Lakes are the northern pair of Montana's graben lakes. The largest of these lakes, Cliff Lake, produced rainbow trout in excess of 20 pounds up to the mid-20th century, and like its neighbor Wade Lake, originally hosted cutthroat trout to equally large sizes. Cliff has a more irregular shoreline than Wade, and this shoreline holds a key to successful fishing. The sooner after ice-out you arrive, the better the fishing. At the slightest hint of warming water, fish begin disappearing into the depths. Contacting the Wilderness Edge Resort can help with timing for a visit.

Once the timing is established, location becomes the next decision to make, and shallow waters will bring the best chances for fishing success. These can be found in abundance on Horn Creek Arm (aka Neeley's Cove), where the Wilderness Edge Resort is located and the adjacent Antelope Arm, and on the extreme north shoreline near Cliff Lake Campground. The resort rents boats and charges a minimal fee to launch private watercraft. Presentations using full-sink and intermediate lines around weed beds and drop-offs are most effective. If you can get there early enough in the season before the water warms and the fish go deep, days having catches of several dozen fish, many of trophy size, are possible.

Early in the twentieth century the Montana record rainbow trout came from Cliff Lake. Record size rainbows are gone from the lake, but just after ice-out, a visiting fly fisher has a chance to encounter a trout of the season here. JOHN JURACEK PHOTO

As the end of June approaches, recreationists begin to appear, making alternate locations to fish more attractive. Warming water also signals the beginning of this human migration on nearby Wade Lake. Surrender the lake to recreationists and to the larger fish now residing in the spacious deep water, and turn your attention to the unbelievable number of nearby locations that offer better fishing during the summer months. But return to Cliff Lake late in autumn to try the same shallows and drop-offs. Larger fish will have returned to greet you.

WADE LAKE

Getting there early and late in the season maximizes the chances for meeting up with the lake's huge brown trout and trophy rainbows.

Access: US Highway 287 to Cliff Lake Road and Wade Lake Road
GPS Coordinates: 44.808347, -111.565115
Equipment: 6- or 7-weight system with floating and full-sink lines; damselfly, dragonfly, and Speckled Dun patterns, and leech, scud, and streamer patterns
Nearest facilities and services: West Yellowstone (Montana), USFS Wade Lake Campground, Wade Lake Resort, Slide Inn
Information resources: West Yellowstone Visitor Center; Custer-Gallatin National Forest; Cliff Lake and Hidden Lake Bench USGS topographic maps
Salmonids present: Brown and rainbow trout

Originally a domain of cutthroat trout, Wade Lake hosts brown and rainbow trout through 20th-century Montana Fish, Wildlife & Parks and private introductions. Back in the 1960s this lake produced what remains the Montana state record brown trout, a bit over 29 pounds. To prove it was not a random act, about a decade later a 28-pound behemoth brown was caught there. Legends are ongoing of browns just as large being present in this relatively compact lake with depths over 100 feet. Resident rainbows do not run as large here, but those reaching several pounds are present in good numbers, and individuals of about half the weight of the record brown trout have been caught.

Encountering these brown and rainbow trout specimens, some of the largest in the Greater Yellowstone Area, is seasonal at best. Ice-out is usually around mid-May, and backcountry road conditions permitting, the lake can be reached soon after this event. Contacting the Wade Lake Resort can help pinpoint ice-out. Large trout are in shallow water at this time and can be encountered by trolling or casting streamer patterns, with the shallower west shoreline being the best location for doing so. How long these large trout remain accessible depends on weather, so unpredictable at this time. There have been years when the road to the lake remains snowbound and not passable until after the opening day of the general

Wade Lake produced the Montana state record brown trout and has potential to produce another such record. The best way to encounter these giants is to fish at night, presenting large streamer patterns with lead-core lines. That way, no recreationists will interfere.

Wade Lake is a popular midsummer destination for various recreationists including fly fishers. The best times for uninterrupted fly fishing, whether wading or boating, is before Memorial Day and after Labor Day. JOHN JURACEK PHOTO

fishing season. For example, I remember arriving in the early 1980s at Wade Lake Campground during an incoming mid-May blizzard and being snowbound there for two days. The fishing was great, if one could withstand the wind and snow out on the rough lake surface, but huddling near a blazing campfire was actually more appealing!

Nevertheless, until the lake warms up, this time of year offers the best chance for encountering the huge resident trout. With warming water comes the social phenomena common to so many regional stillwaters: the onset of recreationists. These usually appear in number by late June and include jet-skiers, kayakers, paddleboarders, rafters, water-skiers, and just plain motorboaters. They can dominate the lake surface during the daytime, and with every right to do so, the serious angler should accept their presence. With their appearance, the nearby Madison River offers less interruptions during the summer as well as some excellent fishing. By now the larger trout have moved to deeper waters, meaning that the fly fisher visiting at this time has a better chance of encountering them through fishing the depths, at night, with lead-core lines and large, brightly colored streamer patterns.

These conditions will last until the Labor Day weekend, after which recreationists increasingly diminish and waters begin cooling with the onset of autumn weather. This double blessing brings on first the gulpers, by late August working in shallow water to feed on emerging Speckled Duns, and then as autumn advances, the return of larger trout to shallower water. A late-season return to the lake is therefore an attractive proposition, with the tactics used for springtime fishing becoming increasingly effective, but keep an eye on the sky for the return of wintry weather.

Red Rock River Drainage

BLAIR LAKE

This small but accessible lake, one of the few in the Centennial Range, sees little pressure and has large cutthroat.

Access: US Highway 20 and Yale-Kilgore Road to the end of Keg Springs Road and the trailhead for the 2-mile walk to the lake
GPS Coordinates: 44.553002, -111.603905
Equipment: 4- or 5-weight system with floating and full-sink lines; traditional attractor nymph, Speckled Dun, and damselfly patterns, and flying ant, leech, and streamer patterns
Nearest facilities and services: Ashton (Idaho), McCrea Bridge Campground on Yale-Kilgore Road, Eagle Ridge Ranch
Information resources: Caribou-Targhee National Forest; Mount Jefferson USGS topographic map
Salmonids present: Cutthroat trout

Blair Lake sits in the Centennial Range at the top of the Missouri River drainage and is essentially the source of Red Rock Creek. It hosts Yellowstone cutthroat

Blair Lake is most easily approached from Idaho's Island Park and hosts Yellowstone cutthroat to trophy sizes. It can be fished from the north and west shorelines; packing in a floatation device permits fishing the entire lake.

trout ranging to 3 pounds. There are two routes to Blair Lake, and neither one can be considered routine. The first begins from South Valley Road in Alaska Basin and follows Hellroaring Creek. It requires bushwhacking up the steep and rocky Hellroaring Canyon for about 5 miles. It's a tough walk, suitable only for those persons in the best of physical condition, and requires dedicated care of one's fly fishing equipment. The other route, a 2-mile walk from the end of the Keg Springs Road, is not strenuous except for the last hundred yards down a steep slope to the lakeshore. It is possible to pack a float tube or other small floatation device along this route if care is taken descending the final slope leading to the lake. Both routes have the disadvantage of being blocked by snows late into June, especially after particularly snowy winters.

Hellroaring Creek leaves from the northeast corner of the lake. Much of the northern and western shore is free enough of obstructions to allow casting; however, using a float tube allows access to the entire lake. Good fishing, even from shore, can be had near inlets from springs or when damselflies and Speckled Duns emerge, mate, and lay eggs.

CULVER POND (AKA THE WIDOW'S POOL)
By Bob Jacklin

This water, having a rich history, is worth a visit for encountering large brook trout. In the future in may be populated by grayling.

Access: Elk Lake Road to Culver Road going east to Culver Spring
GPS Coordinates: 44.652027, -111.657392
Equipment: 4- or 5-weight system with floating and intermediate lines; Speckled Dun, and damselfly patterns, traditional attractor nymph, leech, and streamer patterns, all size 10 and smaller
Nearest facilities and services: West Yellowstone (Montana), Upper Lake Campground on South Valley Road, Elk Lake Resort
Information resources: Red Rock Lakes National Wildlife Refuge Visitor Center; Hidden Lake Bench USGS topographic map
Salmonids present: Montana grayling

This place, where Bill and Lillian Culver homesteaded in the northeast corner of Centennial Valley, is a fishery of legend. Around 1900 they dammed Picnic Creek to form a stock watering pond. They first stocked it with cutthroat trout and grayling from local streams for subsistence, but soon found demand for unusual sportfishing brought a reliable seasonal income. With time they added brook trout and rainbow trout. After Bill's death, it was commonly known as "The Widow's Pool." The first evidence I found about the fishery was a 1913 photograph of two fishermen with a large catch of big trout, apparently rainbows. Pat Barnes told me how his uncle brought him to "Granny's Pond" when he was 10 years old, around 1920. They caught large brook trout and paid a price for the privilege of fishing and keeping the fish they caught. I am sure it must have been the first pay-and-fish preserve in Montana.

Culver Spring was dammed in the 19th century to create a water supply for cattle but later became a famed fly fishing destination. Cutthroat, brook, and rainbow trout as well as grayling have come to inhabit the pond at various times. Proposed reconditioning of Culver Spring would result in a better host for grayling.

Over the years, famed fly fishers such as Howard Back and Jack Hemingway wrote of their successes fishing the pond. In 1959 the U.S. Fish and Wildlife Service broke open the original earthen dam and built a new dam about half a mile farther down Picnic Creek, thereby connecting the original Granny's Pond with another pond. This enlargement made the current pond of about three-quarters of a mile long and around 30 acres. I first fished it, then part of the Red Rock Lakes Wildlife Management Area, in 1968. Since then I've caught and released many 2- to 3-pound brook trout. The largest brookie I caught and released was 5 pounds, in 2000. My largest fish from the pond, caught in 1973, was a 26-inch cuttbow.

These experiences and its serenity are reasons I cherish Culver Pond. I'm sure my experience with these large fish make it sound as if the fishing here is easy—it is not. Over the years, this pond has been dewatered several times that I know of, and I am sure it has hurt the numbers and the size of the remaining brook trout population. Natural progression causes a small lake, or in this case a spring-fed pond, to lose its capability to furnish enough food and offer good reproduction to maintain the high-quality fishery it once had. I believe this factor, plus dewatering, is the cause of the current lower numbers and the size of the brook trout population.

Successful fishing here requires hard work, and many evenings I have gone fishless. My experience is that wet flies such as nymphs and small streamers seem to bring the most success at the pond. My favorite is a size 10 yellow Muddler Minnow. Brook trout still inhabit Culver's Pond, and I encourage fly fishers to visit this historic place.

ELK LAKE

The north end of this lake is idyllic, and its June damselfly emergence dwarfs the good one at the south end.

Access: North on Elk Lake Road from South Valley Road junction
GPS Coordinates: 44.669525, -111.630763
Equipment: 5- or 6-weight system with floating, full-sink, and intermediate lines; damselfly, dragonfly, and Speckled Dun patterns, and leech, scud, and streamer patterns
Nearest facilities and services: West Yellowstone (Montana), Upper Lake Campground on South Valley Road, Elk Lake Resort
Information resources: Beaverhead-Deerlodge National Forest; Elk Springs and Hidden Lake Bench USGS topographic maps
Salmonids present: Cutthroat and lake trout and Montana grayling

Elk Lake is one of the graben lakes, and as with the other of southwestern Montana's graben lakes, it does not have a surface outlet. It is isolated during the winter from all vehicles, except snow machines, until the roads are passable in springtime. It is also one of only two Montana lakes with a native lake trout population. Montana grayling, once abundant, have all but disappeared from this lake, but efforts to restore them are being studied.

For nearly all of the drive up its namesake road, there is no clue that Elk Lake exists. This road passes by Widgeon Pond, into which the males of the controversial cutthroat trout were released after being removed from spawning streams in Centennial Valley. It then proceeds over Elk Spring Creek, which is being reconditioned for the reintroduction of Montana grayling. Next comes a junction with Culver Road, which passes over MacDonald Pond and goes on to Culver Pond and Spring, both of which are being reconditioned for reintroduction of Montana grayling. The history of both these fabled waters and the huge rainbow trout they once hosted is well documented.

Finally, as Elk Spring is approached on the right, a slot in the hills reveals the southern arm of Elk Lake. Beyond the primitive campground on the lakeshore, the famed Elk Lake Resort comes into view. Founded in the 1930s, it is the oldest resort in continuous service in Centennial Valley and has hosted such notables as Jane Russell and Supreme Court Justice William O. Douglas. Open year-round as a full-service destination, the lodge offers boats for fishing the lake and makes a superbly comfortable base for enjoying Centennial Valley salmonids. Fish for cutthroat ranging to trophy size, then enjoy a fine evening meal and comfortable overnight accommodations.

When ice partially covers the lake, there is a chance for the fly fisher to encounter native lake trout running to 20 pounds. Presenting large streamer patterns on full-sink lines around drop-offs is the best way to accomplish this. As ice melts and waters warm, these fish head for the depths, leaving diminishing Yellowstone cutthroat and reintroduced westslope cutthroat to interest the fly fisher. Now the best early-season strategy is to concentrate on the north and south ends of the lake, both of which are shallow but produce a variety of aquatic food forms. The south

Elk Lake hosts the only native lake trout in the Greater Yellowstone Area, and efforts are under way to reestablish grayling. Great action occurs when cutthroat trout respond to late June damselfly emergences in the shallows.

end of the lake is most easily fished where a floatation device such as a pontoon boat or float tube can be easily launched. Anything larger can be launched at the resort for a fee.

The north end of Elk Lake is also worth fishing, and after the road dries out, it offers much more water to be explored than the south end. No boat launch, developed or primitive, is present. One must carry or drag a boat (floatation device) at least 50 yards from the road to the lakeshore. Here the lake is at its widest and is shallow. In the early season, if the waterborne fly fisher ventures to the right (going south), especially if some ice remains, deeper water is encountered, and a streamer presented on a full-sink line, or trolled, might just dredge up one of the large resident lake trout. If that fly fisher remains on the shallows during the same season and presents leech, scud, or damselfly nymph patterns, westslope cutthroat and some of the remaining Yellowstone cutthroat will respond.

The most interesting fishing here occurs around the end of June, when damselflies emerge, mate, and lay eggs. For those fly fishers favoring stillwaters, this is an excellent time to visit the north end of the lake for various reasons. First, the road to the upper end of the lake will be in passable condition, with care, for two-wheel-drive vehicles. Second, nearby and much more accessible Henry's, Hebgen, and Quake Lakes with their well-publicized damselfly emergences will be attracting fly fishers, and both the Madison River and the Henry's Fork will be in the prime of their fly fishing seasons, thus attracting crowds of enthusiasts. Therefore, the chances for solitude on the upper end of Elk Lake are as good as it gets.

The next event here is the Speckled Dun emergence, which can last into late summer. This coincides with the famed emergence and responding gulpers on Hebgen Lake, so few anglers visit Elk Lake at this time. By autumn lake trout begin moving into rocky shallows to spawn. This event attracts boating spin fishers and trollers to these areas, resulting in the most angling interest of the season, but the upper end of the lake with its shallows remains relatively uncrowded because there are no lake trout up there.

HIDDEN LAKE
By Charles Barnes

The reward for visiting Hidden Lake in the early season is solitude and the possibility of landing the largest fish of the season.

Access: North end of Elk Lake Road and trailhead for quarter-mile walk to lake
GPS Coordinates: 44.714134, -111607689
Equipment: 5-weight system with floating and full-sink lines; damselfly, dragonfly, and Speckled Dun patterns, and leech, scud, and streamer patterns
Nearest facilities and services: West Yellowstone (Montana), Upper Lake Campground on South Valley Road, Elk Lake Resort (offers rental boats on lake)
Information resources: Deerlodge-Gallatin National Forest; Cliff Lake USGS topographic map
Salmonids present: Rainbow trout

This Hidden Lake is the largest of all the Hidden Lakes in southwestern Montana. It lies north of Elk Lake, in the Elk-Hidden-Cliff-Wade Lake chain. In the

Some fly fishers consider the rainbow trout to be an invader of area waters. But it and its cuttbow hybrids are the most widespread trout species in the Greater Yellowstone Area.

JOHN JURACEK PHOTO

Hidden Lake, a quarter-mile hike from the nearest road, is a place of legend through hosting large rainbow trout. Being roadless, it is the most tranquil of all the major graben lakes. LEROY COOK PHOTO

early season, you need to be careful on the road when approaching the upper end of Elk Lake. In one place the road slopes to the north through a dense quaking aspen grove and can unexpectedly hold snowdrifts or slippery mud, and occasionally springtime erosion washes out a short piece of the road. Thus in the early season it is prudent to travel in a four-wheel-drive vehicle. Later in the summer this spot is quite passable with any two-wheel-drive vehicle. After this spot, the road drops down to the upper end of Elk Lake, passes it, and proceeds about 2 miles through another forested north-facing slope, which can also be muddy in the early season. At the end of the road, there's space to park several vehicles. You get to the lake by walking about a quarter mile down a well-defined trail. The lake covers 150 acres, and the east shoreline drops off to depth quickly. The west shore has coves and bays with some shallows.

During the time I worked in my father's business (the Pat Barnes Tackle Shop), there were some years when early in the season, all the rivers in the area were running high and dirty and our guides were looking for clean water to take fly fishing clients. Whenever the road was passable, Hidden Lake was a good choice. We either carried canoes down the trail to the lake from the end of the road or rented the padlocked boats owned by the Elk Lake Resort. (Those boats are still available through the resort for a fee.) The reward for visiting Hidden Lake in the early season remains large, energetic rainbow trout of trophy size that will take any Woolly Bugger type of pattern presented on a sunken line. Whether these patterns were taken because they resembled a leech or dragonfly nymph I do not know, but they worked for our clients, and they still work.

Originally westslope cutthroat inhabited Hidden Lake, but just before the mid-20th century the pioneering Neely family introduced rainbow trout into the lake, just as they had done on Cliff Lake a bit farther north. From their lodge on Cliff Lake, the Neelys took clients south on horseback to Hidden Lake to fish for these trout in a wilderness setting. Through hybridization the cutthroats have disappeared, leaving the lively rainbows of the present day.

We still portage canoes down to Hidden Lake not only in the early season but also in July and August to enjoy dry fly fishing on its surface when the usual progression of aquatic insects emerge to bring fish up from the depths. Other fly fishers carry floatation devices to the lake to enjoy the challenge of these rainbow trout. One year I took my family camping at the lake's southeast corner, across the lake from the boat ramp. In the evenings and mornings I found fish feeding close to shore and had success by casting parallel to shore and roll-casting.

The trail from the end of the road to the boat dock forks, with a branch going around the west side of the lake. Where this trail skirts the west shoreline of Hidden Lake, there are areas that can be waded for casting to cruising fish. This trail, being the same one used by the Neely family decades ago, proceeds past Goose and Otter Lakes—both small, with a tendency to moss over in summer, but hosting a few rainbow trout—then goes on to Cliff Lake. Although fishing from the wading locations can be fruitful, boating remains the best way to encounter Hidden Lake's big rainbow trout in solitude.

ODELL CREEK

This is likely the most bypassed water in Centennial Valley, but it gives up large resident cutthroat and grayling to those with a stealthy approach.

Access: Off South Valley Road near Lakeview, Montana
GPS Coordinates: 44.606035, -111.813000
Equipment: 4- or 5-weight system with floating line; caddisfly, BWO, PMD, and Yellow Sally patterns, and terrestrial insect and traditional attractor patterns, all size 10 and smaller
Nearest facilities and services: West Yellowstone (Montana), Upper Lake Campground on South Valley Road, Elk Lake Resort
Information resources: Red Rock Lakes National Wildlife Refuge Visitor Center; Slide Mountain USGS topographic map
Salmonids present: Brook and cutthroat trout and Montana grayling

Traveling from the east along South Valley Road, this Odell Creek—which shares its name with the famed spring creek near Ennis, Montana—first comes into view about a mile from Lakeview, the community that administers the Red Rock Lakes National Wildlife Refuge. Flowing north out of the Centennial Range, it crosses the road in an almost unimpressive manner. Above the road it passes through much private land, mostly posted, until higher reaches. Below the road it is on the refuge and maintained as much as possible in its natural state down to Lower Red Rock Lake. From South Valley Road, it can be fished downstream for

Odell Creek feeds Lower Red Rock Lake and hosts early-season cutthroat and grayling runs featuring trophy-size individuals. Solitude and chances to view wildlife are other rewards when visiting. JOHN JURACEK PHOTO

miles. Just west beyond Lakeview, South Valley Road turns from going north to resume its westerly direction. At this turn a small parking area and gate on the right marks a service road, which after a nearly half-mile walk, bridges Odell Creek and proceeds on into Sparrow Ponds. This road gives access to the middle of the best fishing on the creek.

About two-thirds the size of Red Rock Creek, Odell Creek likewise combines superb spawning gravel with deep holes and plentiful bankside willows and grasses for overhead cover. Also as with Red Rock Creek, its gradient eases as it approaches its confluence, in this case with Lower Red Rock Lake. Silt carried during runoff deposits where gradient eases, compromising the quality of spawning gravel and smothering some of the hosted aquatic insects. Montana grayling and the controversial cutthroat trout run up to the gravel areas to spawn in the springtime. Brook trout are also present and ascend the creek during autumn. Juveniles of all three salmonid species remain in the creek until maturing enough to descend to the lake.

I enjoy fishing this near-pristine creek during July and August. At this time, afternoon caddisfly and diminishing PMD and Yellow Sally emergences attract trout and grayling to the surface. During the early-season PMD emergence, their patterns work well. So do Yellow Sally adult patterns and soft-hackle patterns that represent their emergers. What seems most fun during midsummer is to present terrestrial patterns. Grasshopper patterns in sizes 10 and 12 work best for the small-mouthed grayling. Ant and beetle patterns are also effective.

The size of the grayling in this creek is surprising. They are perhaps the largest in the valley, with individuals approaching 20 inches. These are not as numerous as in nearby Red Rock Creek, but they are worth pursuing. Very large cutthroat are

A large Odell Creek cutthroat trout being released. There are not many of this size in the creek, but a stealthy approach and a proper presentation into a deep hole or pocket can produce fish like this.

also present. Not too long ago I fished Odell Creek with two companions. They went upstream from where the service road crosses the creek. I ventured downstream. After a few hours of successful fishing, I worked my way back upstream to find my companions, Fred and LeRoy, sitting bankside and chatting in an upbeat manner. As I approached, Fred exclaimed, "I spent three years in Alaska and the biggest grayling I caught was 15 inches. Now only 120 miles from home, I land one that is almost 20 inches long!" He had followed that event up with landing a 20-inch cutthroat. Few and far between are the streams that currently offer such fishing!

RED ROCK CREEK

One of the most unique and beckoning streams in the Greater Yellowstone Area. As a host for large cutthroat trout and grayling, it has no equal.

Access: Adjacent to South Valley Road, east of Lakeview, Montana
GPS Coordinates: 44.613317, -111.632904
Equipment: 4- or 5-weight system with floating line; caddisfly, PMD, BWO, and Yellow Sally patterns, and terrestrial insect and traditional attractor patterns, all size 10 and smaller
Nearest facilities and services: West Yellowstone (Montana), Upper Lake Campground on South Valley Road, Elk Lake Resort
Information resources: Red Rock Lakes National Wildlife Refuge Visitor Center; USGS Flow Station Gage 06006000; Mount Jefferson and Upper Red Rock Lake USGS topographic maps
Salmonids present: Brook and cutthroat trout and Montana grayling

A majestic view greets travelers breaking out of the timber when going west off Red Rock Pass. Many stop to marvel at and photograph what is a superb example of "Big Sky Country." This is Alaska Basin, the eastern appendage of Centennial Valley. Continuing west from the pass, within 2 miles Hellroaring Creek, descending from its Centennial Mountains sources, crosses Red Rock Road. One of its tributaries in the Centennial Range to the south begins from Brower's Spring, the ultimate source of the Missouri River. Crossing the road and flowing northwesterly,

Red Rock Creek feeds Upper Red Rock Lake and is the primary water for spawning grayling and cutthroat trout in Centennial Valley. Through hosting a variety of aquatic insects and life-forms, as well as passing through meadows holding bountiful terrestrial insects, the fun of fishing in this beautiful stream is figuring out the taking pattern. JOHN JURACEK PHOTO

Hellroaring Creek fades into a vast meadow in the distance. Here in Alaska Basin, it collects tributaries. Combining with one of these tributaries, Cole Creek, it becomes Red Rock Creek.

Farther west, Alaska Basin pinches down and the road enters Centennial Valley proper, and there Red Rock Creek comes back into sight on the north side of the road. Now it is a beautiful meadow stream about 30 feet wide. Open willows protect banks and provide overhead cover, and grassy banks host plentiful terrestrial insects. But what is its most striking feature now is its substrate. Anyone stopping to observe the dominating gravel realizes the value of this stream as a host for aquatic insects and a salmonid spawning and rearing habitat. Now Red Rock Creek meanders, and with each bend comes enough depth to protect hosted salmonids of all sizes.

Beginning in late April, snow melts on the north-facing slopes of the Centennial Mountains. As May warms, huge quantities of runoff cascade down Hellroaring then Red Rock Creeks. On reaching Upper Red Rock Lake, the cold water signals awaiting grayling and the controversial cutthroat (controversial because of possible past interbreeding with rainbow trout having escaped from private ponds in the valley) to begin their spawning runs to the creek's hospitable gravels. Gravels with an upwelling of water are chosen because eggs deposited there will be exposed to dissolved oxygen in three dimensions, and therefore develop most efficiently. About this time of year, Red Rock Road opens, and travelers can observe spawning activity in the creek, turbidity permitting. The Montana fishing season begins in mid-May, but within the preserve's boundary it opens in mid-June. Here the angler is encouraged to have utmost care for the grayling and obey the special regulations (catch-and-release for grayling, no bait or lead permitted, and barbless hooks encouraged) for fishing refuge waters.

I love my 7-foot, 2-weight fly rod, my choice for fishing small streams where I believe only small salmonids reside. I had heard stories of the large cutthroat trout and Montana grayling residing in Red Rock Creek during summer months, but had the idea that their numbers were quite small and the sizes exaggerated. My experience with grayling in such waters as the North Fork of the Big Hole River and Grebe and Cascade Lakes was that a 13-inch fish was a "braggin' fish." So I proceeded to Red Rock Creek on an early August day taking my favorite small-stream fly rod.

Fishing the creek just inside the upper boundary of the refuge, I fooled a few juvenile brook and cutthroat trout with small grasshopper patterns. When I noticed that Pale Morning Duns were beginning to become active, I switched to an emerger pattern. A few small trout responded, but then came a gentle rise after my pattern that when I set the hook resulted in noticeable resistance. Out of the water came a large grayling. Without a landing net and conscious of not damaging the fish, I finally waded downstream to beach it on a gravel bar. Moving it back into the water, I measured it and found it exceeded in length any grayling I had ever caught, then released it. From that day on, I have taken a 4- or 5-weight rod to this creek to play and land these fish more quickly.

Widgeon Pond, adjacent to Red Rock Creek, hosts large cutthroat trout. However, it is managed by the Red Rock Lakes National Wildlife Refuge primarily as a migratory bird sanctuary, so fishing is allowed only on its shoreline.

I had heard "legends" of better fishing in the more remote reaches of the creek, so on one of my visits, I walked down the creek to approach the lake. I passed beautiful holes and large beaver ponds as I proceeded, and stopped once or twice after observing Yellow Sallys flying and occasional rises to their emergers. I also could not resist the urge to cast small black leech patterns into those beaver ponds. As I approached the lake, noting the easing creek gradient, I had to slog through more bogs to make headway. More significantly, I noticed that the beautiful gravel in the creek bottom was becoming increasingly silty. And when the only fish I could observe were large suckers in spawning colors, I knew it was time to return upstream to the superior habitat running for miles through the refuge and above it.

Yellowstone River Drainage

ABSAROKA-BEARTOOTH WILDERNESS LAKES

Hundreds of these lakes hold salmonids. Be sure to have weather information before deciding to fish the more remote ones.

Access: US Highway 212 to trailheads
GPS Coordinates: 45.944159, -109.591341
Equipment: 5-weight system with floating and full-sink lines; damselfly, dragonfly, midge, and Speckled Dun patterns, and leech, scud, soft-hackle, streamer, and traditional attractor patterns
Nearest facilities and services: Red Lodge (Montana); USFS Greenough, Limberpine, and Parkside Campgrounds; Lazy R-L Ranch
Resources: Custer-Gallatin National Forest, Beartooth Ranger District Office; Red Lodge Visitor Center; Bare Mountain, Black Pyramid, Mount Morris, Silver Run Peak, and Sylvan Peak USGS topographic maps
Salmonids present: Brook, cutthroat, golden, lake, and rainbow trout and splake

To many folks it is known as "the Beartooths," and it is a wilderness expanse like no other in the Greater Yellowstone Area. It lies mainly in the north end of the Absaroka Range and in the Beartooth Range. Access to the south side is from spectacular US Highway 212, where travel over Beartooth Pass is legendary. Just south of the wilderness boundary in Wyoming, Beartooth Lake, offering brook, cutthroat, lake, and rainbow trout, and Island Lake, offering small brook trout, can be easily approached from the highway before ascending Beartooth Pass. Boating is effective for fishing on both lakes.

From the north side, a number of Montana state highways follow major rivers to give access to trailheads going into the Beartooths. Several streams originate here and radiate outward like spokes in a wheel. Beginning in the Montana part of the area are the Boulder River, the Clarks Fork of the Yellowstone River, the Stillwater River, and Rock, Rosebud, and Slough Creeks. All of these eventually feed the Yellowstone River. In Wyoming the Clarks Fork expands to a major backcountry fishery and hosts dozens of alpine lakes.

Twin Lakes at the top of the Rock Creek drainage offers good fishing for brook trout. Expect action from these fish, but because of their relatively small sizes, use lightweight tackle. Pack rain gear when planning to fish any of these lakes.

The Beartooths contain almost a thousand lakes, nearly half of which host salmonids. Lakes hosting salmonids range in elevations from just under 6,000 to just under 11,000 feet. Essentially all the lakes are also in the Yellowstone River drainage, and most are in Montana. Brook, brown, cutthroat, golden, lake, and rainbow trout are variously hosted in these lakes. Some host grayling, and others host splake. Small brook trout are the most numerous and widespread. The season for encountering any of these salmonids in the lakes is short. It begins with ice-out, which varies from June to mid-July depending on elevation, and it can end as early as October. But during the season, interruption can take place because of weather. Thunderstorms are frequent, and they can be violent to the point of being deadly due to hypothermia. Many of the fishing locations are over 8,000 feet, where the partial pressure of oxygen is less than at much lower elevations, so altitude sickness is another situation that can impact physical well-being through headaches and nausea. This does not affect everyone, but is most common for those coming from lower elevations. Thus if you visit from outside of the Rocky Mountains, be aware of this condition.

There are some generalities that apply to fishing lakes in the Beartooths. Fishing near shorelines is usually the most effective strategy, and early and late in the day when salmonids tend to cruise the shore are usually the best times to do so. Making use of shadowed areas can improve fishing success, and so can gentle breezes that riffle the surface. At high elevations shorelines can be particularly fragile, so careful movement is important. A way to avoid damaging shorelines is the use of packable floatation devices, but the inconveniences of bringing them on long hikes is obvious.

With respect to rod and reel, 4- and 5-weight systems apply, and floating lines are effective in most situations because the best fishing is usually in shallow water. My experience fishing alpine lakes is that flies with bodies formed from peacock herl are particularly effective. This applies to both dry and wet patterns. Scud and midge patterns are also effective.

So much for generalities. Dealing with specifics for the lakes would fill a book. No attempt has been made to provide much detail here because that has already been accomplished in superb form by Pat Marcuson. His book *Fishing the Beartooths* offers details on all aspects of fishing these lakes. From accessing the lakes and camping suggestions to specific fishing strategies and which lakes host what salmonids, Marcuson addresses it all.

BOULDER RIVER

The most interesting part of the river from a fishing standpoint courses through the Custer-Gallatin National Forest. Here riffles and fast water runs dominate, but slower water reaches offer more tranquil fishing conditions.

Access: Interstate 90 at Big Timber to Montana Highway 298
GPS Coordinates: 45.550138, -110.210159
Equipment: 4- or 5-weight system with floating and sink-tip lines; caddisfly, BWO, PMD, Golden Stone, and Yellow Sally patterns, and soft-hackle, streamer, terrestrial insect, and traditional attractor patterns
Nearest facilities and services: Big Timber (Montana), several USFS campgrounds along the river, Four Mile rental cabin, Hawley Mountain Guest Ranch
Information resources: Custer-Gallatin National Forest, Big Timber Ranger District Office, Main Boulder River Ranger Station, and Visitor Center; USGS Flow Station Gage 06200000; Chrome Mountain, Big Timber, McLeod, McLeod Basin, and Ross Canyon USGS topographic maps
Salmonids present: Brook, brown, cutthroat, and rainbow trout

Originating in the Beartooth Mountains in the Custer-Gallatin National Forest, the Boulder River descends 7,300 feet and flows 60 miles through varied landscape to join the Yellowstone River near Big Timber, Montana. Most of its drainage lies within the Absaroka-Beartooth Wilderness Area. The river tumbles through Custer-Gallatin National Forest in a breathtaking setting, interspersed by private land, nearly 25 miles through deep glaciated canyons. Rapids, riffles, plunges, and long, wide pools with minor spawning and rearing habitat characterize the river. Here it is being considered for "Wild and Scenic" classification, a reason for its popularity. It leaves the national forest at a natural bridge that collapsed in 1988 and its accompanying nearly 100-foot waterfall, which is a barrier. The Boulder River Ranger Station is a historic presence near the collapsed natural bridge and waterfall. Cutthroat, rainbow, and brook trout live above the waterfall; below it they are joined by brown trout and Rocky Mountain whitefish. Here the gradient lessens, resulting in slow water in places and riffles, runs, and deep pools. Below the falls the river meanders mostly through private agricultural land for about 5 miles to the

The Boulder River offers excellent fishing in a scenic setting. Part of the fun of fishing the upper river is not knowing which of the three resident salmonids will hit a fly. Below the barrier waterfall, five salmonid species are present.

East Boulder confluence. From this point to the mouth, its 28 miles are somewhat steeper and strewn with boulders and cobbles.

The Boulder River drainage offers a wide diversity of fisheries habitats and recreation opportunities, and it also supports the local agricultural economy. The system provides spawning and rearing habitat for fish from the Yellowstone River. It is subject to extreme runoffs, droughts, and the impacts of agriculture and land development. The East and West Boulder Rivers enter the main stem near McLeod. The 20-odd-mile-long smaller East Boulder is being reconditioned to eliminate exotic salmonids (rainbow, brook, and brown trout) in order to reestablish the native cutthroat population. We will discuss the West Boulder separately.

The waterfall also divides the river into two sections with respect to access, the upper being mostly public, and the lower mostly bounded by private land. The river above the falls lives up to its name, flowing quickly with the best fishing in deep holes scattered in giant boulder gardens. Cutthroat ranging to moderate sizes and an occasional rainbow can be encountered.

The Boulder River flows through some alluring private land sections above the Custer-Gallatin National Forest boundary. Be aware of and respect boundaries even though it is legal to fish and walk within the high-water mark.

Below the falls the Boulder spills out onto the plains as it meanders north to its confluence with the Yellowstone. The river flattens out and meanders through hay meadows and ranchland. It's a setting similar to that of eastern Idaho's lower Teton River, where private land dominates the shoreline. Aquatic and terrestrial bug life become abundant, and rainbows and browns to large sizes are present. The lower river is renowned for its hatches, and the dry fly fishing can be spectacular. Some area guiding concerns have working relationships with ranches that allow access to miles of the river's incredible fishing. During high-flow periods, rafts are the best choice for float-fishing the lower river. As water drops due to irrigation drawdowns, pontoon boats are ideal for float-fishing.

Attention from fly fishers, both wading and floating, has increased considerably in the last few years on the river below McLeod. Public access here is limited to two locations, and especially by midsummer low water can be a reason for conflict between floating and wading anglers. The Boulder Forks Fishing Access is just southeast of McLeod on Highway 298 and offers the most water for public use, with a mile of stream access from the confluence of the main stem Boulder and West Boulder River. Resorts, spread from the lower river a few miles from Big Timber to the upper river in Custer-Gallatin National Forest, offer accommodations and single or multiday walk-and-wade guided fly fishing trips.

WEST BOULDER RIVER

This smaller version of the Boulder River is less visited than the main Boulder,
but it has superb fishing for moderate-size trout.

Access: Interstate 90 at Big Timber to Montana Highway 298 to West Boulder Road and
West Boulder Meadows trailhead
GPS Coordinates: 45.548404, -110.306793
Equipment: 4- or 5-weight system with floating and sink-tip lines; caddisfly, BWO, PMD,
Golden Stone, and Yellow Sally patterns, and soft-hackle, streamer, terrestrial insect,
and traditional attractor patterns
Nearest facilities and services: Big Timber (Montana), USFS West Boulder
Campground, West Boulder rental cabin, McLeod Resort
Information resources: Custer-Gallatin National Forest, Big Timber Ranger District
Office; Mount Rae, Springdale, and West Boulder Plateau USGS topographic maps
Salmonids present: Brown, cutthroat, and rainbow trout

The West Boulder meets the Boulder River 15 miles south of Big Timber near
McLeod, Montana. Likewise, its sources are in the Absaroka-Beartooth Wilderness
Area. Essentially a smaller version of the Boulder, it offers no interruptions from
float-fishers or boaters. It's similar to the tranquility the North Fork of the Teton
River offers compared to the summer daytime passage of boating recreationists and
float-fishers on east Idaho's Teton River in Teton Basin. Its approach is also similar to that of the Boulder River, with travel through ranch and farm land in lower
reaches and the Custer-Gallatin National Forest in upper reaches.

Meadows on the West Boulder River feature early-season wildflowers. It's another reason
to bring a camera capable of preserving the colors.

The trailhead for accessing the upper river, parking area, rental cabin, and campground, surrounded by private land, is inside the Custer-Gallatin National Forest boundary. Here hikers, photographers, horse packers, and backpackers gear up for visits to the spectacular country above. The road beyond the trailhead is private, but those using the trail have passage rights until the trail diverts from the road.

Within about 3 miles above a canyon holding faster water, the river flows more gently though the West Boulder Meadows, a most attractive location to fish and popular with anglers. On reaching this meadow section, one is reminded of Slough Creek in the first meadow above the campground. Clear, nearly still water reveals cruising cutthroat trout, giving a hint that stealth will be needed to encounter them. True, these trout range to smaller sizes than their Slough Creek brethren, but they can be as wary.

The upper river is in another canyon hosting cutthroat trout, with a few individuals approaching moderate size. Lightweight tackle is ideal for fishing throughout the river. The lower river outside the national forest hosts browns and rainbows to moderate sizes. As one travels downstream during summer irrigation season, dewatering impacts fishing. Downstream access is limited mostly to bridges and roadsides allowing passage to the high-water mark.

MILL CREEK
By Satoshi Yamamoto

Close to Livingston, this stream offers miles of lightweight tackle water and a quality small-stream experience where it runs through the Custer-Gallatin National Forest.

Access: US Highway 89 to Mill Creek Road
GPS Coordinates: 45.426665, -110.645753
Equipment: 4-weight system with floating and sink-tip lines; caddisfly, BWO, PMD, Golden Stone, and Yellow Sally patterns, and soft-hackle, streamer, terrestrial insect, and traditional attractor patterns
Nearest facilities and services: Livingston (Montana), USFS Snowbank Campground, Mill Creek rental cabin, Chico Hot Springs Resort
Information resources: Custer-Gallatin National Forest, Yellowstone Ranger District Office; Livingston Visitor Center; Knowles Peak and The Pyramid USGS topographic maps
Salmonids present: Cutthroat and rainbow trout and Rocky Mountain whitefish

So much of the fishing in Paradise Valley centers, for good reason, on the famed spring creeks and the Yellowstone River. These can be crowded or subject to reservations, making available fishing time not always satisfying during the best of the season. Mill Creek is an alternative that can provide you with some wonderful fishing.

Mill Creek flows west out of the Absaroka Mountains and joins the Yellowstone River in the middle of Paradise Valley. The lower creek (approximately 7 miles) is bordered by private lands, so access is difficult, if not impossible, to achieve. However, driving approximately 6 miles east from the Mill Creek Road–East River

Mill Creek, a major Yellowstone River tributary, offers miles of lightweight tackle water where it runs through the Custer-Gallatin National Forest. SATOSHI YAMAMOTO PHOTO

Road intersection will take you to the national forest boundary (look for the sign). Upstream from there, the creek and its tributaries are easily accessed for miles, along with parking spaces. The public campground is about 4 miles from the boundary sign and 10 miles from the intersection.

As is typical of mountain streams, the farther upstream one goes, the smaller the creek gets. Around the campground to the mouth, the 20- to 25-foot wide creek consists of pocketwater, deep pools, and riffles. During summer months, the lower creek is diverted for irrigation use on private lands. Therefore, the flow tends to be low through the lower creek to the mouth, warming the water to a point where fish mostly move out. Just like any other small mountain stream, small yet feisty fish will attack your well-presented dry flies. The phrase "numbers make up for size" is true here, but there are also some individuals that catch anglers by surprise! Although dry fly fishing is a major part of the action, don't forget to search deep pools and pockets with nymphs.

The Montana general fishing season, the third Saturday of May to November 30, applies to Mill Creek. Runoff usually subsides toward the end of June. As with any other area stream, mayflies, caddisflies, stoneflies, and terrestrial insects are important food sources at Mill Creek. Rather than specific match-the-hatch patterns, my fly selection consists of traditional attractor dry flies and nymphs. Nymphs such as small bead-head patterns should imitate most mayfly and stonefly nymphs and caddis larvae. A small black Woolly Bugger can be effective.

Do you have a Yellowstone River float trip planned that goes by the mouth of Mill Creek? This is a good place for a lunch break as well as for fishing. Typically, my clients and I get out of the boat and fish along the bank. Then we venture upstream to the East River Road bridge. When flow in the creek is good, there is a possibility that some trout from the Yellowstone River will be there. Friendly advice: Oftentimes we end up enjoying this nice setting and forget our time frame. In that case, it will be a long day till we reach the takeout. So plan accordingly!

ROCK CREEK

A stream with picturesque surrounding in its upper reaches where fast action is possible after run-off.

Access: Pull-outs and parking areas along US Highway 212 paralleling the creek
GPS Coordinates: 45.037334, -109.355208
Equipment: 3- or 4-weight system with floating line; caddisfly, BWO, PMD, Golden Stone, Trico, and Yellow Sally patterns, and soft-hackle, streamer, terrestrial insect, and traditional attractor patterns
Nearest facilities and services: Red Lodge (Montana); USFS Greenough Lake, Limberpine, and M-K Campgrounds; Lazy E-L Ranch
Information resources: Custer-Gallatin National Forest, Beartooth Ranger District Office; Red Lodge Visitor Center; USGS Flow Station Gage 06209500; Black Pyramid, Cooney Reservoir, Mount Morris, Red Lodge East, Red Lodge West, and Roberts USGS topographic maps
Salmonids present: Brook, brown, cutthroat, and rainbow trout and Rocky Mountain whitefish

Rock Creek upstream of Red Lodge offers fast lightweight tackle fishing. Almost any floating fly in small or medium sizes will be struck by resident trout as it quickly drifts downstream.

Montana has several Rock Creeks, and the upper part of this one is in the most spectacularly scenic country in Montana. It's a freestone stream, near 60 miles long, flowing almost north out of the Beartooth Plateau then curving northeast to eventually empty into the Clarks Fork of the Yellowstone River. As with its larger neighbors to the west, the Stillwater and Boulder Rivers, Rock Creek's upper portion is in beautiful mountain country, mainly public land, while its lower portion flows through private farming and ranching country. A difference is that much of Rock Creek worth fishing is adjacent to a major highway and therefore easily accessible. Above Red Lodge, Montana, it is of its highest gradient, has ample access, and hosts small brook, cutthroat, and rainbow trout and Rocky Mountain whitefish. It is a stream meant for lightweight tackle, Tenkara, wet wading, and dry fly fishing. The small, eager trout present in good numbers are opportunistic enough not to pass any surface offering that resembles a food item. Thus dry attractor patterns in small and moderate sizes work well, along with caddisfly and stonefly imitations.

Downstream of Red Lodge, Rock Creek flows through farming country with access limited to bridges and four public fishing access areas between Red Lodge and the town of Roberts. Each of these is easily reached from Highway 212. Here the creek retains its rocky substrate and flows in brushy meanders through hay meadows bordered creek-side by cottonwood groves. Wading is easy. Cutthroat trout diminish and brown trout increase. By midsummer terrestrial insects abound, but irrigation diversion dewaters the creek somewhat to slow daytime fishing success. Downstream at Boyd, Boyd Cooney Dam Road takes one to Cooney Reservoir, filled with summertime boaters, water-skiers, and other recreationists.

STILLWATER RIVER
By Harley W. Reno, PhD

The lower Stillwater's placid currents are prime for dry fly fishing, but in the fall it shines for streamer fishing.

Access: Montana Highway 78 to Nye Road (Highway 420) and Highway 419 to Stillwater trailhead
GPS Coordinates: 45.351008, -109.903407
Equipment: 5- or 6-weight system with floating and sink-tip lines; caddisfly, BWO, PMD, Golden Stone, and Yellow Sally patterns, and soft-hackle, streamer, terrestrial insect, and traditional attractor patterns
Nearest facilities and services: Columbus (Montana), USFS Woodbine Campground, Meyers Creek rental cabin, Berry Creek Ranch
Information resources: Custer-Gallatin National Forest, Big Timber Ranger District Office; USGS Flow Station Gage 06205000; Absarokee, Beehive, Cathedral Point, Cow Face Hill, Nye, Sanborn Creek, and White Bird Hill USGS topographic maps
Salmonids present: Brook, brown, and rainbow trout and Rocky Mountain whitefish

My fly fishing experience on the Stillwater River began when I was a doctoral candidate at Oklahoma State University. My uncle invited me to join his group on a big-game hunt in the Absaroka Mountains of Custer National Forest. Our hosts, the Ralph Mitchell family, owned property along the Stillwater River, about midway between Absarokee and Nye. While hunting the mountainous country around their property, my attentions wandered toward fishing the Stillwater River, coursing along Highway 420 in front of their property. The river there was narrow, swift, deep, and strewn with boulders—some as big as automobiles. That's my kind of water, so it was love at first sight. I am a streamer specialist using short fly rods to cast big, heavily weighted flies. I revisited the Stillwater maybe four times to successfully fish the swift water in front of or a few hundred yards downstream of the Mitchell ranch. Sad that the famous tributaries and upper stretches of the Missouri and Yellowstone Rivers are becoming ever so crowded, but glad to know that the Stillwater still looks and fishes the same as in those days of yore, notwithstanding the rafters who float the river during the spring and early summer runoff.

The Stillwater River, about 70 miles long, begins in the mountainous Absaroka-Beartooth Wilderness Area and ends at the Yellowstone River near Columbus, Montana. Cutthroat trout, with samplings of rainbow and brook trout, are the principal piscine residents of the "high country." The mountainous section of river is swift and punctuated with meadows. In that 20-mile section, access is almost unlimited. One can hike, backpack, ride horseback, and in a limited sense use motorized vehicles to reach hidden jewels in the form of isolated lakes and small streams. In short, the Stillwater River in the wilderness country is the consummate freestone stream, and its name belies its overall character. Within upstream national forest land, a natural flow in the river predominates throughout the season.

Moose are common riparian zone inhabitants throughout the Greater Yellowstone Area. Females can be aggressive when their young seem threatened, so keep your distance. Give plenty of room to bulls during the autumn rutting season. JIMMY AND MILLI GABETTAS PHOTO

Brown trout are known for adaptability. Thus they are well suited for lower reaches of streams experiencing drawdown for agricultural purposes. JOHN JURACEK PHOTO

Downstream of the wilderness area, the Stillwater flows for about 45 miles through a mixture of canyons, prairie, agricultural land, and forest before intersecting the Yellowstone River. There are narrows with fast-flowing water, shallows with rocks of all sizes, and serene and placid areas. Fly fishing in those areas begins with looking for deeper water or sheltered areas in which trout can hide. Rocks are slick and loose and the bottom is uneven everywhere, both of which make for uneasy wading. Felt-soled water shoes and a wading staff lessen the chance of a dunking. Accurate casts in holes, runs, riffles, pockets, and sheltered areas are requisite. Trout in this section of the river are not picky; however, sloppy presentations can make for unhappy experiences.

The first 8 miles downstream of Nye is mostly canyon. The west side of the canyon is steep cliffs, with Nye Road cut therein. Experienced kayakers and white-water enthusiasts, and a few fly fishers, especially enjoy this stretch. However, the river can be fished from the road and bridges and at nine designated access points across private lands. The canyon ends a short distance downstream of Cliff Swallow Fishing Access site.

The remaining 37 miles of river is relatively placid and hosts cutthroat, rainbow, and brown trout, with fish ranging from a few inches to about 20 inches. Here it is favored by rafters and by anglers who enjoy casting small dry flies. I understand why fly fishers enjoy casting to trout feeding on the surface. There is nothing more exhilarating than watching trout come from the depths to take one, especially if the fly has been designed and tied by the caster. Virtually any imitation or attractor pattern will work every day during the summer and early fall. The key is proper presentation and drift. However, as soon as the Stillwater valleys frost in early fall, dominance swings to the brown trout, many pushing the ruler beyond 24 inches. This is when I concentrate on presenting my season-long fly fishing preference, that of presenting streamer patterns in deeper water.

The Yellowstone River enters the southeast arm of Yellowstone Lake. This location is one of the more remote places to fish in the Greater Yellowstone Area.

The Stillwater River has one major tributary, Rosebud Creek to the east. If you visit the Stillwater but are stymied by high water or landslides, or are trapped by multitudes of recreational boaters, drive back to Absarokee, turn south on Highway 78, and course along Rosebud Creek. The Rosebud and especially its three tributaries (from east to west, East Rosebud Creek, West Rosebud Creek, and Fishtail Creek) are ideal for wading, dry fly fishing, and catching medium-size trout.

PART 4

NORTHWESTERN WYOMING

Whereas Greater Yellowstone waters in Idaho are solely in the Pacific drainage and those in Montana are in the Atlantic drainage, the Continental Divide splits Wyoming's Greater Yellowstone Area into both drainages. The same happens with Yellowstone National Park waters, the park being mostly in Wyoming. Beyond park boundaries these Wyoming waters are only in the Yellowstone River drainage and the Snake River drainage. We will discuss each in turn. Beforehand,

Colorful scenery combined with a better chance for solitude makes autumn a particularly attractive time to visit Greater Yellowstone Area waters. JOHN JURACEK PHOTO

it is worth noting that compared to Idaho, Montana, and Yellowstone National Park waters, Greater Yellowstone waters in Wyoming hosting salmonids are generally lesser known than those in the other three places.

By the early 20th century, railroads reached the borders of Yellowstone National Park, coming through Island Park in Idaho to West Yellowstone, Montana, and up the Yellowstone River Valley to Gardiner, Montana. These were the basis for discovering the quality of and then promoting the Henry's Fork drainage, the Madison River drainage, and the Yellowstone River drainage above Gardiner. To this day, no railroads reach the park borders from the Wyoming sector of the Greater Yellowstone Area, and are somewhat distant on the eastern side. Other infrastructure was also slower in coming to Wyoming's portion of the Greater Yellowstone Area. For example, paved roads and electrification did not come to Star Valley until just before the mid-20th century. A road connecting Alpine and Hoback Junction through the Snake River Canyon was not completed until the mid-20th century.

The effect of such late development was to limit knowledge of and angling experience on many quality backcountry waters, both public and private, in western Wyoming. With the exception of Jackson Hole waters being promoted as quality fisheries by renowned local angling retailers Bob Carmichael and Boots Allen (the elder), beginning in the mid-20th century, nothing of major notice had been produced until Jack Dennis and Curt Gowdy in a *Wide World of Sports* television series feature revealed the Snake River fishing quality—in Jackson Hole. Presently, Boots Allen's (the younger) informative books promote fishing in the Snake River, but little is offered on other waters. Within this work, the quality of some Wyoming waters in the Greater Yellowstone Area will be revealed for the first time.

Nevertheless, the Wyoming Game & Fish Department takes care of their coldwater fisheries. A good example of this stewardship is the X-Stream Angler Program. In July 2012 the department began this program to showcase some of the state's most important streams and the work done to protect their waters for the public. The program was created to encourage anglers and anyone else who values flowing waters to seek out the many popular, and not so popular, streams where instream flow water rights to protect fisheries have been obtained over the past quarter century. An instream flow water right refers to the legal means to protect water in streams for the benefit of fish and is based on the same laws used for other kinds of water rights. Once an instream flow right has been obtained in Wyoming, it lasts forever. At present, the list of streams with instream flow water rights includes 130 stream segments and it's growing every year. Go to the Wyoming Game & Fish Department website to see the complete list of streams with instream flow water rights. It's a start in focusing on which backcountry streams are worth visiting. Several of those streams with instream flow water rights are discussed in this book.

In Idaho, Montana, and Wyoming the public can legally pass through private land to access fishing only with permission from the landowner. Also in all three states, access to public lands is legal only if these lands can be reached by an existing public road or easement or border other public lands. Once within an Idaho or Montana public water body, a visitor has legal access within the high-water mark. Here is where the Wyoming landownership laws differ from the other two states. In Wyoming, the streambed is the property of the adjacent landowner. It is legal to

The Hoback River within the Bridger-Teton National Forest offers roadside fly fishing. It is not as crowded as one might think because the Snake River is nearby. Snake River fine-spotted cutthroat rule the roost here, and they offer excellent dry fly action.

float a river through private land, but those doing so must stay in their watercraft at all times unless permission to debark has been given by the landowner. Thus wading, debarking, or anchoring without permission is trespassing. For the purpose of personal safety, state trespass law allows leaving a watercraft only to make short portages around such non-navigable obstacles as irrigation diversions. More details on trespass are available on the Wyoming Game & Fish Department website. The website also identifies public access locations on waters outside public lands. Knowledge of these locations can be crucial to enjoying a visit to Wyoming waters surrounded by private land.

Snake River Drainage

ASHTON–FLAGG RANCH ROAD WATERS

For the relatively few fly fishers in the know, Ashton–Flagg Ranch Road, which parallels the western part of Yellowstone National Park's south boundary, is a "stairway to heaven."

Access: Adjacent to or from trails and primitive roads from Ashton–Flagg Ranch Road
GPS Coordinates: 44.106688, -110.666379 (West end); 44.056970, -111.468802 (East end)
Equipment: 3- to 6-weight systems with floating, full-sink, and sink-tip lines depending on water targeted; damselfly, caddisfly, BWO, Golden Stone, Gray Drake, Green Drake, PMD, Speckled Dun, Trico, and Yellow Sally patterns, and streamer, terrestrial, and traditional attractor patterns
Nearest facilities and services: Ashton (Idaho), Jackson (Wyoming), USFS Sheffield Campground, primitive campgrounds at east end of road, Squirrel Meadows Guard Station rental cabin, Flagg Ranch Resort
Information resources: Caribou-Targhee National Forest, Ashton Ranger Station; Bridger-Teton National Forest, Jackson Ranger District Office; Ashton Visitor Center; Jackson Visitor Center; Wyoming Game & Fish, Jackson Regional Office; Flagg Ranch, Grassy Lake Reservoir, Hominy Peak, and Survey Peak USGS topographic maps
Salmonids present: Brook, cutthroat, cuttbow, lake, and rainbow trout and Rocky Mountain whitefish

Also known as "The Reclamation Road" and in Jackson Hole as "The Grassy Lake Road," there is nothing else in the Greater Yellowstone Area quite like this road with respect to offering access to quality streams and stillwaters. Built to transport construction materials and personnel by mule and ox train from the Union Pacific railhead in Marysville, Idaho, to the Jackson Lake Dam site over a hundred years ago, it was also a notorious escape route out of Jackson Hole into Idaho for elk ivory poachers and illegal trappers. Now it offers access to a superb array of fisheries, picturesque waterfalls, stunning views, and a wilderness setting.

Ashton–Flagg Ranch Road begins just a mile south of Ashton off US Highway 20, courses several miles due east through farmland, and is adjacent to Fall River Canyon. Next, it enters Caribou-Targhee National Forest then crosses the Idaho-Wyoming state line. The road itself is deceptive because each end is paved, albeit for only a few miles, to the Polecat Creek crossing at the east end from US Highway 89 just above Flagg Ranch Resort. The west end of the road is paved for several miles going east, from where it exits Highway 20 to the Caribou-Targhee National Forest boundary. From here, going about 8 miles east, it is an improved gravel road that is dusty and "washboardy" in places but easily passable with care and offering beautiful views of the Teton Range west slope.

At the South Boone Creek crossing, the road narrows to begin living up to its reputation for converting the newest and most rugged vehicle into a rattle trap. Moving through Squirrel and Gibson Meadows, it hardly gains elevation. But on climbing Calf Creek Hill, just east of the North Boone Creek crossing, it becomes almost primitive for many miles. From here on to the Polecat Creek crossing, it is not recommended for trailers, low-clearance vehicles, or large RVs. Beyond Calf Creek Hill on east to Grassy Lake Reservoir, it may be blocked by snowdrifts until around the first of July. And why not? Much of this stretch is around 7,000 feet in elevation. Narrow at places, it is dusty when dried out, full of chuckholes and boulders, muddy in places after a drenching thundershower, winding with blind corners, and closed frequently before the end of October by blinding blizzards. But it is passable in season with care for even sedans grinding away at around 20 miles an hour.

There are no developed campgrounds or resorts along the entire length of the road. Several pullouts on the east end, some adjacent to the Snake River, serve as primitive campgrounds. During midsummer these can be filled with overflow campers from both Yellowstone and Grand Teton National Parks, but when vacant, they offer bases from which to fish. To the north, Yellowstone Park hosts the best part of the Fall River with its stair-step meadows, Mountain Ash Creek, Proposition Creek, and Beula and Hering Lakes. These waters were addressed in the Yellowstone National Park section, and the Fall River outside Yellowstone Park was discussed in the Eastern Idaho section. Now let's look at the other quality waters outside the park that are accessed from Ashton–Flagg Ranch Road.

At its east end Ashton–Flagg Ranch Road crosses lower Polecat Creek, which begins in Yellowstone Park and hosts brook, brown, and cutthroat trout. This meadow reach in Wyoming offers wonderful dry fly fishing during terrestrial insect season.

Only native grayling exceed cutthroat trout in being endangered. Once the only trout species in the Greater Yellowstone Area, excepting Elk Lake's native lake trout, it is increasingly protected in order to counter its decreasing numbers. JOHN JURACEK PHOTO

Waters worth visiting begin near the Idaho-Wyoming state line. These, going east into Wyoming on either side of the road, are among the manifold fisheries of the Fall River Basin. With forks converging just north of the road and flowing into Idaho to meet the Fall River, Boone Creek becomes an isolated brook and cutthroat trout fishery replete with numerous beaver ponds holding individuals exceeding a foot in length. This creek can be reached around the state line from a few rough trails going north on either side of the line. It can also be reached from Fish Lake–Loon Lake Road leaving Ashton–Flagg Ranch Road at the North Boone Creek crossing.

There is, however, a much more interesting place, albeit seasonal, to fish from Fish Lake–Loon Lake Road, which ends at the Winegar Hole Wilderness boundary. From here, Fish Lake is a walk of about a mile. It hosts brook trout that range in size to over 20 inches, and how they came to be here is lost to time. The Wyoming Game & Fish Department recently tried to replace them with cutthroat trout, but this action met with some success and the brook trout remain. They are most easily caught early in the season after ice-out, when dragonfly nymphs seem to be their main food item. As springtime advances, Fish Lake develops an algae bloom as thick as any stillwater can, and these fish become difficult to encounter. The lake is also the source of brook trout going down through a nearby, and fishable, beaver pond and then into the Fall River.

East of Calf Creek Hill, a series of fisheries begins that extends to where the Snake River drainage relieves the Fall River drainage. The first of these, Lake of the Woods, is just south of the road and hosts a major Boy Scouts of America summer camp. From here boats can be launched to encounter large cuttbows within the deep, mile-long lake. In season, ant hatches from the surrounding pine forest interest trout, but presenting streamer patterns brings season-long responses. Early in the season they can be caught at the east-end outlet, which goes on to enlarge Cascade Creek. The creek flows into Tillery Lake, and both hold unusually colorful cuttbow trout.

Below Tillery Lake, Cascade Creek flows through beaver ponds adjacent to Ashton–Flagg Ranch Road and hosts large cuttbow trout, then proceeds on to the Fall River within Yellowstone National Park. A few miles east the Ashton–Flagg Ranch Road crosses Grassy Lake Dam, which impounds water for downstream Idaho irrigators. This 2-mile long reservoir hosts lake and rainbow trout growing to large sizes. A boat ramp near the dam provides access for boaters to troll or present streamers for the large trout. Some walk-in wade fishing and fishing from floatation devices is available along the north shore, where primitive camping is possible along the road. Just beyond is the barely discernable divide on the other side, which is part of the Snake River drainage. Glade Creek in Bridger-Teton National Forest, enhanced by a picturesque spring, begins here and hosts colorful brook trout. Less than a mile east the Berry Creek Trail leaves to the south providing a 4-mile-or-so walk to some of the best small-stream fishing for cutthroat trout in Grand Teton National Park.

Soon the road parallels the Snake River, offering several primitive camping locations and opportunities for walk-in wade fishing to encounter Snake River fine-spotted cutthroat and brown trout. Finally at the Polecat Creek (discussed in the Yellowstone National Park section) crossing, the road is paved for a few miles until ending at US Highway 89/191 in the John D. Rockefeller Jr. Memorial Parkway.

Essentially a whole season can be spent fishing the waters accessed by this road, and even then, all will not be completely visited. From July through September, this road opens the gate to fishing experiences that surpass those on more renowned waters.

BUFFALO FORK OF THE SNAKE RIVER
By Dave Brackett

One of the last major streams in the area to clear enough for fishing, the Buffalo Fork is often bypassed, yet it is a superior Snake River fine-spotted cutthroat trout fishery.

Access: US Highway 26/287 east from Moran Junction to Buffalo Valley Road
GPS Coordinates: 43.856825, -110.263328
Equipment: 5-weight system with floating and sink-tip lines; caddisfly, BWO, Golden Stone, Mahogany Dun, PMD, Trico, and Yellow Sally patterns, soft hackle and streamer, terrestrial, and traditional attractor patterns
Nearest facilities and services: Jackson (Wyoming), Turpin Meadow Campground, Turpin Meadow Ranch
Information resources: Bridger-Teton National Forest, Black Rock District Ranger Office; Jackson Visitor Center; Wyoming Game & Fish, Jackson Regional Office; USGS Flow Station Gage 13011900; Angle Mountain, Davis Hill, Moran, and Rosie's Ridge USGS topographic maps
Salmonids present: Brown and cutthroat trout and Rocky Mountain whitefish

Going north just before reaching Moran Junction between Grand Teton and Yellowstone National Parks, one crosses the Buffalo Fork, which feeds into the Snake River just south of the junction in Grand Teton National Park. The Buffalo Fork and its drainage receive little fishing pressure when compared to other Jackson

The Buffalo Fork of the Snake River is a major Snake River fine-spotted cutthroat trout fishery. These trout ranging to trophy size dominate throughout with a few brown trout in the extreme lower reach.

Hole watersheds. Why? The Buffalo Fork headwaters are in the Teton Wilderness on the west slopes of the Absaroka Mountains, which usually receive heavy snows that melt to supply abundant early-season water. The two branches of the river, the North Fork and the South Fork, flow though unstable hillsides that erode during high water to introduce huge amounts of silt into the river. Because of the high elevation of these drainages, runoff requires much time to complete, meaning the Buffalo Fork is one of the last major streams in the area to clear enough for fishing. So while fishing is great on other Jackson Hole streams, the Buffalo Fork is bypassed because of discolor from mid-June to mid- July. "Every time I go over the Buffalo Fork in June or early July, it looks like a milkshake," Bruce Staples complains. My response is "Be patient!" Soon after mid-July this river clears enough to offer good fishing.

Another major reason for less traffic on the Buffalo Fork are the few put-in and take-out facilities, meaning the river experiences little boat traffic and guided trips. Also, floatation craft are not allowed on the portion of river within Grand Teton National Park. Visible fishing traffic on the river is therefore small in a relative sense, thus begging the question: Is this river a poor fishery? In my experience, it is a superior Snake River fine-spotted cutthroat trout fishery. All a person needs to enjoy it on Grand Teton National Park, Bridger-Teton National Forest, or BLM land is a Wyoming fishing license and some information.

Heading east next to the river on US Highway 26/89 within Grand Teton Park, the old highway bridge site comes into view about a mile upstream. One of my fishing buddies revealed this location to me and posted it on his blog. If a visitor parks here, great-looking water is in view, but few visitors stop to try it. Cutthroat trout populate the river here, and during late summer encountering a brown trout is possible because they inhabit the Snake River just below. These trout do not seem to proceed upstream from here, perhaps because the river cools to their discomfort in upper reaches.

On leaving the park, traveling east on US Highway 26/287, ranches come into view. The first road going north is Buffalo Valley Road. The river off this road flows through a mixture of private, national forest, and BLM land. On passing Heart Six Dude Ranch, access roads lead to the river, where some large cutthroat reside. My fellow United Parcel Service driver, Nick Centrella, would stop here on his route during lunch break to fish. Always running late when substituting while he was on vacation, I never had time to enjoy them.

The next public access road from Buffalo Valley Road is USFS Road 30069, which ends at the river. It avoids the homes and private land along Buffalo Valley Road. This Forest Service road proceeds through Turpin Meadow and ends at a public campground with a Teton Wilderness trailhead. From here, the road ascends and returns to Highway 26/287. Years ago I took my family to this campground. I noticed fish in the river taking Mahogany Duns, so they allowed me to fish. I caught a few, then noticed a large fish rising underneath an overhanging tree. He took my first offering and headed downstream. I ran after him, landed him, and measured his length at 21 inches. On returning to my awaiting family, my wife, Cindy, asked why I ran down the bank. Who would not do the same for a cutthroat that large!

If one bypasses Buffalo Valley Road and stays on the highway going east, this road passes an RV park and then a pasture, all on the south side of the road. On the north side of the highway the river is close to the road, and a large buck rail fence on Forest Service land marks access to an outstanding reach of the river. I have fished here many times with excellent results, and the only other angler I saw came through in a pontoon boat. The Hatchet Motel and Restaurant and the Black Rock Ranger Station are farther east on the south side of the highway. A road going north here from the highway across from the ranger station leads to Forest Service housing right on the river. You can park here and fish.

Black Rock Creek crosses the highway just beyond the ranger station. Large Buffalo Fork cutthroat spawn in this stream and remain until water drops to base level during late summer. It's a wonderful little creek that no one seems to fish. Farther up Togwotee Pass, the Togwotee Mountain Lodge marks a trailhead for summer fly fishing on both forks of the Buffalo Fork. The hike to each is only a few miles, but the rewards are spectacular views and smaller but active cutthroat trout.

Timing of insect hatches here vary year to year, with clearing of the drainage from runoff and summer weather impacting water temperature. Streamer patterns work well in the slow water of the lower river. Hatches here mirror those in other Jackson Hole streams in that they may be active in only a short section of the river, thus the need to carry a variety of patterns and to fish a hatch hard on its discovery. If there is no surface activity, try leech, streamer, and damselfly and dragonfly nymph patterns. I recommend taking time to explore this wonderful river and its drainage. I believe it will never be overfished. One more thought: If you are going to visit, be sure to pack that high-resolution camera, a claxon horn, and reliable bear spray.

Grand Teton National Park Waters

Without a doubt, floating or wading the Snake River and trying for lake trout in Jackson Lake and wily trout in Blacktail Ponds are the major fly fishing attractions in Grand Teton National Park. Not only is the river a stronghold of the Snake River fine-spotted cutthroat trout, ranging to sizes over 20 inches, but the scenery is absolutely out of this world. Jackson Lake features not only cutthroat and brown trout but also lake trout ranging to more than 20 pounds. A Wyoming record lake trout, 50 pounds, came from Jackson Lake in the early 1980s. Streams within the park are another story. Renowned author, fly tier, and fly fisher Scott Sanchez offers: "The Snake River offers far and away the best stream fishing for cutthroat trout within the park." Much of Pacific Creek is nearly roadside here and easily approached, but fishing Berry Creek requires boating across the upper end of Jackson Lake or a 4-mile walk south from Ashton–Flagg Ranch Road.

Fishing within the park is subject to all Wyoming Game & Fish requirements, which in some cases are more restrictive in order to protect resident cutthroat trout, especially under spawning conditions. Nonmotorized boats (canoes, drift boats, kayaks) are subject to a $10 fee. Personal watercraft are not allowed on park lakes. Alpine conditions of extreme weather, a short growing season, and strenuous access to waters away from the river and lake further limit angling in the park. Nevertheless, some locations offer quality fishing, scenery, and solitude. A look at the best of these follows.

The Snake River running through Grand Teton Park is an important part of the Jackson Hole economy. Anglers, sightseers, boaters, wildlife enthusiasts and photographers are among the numerous visitors. JOHN JURACEK PHOTO

The Teton Range is the source of several quality fly fishing streams and contains numerous lakes hosting salmonids. On the east is upper tributaries of the Snake River drainage, and directly to the west is the Teton River drainage.

BRADLEY AND TAGGART LAKES

These lakes offer stunning scenery more than anything else. Taggart, with the most open shoreline, is the easier of the two to fish.

Access: Moose Junction from US Highway 26/89/191 and Teton Park Road to Bradley–Taggart Lake trailhead
GPS Coordinates: 43.693263, -110732902
Equipment: 5- or 6-weight system with floating and sinking lines; damselfly, midge, and Speckled Dun patterns, and flying ant, terrestrial insect, soft hackle and streamer patterns
Nearest facilities and services: Jackson (Wyoming), Jenny Lake Campground, Jenny Lake Lodge
Information resources: Grand Teton National Park Visitor Center and Jenny Lake Ranger Station; Grand Teton USGS topographic map
Salmonids present: Cutthroat trout

Situated on a bench just south and east of the main Teton peaks, Taggert Lake lies just under 7,000 feet in elevation, while nearby Bradley Lake is 100 feet higher. Both are of glacial origin. Their trailhead is about 2 miles north of the Moose Entrance to the park. It's a popular trail with hikers and photographers from all parts of the world during the summer. Fly fishers heading to either lake are far less numerous, and so are bears because of the human traffic volume.

After a bit more than a mile, the trail splits, with Taggart Lake a nearly flat half mile away on the left-hand fork and Bradley Lake a mile away on the more uneven

Taggart Lake is an easy hike and offers several locations where fly casting can be done without obstruction. Try it, or nearby Bradley Lake, in June when flying ants fall onto its surface and resident trout respond with vigor.

right-hand fork. The only way to fish is from the shoreline because boats of any kind are not allowed on either lake. Lakeside meadows, especially those with inlet creeks and points, are the best locations for fishing. Other than these locations, shorelines are mostly timbered, making wading necessary for an effective backcast or to reach cruising fish. If wading, reliable insulation is required for any enthusiast wishing to remain in the water for any length of time. Both lakes host cutthroat trout, and Taggart Lake also holds a few brook trout. Taggart cutthroat range to larger sizes, approaching 18 inches, than their Bradley Lake brethren.

Fish in both lakes tend to cruise shallows early and late in the day. Their courses are easily visible in the unusually clear waters, thus when sparse Speckled Duns or damselflies are on the surface, some action results. Without a doubt, the best time for surface fishing is, as with Jenny Lake, during the flying ant emergence in late June. Wind commonly picks up midday or during incoming or outgoing storms, lowering surface visibility for both fish and anglers. Switching to wet patterns such as small leeches and bead-head nymphs during these times may bring a return to action. All of this applies to larger Phelps Lake a few miles farther south and accessed by trails including the Death Canyon Trail off Moose-Wilson Road. As with Jenny and Leigh Lakes, it hosts lake trout.

JENNY LAKE
By Dr. Joe Burke

It is difficult to find a more beautiful setting than that of Jenny Lake. There will be many visitors during fishing season, so include tolerance with your fly gear if you intend to visit.

Access: Moose Junction from US Highway 26/89/191 and Teton Park Road to Jenny Lake Drive
GPS Coordinates: 43.692904, -110.732618
Equipment: 5- or 6-weight system with floating and sinking lines; damselfly, midge, and Speckled Dun patterns, and flying ant, terrestrial insect, and streamer patterns
Nearest facilities and services: Jackson (Wyoming), Jenny Lake Campground, Jenny Lake Lodge
Information resources: Grand Teton National Park Visitor Center and Jenny Lake Ranger Station; Jenny Lake USGS topographic map
Salmonids present: Brook, cutthroat, lake, and rainbow trout and Rocky Mountain whitefish

Being within Grand Teton National Park, Jenny Lake is essentially totally accessible. The quickest way to reach it is given above. Alternatively, a visitor can stay on the highway to Moran Junction and turn left onto Teton Park Road, proceed south over Jackson Lake Dam and on to North Jenny Lake Junction, then turn right to Jenny Lake Lodge. From there a one-way loop road going south skirts the east

Jenny Lake offers five salmonid species, each requiring specific fishing strategies. The lake also offers distracting scenery.

shoreline to South Jenny Lake Junction. This road offers a few places where the lakeshore can be waded and fished.

There is a public boat dock near the south end of the lake at the end of the Lupine Meadows access after crossing Cottonwood Creek and turning right. A park boating permit as well as a Wyoming fishing license are required, both of which are conveniently obtained at the Moose Entrance or at the Jenny Lake Ranger Station. Wyoming fishing regulations apply. Motorized boats on the lake are limited to less than 10 horsepower, and any floatation devices are prohibited. Boat rentals are also available at the marina next to the visitor center. The trail that surrounds the lake can be accessed at this boat dock as well as from parking areas along the east shoreline.

Because the shoreline drops off steeply, hiking anglers have limited wading locations along the lakeshore. To shorten the time required to reach the far (western) shore where there are a few locations suitable for wading, the shuttle boat can be taken, round trip for a fee, from the visitor center. Presenting streamer patterns from the western shore Cascade Creek delta can be effective.

Cutthroat and lake trout are the dominant salmonids in the lake, which is up to 200 feet deep, but lesser populations of rainbow and brook trout are present as well as Rocky Mountain whitefish. Cutthroat trout, in a concentration greater than in Jackson Lake, and Rocky Mountain whitefish are native to the lake.

Ice-out usually occurs by the middle of May. From ice-out until the lake water warms, presenting leech, streamer, and Woolly Bugger patterns are most effective for encountering resident trout, and these patterns remain effective throughout the fishing season. As the water warms, fish respond to increasing midge activity. Around the mudflats just south of the Cascade Creek confluence, I have watched trout in the ultra-clear waters nose bump a midge pupa pattern. My response is to let the pattern drop, then use a slow retrieve. This triggers trout to respond with a strike at the pattern.

Because of the year-round cold water temperature in most of Jenny Lake, aquatic insect life is somewhat limited. This means damselfly and Speckled Dun populations are minor and their emergences scattered. But when the flying black ants assemble in mid to late June, the surface fishing on the lake can be excellent. Wind blows ants from shoreline pines onto the lake surface, and cutthroat and juvenile lake trout respond, providing great dry fly fishing. Any dark-colored ant pattern in sizes as large as 12 will do.

Boating anglers should keep an eye on the sky because wind can quickly come off the mountains to whip the surface into waves up to several feet in a matter of minutes. Remember this because during the summer, the best fishing is along the far (west) side of the lake. At this time presenting terrestrial insect patterns, particularly hoppers and floating rubber leg patterns, around shoreline overhead cover can attract cruising trout. Attaching a small trailing nymph pattern to these can also be effective. Points along the west shoreline also become ambush locations for trout seeking forage minnows, so streamer patterns can work well. But again, watch for wind!

Some of the best shoreline fishing shifts to the east side of the lake during autumn. Here's why: Lake trout move to the east side's rocky shallows during this time to spawn. Egg incubation is helped because wave action adds dissolved oxygen to the hosting water. Trout and Rocky Mountain whitefish follow the migrating lake trout to feast on released eggs and the forage minnows doing the same. Their presence means presenting streamers along the shallows is also effective here this time of the season.

LEIGH LAKE

A fairly remote lake in a beautiful setting that offers fishing for cutthroat and lake trout that reach good sizes.

Access: US Highway 26/89/191 to Teton Park Road at Moose Junction to String Lake–Jenny Lake Drive to Leigh Lake trailhead
GPS Coordinates: 43.788717, -110.730690
Equipment: 5- or 6-weight system with floating and sinking lines; caddisfly, damselfly, midge, and Speckled Dun patterns, and flying ant, terrestrial insect, and streamer patterns
Nearest facilities and services: Jackson (Wyoming), Jenny Lake Campground, Jenny Lake Lodge
Information resources: Grand Teton National Park Visitor Center and Jenny Lake Ranger Station; Jenny Lake and Mount Moran USGS topographic maps
Salmonids present: Cutthroat and lake trout and Rocky Mountain whitefish

From the trailhead, Leigh Lake is easily accessed by a 1-mile trail over flat terrain. The most popular way to fish Leigh is by boating up String Lake from its

Leave beautiful String Lake to recreational boaters. It is too shallow and without enough overhead cover to host a significant salmonid population. Leigh Lake offers an escape from motorized recreation similar to that offered by Shoshone Lake in Yellowstone Park.

parking lot and picnic area. String Lake, no more than a channel, offers little as a fishery, as it is shallow and therefore warms quickly, but it is a popular location for recreational boating.

The incredible sight of Mount Moran greets the visitor arriving at the lake, where you are almost certain to enjoy solitude relative to Jenny Lake with its numerous visitors. The last few hundred yards below Leigh Lake must be portaged; therefore, canoes or kayaks are most suitable for reaching the lake, which is nonmotorized. Wading to fish is possible at some locations. Permits must be obtained for the primitive campsites on Leigh Lake and on cutthroat-populated Bear Paw and Trapper Lakes about 2 miles by trail to the north. These are available at the Jenny Lake Ranger Station or at the Moose Entrance.

Leigh Lake offers fishing for cutthroat and lake trout that reach good sizes. They are most successfully fished for in deep water with streamer and Woolly Bugger patterns. Sporadic Speckled Dun and caddisfly emergences offer some topwater fishing. These mostly occur along the shallows of the east shoreline. A better chance for fishing on the surface takes place during the late June flying ant hatch, which is not as widespread as that on Jenny Lake. Thus to enjoy it, shorelines where pines dominate must be visited. Some success with nymph and streamer patterns is possible at west-side creek inlets, as fish stage here to feed on items drifting into the lake. The weather warnings given for Jenny Lake also apply to Leigh Lake, since winds can arrive in an instant and make the lake surface perilous.

Gros Ventre Wilderness Waters

CRYSTAL CREEK

By Boots Allen

There is no better or more beautiful stream in the Gros Ventre Wilderness than this to watch 18-inch cutthroat trout rise to your fly.

Access: US Highway 26/89 to Lower and Upper Gros Ventre Roads to Red Rock Ranch Road
GPS Coordinates: 43.610972, -110.427243
Equipment: 5-weight system with floating line; caddisfly, Golden Stone, and Yellow Sally patterns, and soft-hackle, terrestrial insect, and traditional attractor patterns
Nearest facilities and services: Jackson (Wyoming), USFS Crystal Creek Campground, Red Rock Ranch
Information resources: Bridger-Teton National Forest; Jackson Visitor Center; Wyoming Game & Fish, Jackson Regional Office; Grizzly Lake USGS topographic map
Salmonids present: Cutthroat trout and Rocky Mountain whitefish

Flowing north out of the Gros Ventre Range, Crystal Creek is a major tributary of the Gros Ventre River. Pavement on Upper Gros Ventre Road ends not quite 2 miles from the Crystal Creek crossing. From the parking area off Red Rock Ranch Road, anglers can access most of the stream up to its headwaters. Much of lower Crystal

Lower Crystal Creek, a major Gros Ventre River tributary, offers excellent mid- and late summer dry fly fishing. From where it crosses the Gros Ventre Road on downstream to the river, it offers the best fishing for cutthroat ranging to trophy size.

Creek flows through meadows where undercut banks, runs, and small riffles can be fished. Higher up, pocketwater and small pools make for fun fishing.

Fishing Crystal Creek is all about the dry fly. From the time it clears in early July until late September, cutthroats are taken on a variety of size 8 to 12 attractor and terrestrial patterns. These flies produce not so much because the fish are hungry and not pressured, but because Crystal Creek has a healthy population of *Claassenia* stoneflies and its banks can be littered with a variety of terrestrial insects, especially grasshoppers. Cutthroat trout have a reputation for taking a floating pattern with a slow, deliberate rise, and Crystal Creek is an ideal stream for observing this.

GRIZZLY LAKE

You can fish this lake all day and have a great chance of not seeing another person, though you may run into wildlife.

Access: US Highway 26/89 to Lower and Upper Gros Ventre Road to trailhead
GPS Coordinates: 43.619770, -110478375
Equipment: 5- or 6-weight system with floating and intermediate lines; caddisfly, damselfly, dragonfly, midge, and Speckled Dun patterns, and leech and streamer patterns
Nearest facilities and services: Jackson (Wyoming), USFS Crystal Creek Campground, Gros Ventre River Ranch
Information resources: Bridger-Teton National Forest; Jackson Visitor Center; Wyoming Game & Fish, Jackson Regional Office; Grizzly Lake USGS topographic map
Salmonids present: Cutthroat trout

The Red Hills are a beautiful distraction for fly fishers visiting the Gros Ventre River above Lower Slide Lake. An almost surreal presence, they command attention as they come into view around a bend of the Gros Ventre Road above the lake. Take care to safely pass the numerous photographers along the road snapping electronic mementos of this striking land feature.

Just east of Slide Lake, the road leading up the Gros Ventre Valley turns from asphalt to dirt. This reach of the Gros Ventre River remains channelized but has a lower gradient than that part immediately below the lake. Fishable tributaries are numerous, as are small, intimate lakes. One of the lesser visited but more productive of these is Grizzly Lake. As its name implies, grizzlies frequent the area.

The trail to Grizzly Lake begins at a turnout with parking approximately 1.5 miles east from where the asphalt ends. Getting to the lake from the trailhead requires a relatively short hike to the south with crossings of the Gros Ventre River and some small creeks. Therefore, visits should be considered only after runoff is finished. I have packed in a float tube, fins, and waders on a couple of occasions. Cutthroat trout in the lake range from fun 12-inchers to impressively thick 18-inch individuals. Damsel and dragonfly larva imitations have been my go-to patterns. Evenings surface fishing can be worthwhile with chironomid adult imitations.

LOWER GROS VENTRE RIVER

One can spend a week traversing its 75-mile distance and barely touch the diverse prospects presented by this tucked-away stream.

Access: US Highway 26/89 to Lower and Upper Gros Ventre Roads
GPS Coordinates: 43.597655, -110.697764
Equipment: 5-weight system with floating and sink-tip lines; caddisfly, BWO, Golden Stone, PMD, Trico, and Yellow Sally patterns, and soft-hackle, streamer, terrestrial insect, and traditional attractor patterns
Nearest facilities and services: Jackson (Wyoming), USFS Atherton Creek Campground, Grand Teton National Park Gros Ventre Campground, Gros Ventre River Ranch
Information resources: Grand Teton National Park Visitor Center; Bridger-Teton National Forest; Jackson Visitor Center; Wyoming Game & Fish, Jackson Regional Office; USGS Flow Station Gage 13014500; Gros Ventre Junction, Moose, and Shadow Mountain USGS topographic maps
Salmonids present: Cutthroat and rainbow trout and Rocky Mountain whitefish

The Gros Ventre River flows into the Snake approximately 3 miles upstream of Highway 22 and Wilson Bridge. It is part of the eastern flank drainage of the Jackson Hole Valley and is a fishing paradise unto itself. The term *Gros Ventre* derives from the French words meaning "big belly," a name that early trappers and explorers gave to a Native American tribe closely linked to the Arapaho. Pronunciations range from the more commonly used "Grow-vaunt" to the perhaps more correct "Grow-venture." Locals get quite a kick out of listening to visitors' attempts at pronunciation.

The confluence is home to important spring creeks for spawning Snake River fine-spotted cutthroat trout. Like most of Jackson Hole, European settlement along the river did not occur until the 1890s. Many of these settlements were cattle ranches, including the Taylor Homestead, which served as a site for the film *Shane*. Some of these early ranches remain, but almost all now operate as high-end guest ranches.

Fishing is fabulous along this reach of the Gros Ventre, though the land here is private and not accessible to anglers unless they have permission from adjacent landowners. Only 5 miles upstream, the river is within the boundaries of Grand Teton National Park and, farther upstream, Bridger Teton National Forest. Almost all of the land here is designated as wilderness, and public access is just about limitless. The Gros Ventre drainage, and all the amazing water it has to offer, is wide open to the fly fisher.

The lower river parallels Gros Ventre Road from its junction with Highway 26/89 to the town of Kelly. Here it is a classic freestone stream, with braided channels, small seams, and scores of intimate little riffles. A healthy population of fine-spotted cutthroats call this part of the Gros Ventre home. Gros Ventre Campground is a prime jumping-off point to explore the river, but there are several turnouts where a fly fisher can park, prep gear, and head down to the streambed. Wade-fishing is rather easy after runoff subsides in late June and early July. Anglers share the river with moose throughout the summer, and during autumn it is easy to spot elk and bison as they migrate to their winter grounds.

The Gros Ventre River above and below Lower Slide Lake offers miles of excellent fly fishing. There are stretches of private land here, so be aware of posted areas. A few rainbow trout reside in the lower river, and they are the only such trout found in Jackson Hole streams.

Upstream of Kelly, the Gros Ventre becomes channelized and has a noticeably higher gradient. This part of the river is populated by cutthroats, as well as a remnant population of rainbow trout. These fish are the last remaining descendants of a state-run stocking program that introduced hundreds of thousands of McCloud-strain rainbows into the Snake River watershed from 1928 to 1964. In the early 1950s, rainbows comprised a full 20 percent of all fish caught in Jackson Hole. In J. Edson Leonard's *Trout*, Bob Carmichael notes their presence in the Gros Ventre River. Today, it is rare to catch rainbows anywhere in Jackson Hole, unless one is fishing on the lower Gros Ventre.

GROS VENTRE HEADWATERS

A small-stream paradise mainly populated by cutthroat trout. Road conditions can degrade in the upper drainage after storms, so pay attention to weather reports.

Access: US Highway 26/89 to Lower and Upper Gros Ventre River Roads to trailhead
GPS Coordinates: 43.470022, -110.196335
Equipment: 5- or 6-weight system with floating and intermediate lines; caddisfly, damselfly, dragonfly, midge, and Speckled Dun patterns, and leech, soft-hackle, streamer, terrestrial insect, and traditional attractor patterns
Nearest facilities and services: Jackson (Wyoming), USFS Crystal Creek Campground, Gros Ventre River Ranch
Information resources: Bridger-Teton National Forest; Jackson Visitor Center; Wyoming Game & Fish, Jackson Regional Office; Burnt Mountain, Darwin Peak, Double Top Peak, Ouzel Falls, Sheridan Pass, and Upper Slide Lake USGS topographic maps
Salmonids present: Brook and cutthroat trout

The Gros Ventre Road continues upstream from Soda Lake for another 7 miles before it dead-ends at the site of the now-defunct Horn Ranch. Prior to the 1960s, the road continued over the divide near the Darwin Ranch and vehicles could make their way down into the Green River drainage. Today, fly fishers wishing to access the upper reaches of the Gros Ventre River must hike in from where the road now ends.

The upper Gros Ventre hosts two stunning waterfalls: Ouzel Falls and Upper Gros Ventre Falls. Ouzel Falls is approximately a 6-mile hike upstream from the Horn Ranch. These falls are separated by approximately 2 miles of river meandering through a willow-filled meadow. Wildlife is abundant here, and the meadow is prime summer grounds for elk and moose. A small population of brook trout share the stream with cutthroat ranging from 10 to 16 inches. It is a 7-mile round-trip hike to the best fishing on the upper Gros Ventre River. A more enjoyable experience can be had here by camping for a night or two. This allows one to truly take in the scenery, wildlife, and fishing this part of the drainage has to offer.

Continuing up the Gros Ventre from Crystal Creek, the road passes by a marshy body of water known as Upper Slide Lake. This is summer grounds for what is sometimes dozens of trumpeter swans and can be easily seen from nearby turnouts. Farther upstream, the Gros Ventre is joined by two small and nearly adjacent streams: Cottonwood Creek and Fish Creek. Both have impressive numbers of cutthroat trout. I have had days fishing them where a long lull in activity might be 20 minutes. A day with several dozen cutthroat caught and released can be had on both streams. The trails that parallel these creeks can be hiked well over 10 miles upstream, with fishable water almost everywhere. As with Crystal Creek, both streams become fishable once runoff subsides in early to mid July. They will fish into autumn with a variety of dry patterns. Because of the sheer number of cutthroat in Cottonwood and Fish Creeks, fishing a tandem dry fly rig can result in more than a few double hookups.

In many places the Gros Ventre River above Lower Slide Lake is easily approached. Cutthroat trout here respond reliably to the aquatic insect emergence sequence and to terrestrial insects but keep an eye on the sky for thundershowers.

A number of trails ascend from the upper Gros Ventre River to the mountains above. These paths can be followed around Triangle and Darwin Peaks and then down into the Hoback River watershed. A number of small, fishable stillwater bodies are located at these higher elevations, and they fit the definition of "high alpine" perfectly. Chateau Lake is located just above and to the southeast of Upper Gros Ventre Falls. The hike from the trailhead to the lake is 11 miles. It is about the size of two basketball courts, with ample room for sight-casting to a healthy population of brook trout, some of which exceed 18 inches.

Hiking another 3 miles up from Chateau Lake through the steep Grizzly Basin takes the fly fisher to the much larger Brewster and Lunch Lakes. Brewster feeds Lunch, and their combined flow creates the Dry Fork, which joins Clear Creek, which soon flows into the Gros Ventre River below Ouzel Falls. Casting dry and wet flies to cutthroat trout on these lakes is easy from shore, but those with stamina to carry in a float tube such a distance (at least 9 miles from the Horn Ranch trailhead) will be rewarded with an experience full of solitude and raw beauty.

SLIDE LAKE

Good fishing for fine-spotted cutthroat and lake trout on a young lake. Expect some summertime recreational boating and such.

Access: US Highway 26/89 to Lower and Upper Gros Ventre Roads
GPS Coordinates: 43.636518, -110.523356
Equipment: 5- or 6-weight system with floating, intermediate, and sinking lines; caddisfly, damselfly, midge, and Speckled Dun patterns, and leech and streamer patterns
Nearest facilities and services: Jackson (Wyoming), USFS Atherton Creek Campground, Gros Ventre River Ranch
Information resources: Bridger-Teton National Forest; Jackson Visitor Center; Wyoming Game & Fish, Jackson Regional Office; Mount Leidy and Shadow Mountain USGS topographic maps
Salmonids present: Cutthroat and lake trout

In 1925 one of the largest modern-day landslides in North America occurred along the southern flank of the Gros Ventre River. Fifty million cubic yards of sediment tumbled into the valley below and blocked the flow of the river. The water that accumulated behind this natural impoundment formed what is now Slide Lake.

The submerged forest at the upper end of Lower Slide Lake is a good location to fish for foraging cutthroat trout. These trees host a rich array of aquatic insects on submerged portions and numerous terrestrial insects above.

Engineers who were working on Jackson Lake Dam at the time inspected the slide and found it to be structurally sound. But only two years later, a portion of the slide gave way. A wall of water rushed into Jackson Hole, flooding the nearby community of Kelly and killing six people. Today, the slide is a historic site and studied by geologists from around the world.

Lower Slide Lake is the only stillwater in the drainage with a developed boat launch. This is at Atherton Creek Campground on the lake and is accessed from the main road which runs along northern lakeshore. This campground can be a base from which to explore the upper Gros Ventre River drainage. It's a full-service campground catering to boating anglers and recreationists.

Snake River fine-spotted cutthroat trout dominate the lake. The lake also hosts a small population of lake trout resulting from Wyoming Game & Fish releases decades ago. These tend to remain in deep water except for a while after ice-out and again in late autumn when they migrate to rocky shorelines to spawn. A variety of weighted and unweighted streamers, trolled or cast with floating and intermediate lines along flats, shorelines, and submerged structure, will bring responses from foraging cutthroat trout.

The real draw, however, are the caddis and *Callibaetis* mayfly hatches in the evening from late June through September. Enticing dimples made by cutthroat feeding on emergers and adults of these insects can be seen all along the lake surface on windless days. The late-evening pink alpenglow cast upon Sheep Mountain to the south is an added bonus. So is the looming landslide that brings on the hope that another will not occur, at least not while the fly fishing observer is on the lake!

SODA LAKE

Soda Lake offers the best opportunity for a shot at trophy trout in the Gros Ventre Wilderness. Cutthroats well over 20 inches call this lake home.

Access: US Highway 26/89 to Lower and Upper Gros Ventre Roads to trailhead on USFS Road 30437
GPS Coordinates: 43.538660, -110.256651
Equipment: 5- or 6-weight system with floating and intermediate lines; caddisfly, damselfly, dragonfly, midge, and Speckled Dun patterns, and leech, streamer, terrestrial insect, and traditional attractor patterns
Nearest facilities and services: Jackson (Wyoming), USFS Atherton Creek Campground, Gros Ventre River Ranch
Information resources: Upper Slide Lake USGS topographic map
Salmonids present: Brook and cutthroat trout

Sight-fishing is the name of the game on Soda Lake. To get there, take the rough 1-mile-long dirt double-track from the Upper Gros Ventre Road leading to Soda Lake. You can only fish from shore in a few places due to high banks and tall lodgepole pines that ring most of the water, so float tubes and kick boats make for a better experience. Drift boats and rafts can be trailered in, but there is no developed boat ramp.

Damsel and dragonfly larva imitations work well, and my favorites include locally created patterns. A number of years ago a friend of mine turned me onto the effectiveness of Zug Bugs and Soft-Hackle Prince Nymphs on Soda Lake. These are now my go-to patterns. All of these are fished best with slow hand twist or pinch retrieves on floating, hover, and intermediate lines. There are times, however, when faster retrieves with moderately sized streamers is the way to go. It's a lot of fun watching a 20-inch stillwater cutthroat chase a size 8 baitfish imitation and make its grab within a few yards of your rod tip.

The largest cutthroat I have seen taken on Soda Lake was a 24¼-inch specimen in 2008. This size outpaces that of any cutthroat taken by the several bald eagles that nest along the shore.

GREYS RIVER DRAINAGE

Flowing almost totally through Bridger-Teton National Forest, the Greys River offers excellent fishing for Snake River fine-spotted cutthroat trout.

Access: Greys River Road off US Highway 89 in Alpine, Wyoming
GPS Coordinates: 43.163554, -111.017845
Equipment: 4- or 5-weight system with floating and sink-tip lines; caddisfly, BWO, Golden Stone, PMD, Trico, and Yellow Sally patterns, and soft-hackle, streamer, terrestrial insect, and traditional attractor patterns
Nearest facilities and services: Jackson and Alpine (Wyoming); USFS Forest Park, Lynx Creek, Moose Flat, and Murphy Creek Campgrounds; USFS Cazier, Deer Creek, and Meadows Guard Station rental cabins; Box Y Guest Ranch
Information resources: Bridger-Teton National Forest, Greys River Ranger District; USGS Flow Station Gage 13023000; Blind Bull Creek, Box Canyon Creek, Deer Creek, Mann Peak, Park Creek, and Pine Creek USGS topographic maps
Salmonids present: Brown and cutthroat trout and Rocky Mountain whitefish

Whereas the adjacent Salt River runs mostly through private land but with several public access sites, the Greys River courses about 60 miles through Bridger-Teton National Forest land with the exception of about 2 miles of private land belonging to the Box Y Ranch about 30 miles upstream from Alpine, Wyoming. There are other major differences between these adjacent rivers. The Salt River meanders mainly through meadows of pastoral beauty, while the Greys River descends a forested valley in a series of riffles, runs, cutbanks, pockets, and pools. Islands and side channels are present, along with logjams, boulders, willowed meadows, and timbered banks.

Except for a few brown trout in its lower portion near Alpine, the Greys River is a Snake River fine-spotted cutthroat and Rocky Mountain whitefish stronghold. Whereas a major highway follows the Salt River and passes through some towns, Greys River Road closely parallels the river. Because of recreational traffic, the section of this road below the Murphy Creek Road intersection can become a bit rough during summer months. Professional guide services are not offered for float-fishing here, as on the more easily approached Salt River, and most fly fishers are

During midsummer the Greys River offers superb dry fly fishing opportunities. As waters warm past midday, caddisfly activity increases and terrestrial insects have absorbed enough heat to become active. Resident cutthroat take notice, and the fun of encountering them begins.

local enthusiasts. Four developed and beautifully sited campgrounds are on the river above the Little Greys River confluence.

The Little Greys River is a smaller version of the main river, replete with a well-maintained road and smaller Snake River fine-spotted cutthroat trout in abundance. Above the Murphy Creek confluence to Corral Creek, a distance of over 30 miles, the Greys River is managed as a wild trout fishery with only artificial flies and lures permitted. Whereas below the Little Greys River confluence recreational boating and rafting is popular, above this point only an occasional raft, usually occupied by anglers, will be encountered. A few fishable alpine lakes are in the drainage to tempt the fly fisher wishing to combine fishing with hiking.

With the Wyoming Range to the east and the Salt River Range to the west, the Greys River is a major runoff stream, usually clearing around the first of July. By then aquatic insects become abundant. As July advances, terrestrial insects become numerous enough to be a significant part of the salmonid diet. My best experiences fishing this beautiful river begin in August and continue through mid-September. By midday aquatic and terrestrial insects become active and trout respond, often feeding with gusto.

These events and natural beauty make the Greys River an ideal dry fly stream. Most of my visits are day trips, but stays in one of the well-maintained riverside campgrounds have been rewarding for me. On a few occasions, copious rain from a thundershower has muddied the river, but I have found it possible to travel upstream far enough to fish above discolored water. Fishing dry caddisfly, terrestrial, and traditional attractor patterns, I had not encountered any Greys River cutthroat exceeding 16 inches, but Jack Dennis recommended to me to fish soft hackled patterns during the hatches, which resulted in cutthroats exceeding 20 inches. Jack and other Jackson Hole enthusiasts also suggest that not using a Humpy on the Greys River is not only close to being criminal, but also a mistake in presentation strategy!

With the South Fork reach below and the Snake River in Jackson Hole above, most visiting anglers are attracted away from the Greys River. In addition, this river, particularly the wild trout section, is not well-suited for drift boats. An advantage of fishing in September is that many local anglers who visit the river earlier in the season are now hunting. Another advantage of a September visit are the oranges, reds, and yellows from cottonwoods, mountain mahogany, and quaking aspens complementing the blue skies and green conifer forest.

Wyoming waters host four species of cutthroat trout: Bonneville, Colorado River, Snake River fine-spotted, and Yellowstone. To promote this enviable ensemble, Wyoming Game & Fish offers the "Cutt Slam" to develop appreciation and support for the department's trout management programs. On providing dates, locations, and photographic evidence that a person has caught (and hopefully released) each cutthroat subspecies in their native Wyoming range, a Wyoming Game & Fish fisheries biologist will verify the species identification. Once verified,

The Little Greys River and its tributaries are ideal for lightweight tackle. Resident cutthroat trout are active and solitude prevails. Only the occasional thundershower can interfere. PIONEER ANGLERS PHOTO

the submitting angler will receive a certificate in recognition of accomplishing the Cutt Slam. Of all Wyoming waters, none is more suited to conveniently accomplishing the Cutt Slam than the Greys River. Here's why: Yellowstone cutthroat trout abound in nearby Yellowstone Park waters. The Tri-Basin Divide is at the top of the Greys River; to the east, streams in the Green River drainage host the Colorado River subspecies, and to the west, streams in the Great Basin drainage host the Bonneville species. In the midst of these is the Greys River hosting the Snake River fine-spotted subspecies. Thus it is possible within only a few days of fishing the Greys River to encounter the four cutthroat trout subspecies and qualify for a Cutt Slam certificate.

Hoback River Drainage

CLIFF CREEK

A great candidate if you seek solitude, active trout, and easy access. The trout run small, but they are eager.

Access: US Highway 189/191 to Cliff Creek Road
GPS Coordinates: 43.248616, -110.495002
Equipment: 3- or 4-weight system with floating line; caddisfly, Golden Stone, PMD, Trico, and Yellow Sally patterns, and soft-hackle, streamer, terrestrial insect, and traditional attractor patterns
Nearest facilities and services: Jackson (Wyoming), USFS Hoback and Kozy Campgrounds, Hoback Guard Station rental cabin, Black Powder Guest Ranch
Information resources: Bridger-Teton National Forest, Jackson Ranger District Office; Jackson Visitor Center; Wyoming Game & Fish, Jackson Regional Office; Clause Peak USGS topographic map
Salmonids present: Cutthroat trout and Rocky Mountain whitefish

As with the Hoback River, Cliff Creek begins in the Wyoming Range in Bridger-Teton National Forest to the south, but unlike the river, it flows entirely through the forest. The river begins to the east in the same forest, leaves it quickly southeast of Bondurant, and then flows several miles through private land until it comes adjacent to US Highway 189/191 west of town. After several miles along the highway, where it is heavily fished, it goes back to private land and its Snake River confluence.

Cliff Creek is the smallest of the Hoback River tributaries we will discuss and is lightly fished. It flows mostly through a meadow of broken willow thickets, and its eager Snake River fine-spotted cutthroat make it ideal for the lightest weight tackle and traditional attractor patterns or Tenkara techniques. The well-maintained road going south from Highway 189/191 parallels the creek for miles and offers much solitude. About the wildest animal to be expected along most of Cliff Creek would be a Black Angus bull looking for his favorite cow.

Cliff Creek is another ideal stream for using the lightest tackle available. A forest road parallels the stream for miles, making it a good candidate for a daylong visit.

GRANITE CREEK

This is the most visited of the Hoback River tributaries. But with water types varying from freestone stretches to beaver ponds, it is the most interesting of the tributaries to fish.

Access: US Highway 189/191 to Granite Creek Road
GPS Coordinates: 43.283093, -110.534077
Equipment: 3- or 4-weight system with floating line; caddisfly, Golden Stone, PMD, Trico, and Yellow Sally patterns, and soft-hackle, streamer, terrestrial insect, and traditional attractor patterns
Nearest facilities and services: Jackson (Wyoming), USFS Granite Creek Campground, Hoback Guard Station rental cabin, Black Powder Guest Ranch
Information resources: Bridger-Teton National Forest, Jackson Ranger District Office; Jackson Visitor Center; Wyoming Game & Fish, Jackson Regional Office; Crystal Peak and Granite Falls USGS topographic maps
Salmonids present: Cutthroat trout and Rocky Mountain whitefish

Of the four tributaries, Granite Creek is likely the most visited, and being the largest tributary, noticeably increases the size of the river. An adjacent well-maintained gravel road leaves US Highway 189/191 at The Meeting Place, a local name for this intersection and a Hoback River Bridge, 10 miles southeast of Hoback Junction, and follows it for several miles to Granite Hot Springs Resort. Safari Club International's Granite Creek Ranch is about halfway between the highway and the resort, and a popular campground and a trailhead to the south side of the Gros

Granite Creek offers fishing for Snake River fine-spotted cutthroat and Rocky Mountain white-fish along with a hot spring resort and campground. Expect recreational and tourist traffic on the road paralleling the creek. So be sure to use pullouts that give access to the stream.

Ventre Wilderness Area is adjacent to the resort. Mountain scenery and Granite Creek Falls attract visitors and photographers.

Although frequently fished, Granite Creek offers miles of good pocketwater, a few deep holes, small-stream riffles and runs coursing through willow patches, a few beaver ponds, and easy access. Snake River fine-spotted cutthroat trout up to moderate sizes reside mostly in the deeper holes. Rocky Mountain whitefish are also present, and encountering one over 14 inches is an event. Traditional dry fly patterns in small and medium sizes are ideal for enticing the resident salmonids.

SHOAL CREEK

On this newly designated Wild and Scenic River, solitude reigns and the cutthroat range to moderate size.

Access: US Highway 189/191 to Shoal Creek trailhead
GPS Coordinates: 43.271734, -110.522833
Equipment: 3- or 4-weight system with floating line; caddisfly, Golden Stone, PMD, Trico, and Yellow Sally patterns, and soft-hackle, streamer, terrestrial insect, and traditional attractor patterns
Nearest facilities and services: Jackson (Wyoming), USFS Hoback and Kozy Campgrounds, Hoback Guard Station rental cabin, Black Powder Guest Ranch
Information resources: Bridger-Teton National Forest, Jackson Ranger District Office; Jackson Visitor Center; Wyoming Game & Fish, Jackson Regional Office; Bondurant and Double Top Falls USGS topographic maps
Salmonids present: Cutthroat trout and Rocky Mountain whitefish

Shoal Creek enters the Hoback River just above the Kozy Campground. Its trailhead is about a quarter mile downstream where the highway crosses the river, thus it is on the far side of the river from the campground. After runoff season, this creek offers some fine fishing for Snake River fine-spotted cutthroat to moderate sizes. Its lower reach receives the most pressure, albeit light.

About 2 miles north of Bondurant, Dell Creek Road (USFS Road 30600) leaves US Highway 26 and trends northeasterly. After about 4 miles, USFS Road 30590 turns left (north) and enters Riling Draw, where it degrades. Shoal Creek is about a mile northwest on the rough road, better for walking than driving, and offers a greater chance of solitude and undisturbed cutthroat trout than the access off Highway 189/191. It is also a shortcut for reaching Shoal Creek Falls compared to the distance from the trailhead on the highway below Kozy Campground. Just a look at Shoal Creek hints that it is a perfect example of dry fly water. Any small or medium-size pattern drifted into pockets and pools will be accepted by resident cutthroat trout. The Hoback Guard Station can be rented from Bridger-Teton National Forest to serve as a base for exploring the Hoback River drainage, including the upper reach of Shoal Creek.

WILLOW CREEK

Tough to get to, but offers near-certain solitude and eager cutthroat trout ranging to trophy size.

Access: US Highway 189/191 and Bryan Flats Road to Willow Creek trailhead
GPS Coordinates: 43.275697, -110646676
Equipment: 3- or 4-weight system with floating line; caddisfly, Golden Stone, PMD, Trico, and Yellow Sally patterns, and soft-hackle, streamer, terrestrial insect, and traditional attractor patterns
Nearest facilities and services: Jackson (Wyoming), USFS Hoback and Kozy Campgrounds, Hoback Guard Station rental cabin, Black Powder Guest Ranch
Information resources: Bridger-Teton National Forest, Jackson Ranger District Office; Jackson Visitor Center; Wyoming Game & Fish, Jackson Regional Office; Bailey Lake and Camp Davis Falls USGS topographic maps
Salmonids present: Cutthroat trout and Rocky Mountain whitefish

As with the Hoback River and Cliff Creek, Willow Creek begins in the Wyoming Range to the south, and like the river, ends flowing on private land. The trailhead for the lower part of the creek, surrounded by private land, is reached off the highway by a stock bridge crossing the river. Its upper reaches are accessed from Bryan Flats Road off Highway 189/191 about 4 miles east of Hoback Junction. This road crosses the Hoback River and proceeds to the trailhead, from which the creek is accessed just before reaching the Bryan Flats Guard Station. From here, be ready to walk about 3 miles to access the creek. Bring potable water and bear spray.

The alternative is getting to know the landowners above the guard station to obtain access, because the road that eventually approaches upper Willow Creek is private. Being able to drive to the creek using this road to encounter its fine Snake River fine-spotted trout population would be more than convenient. But knowing how precious property rights are in Wyoming, the chances of trespass permission on it are certainly small at best.

PACIFIC CREEK DRAINAGE

A stronghold for Snake River fine-spotted cutthroat trout, but it is best to rely on its upstream reaches for tranquility. Observe grizzly bear protocol.

Access: US Highway 89/191 to Pacific Creek Road to Pacific Creek trailhead
GPS Coordinates: 43.940753, -110.440872
Equipment: 3- or 4-weight system with floating line; caddisfly, Golden Stone, PMD, Trico, and Yellow Sally patterns, and streamer, terrestrial insect, and traditional attractor patterns
Nearest facilities and services: Jackson (Wyoming), Pacific Creek Campground, Turpin Meadow Ranch
Information resources: Bridger-Teton National Forest, Black Rock District Ranger Office; Jackson Visitor Center; Wyoming Game & Fish, Jackson Regional Office; USGS Flow Station Gage 13011500; Gravel Mountain and Whetstone Mountain USGS topographic maps
Salmonids present: Cutthroat trout and Rocky Mountain whitefish

Like its neighbor to the south, the Buffalo Fork of the Snake River, this freestone stream has runoff of major proportions. Its renown, rather than being an outstanding

North Two Ocean Creek splits into Atlantic and Pacific Creeks. This remote fork forms the ancient water trail by which cutthroat trout migrated from the Pacific to the Atlantic side of the Continental Divide.

fishery, is for being the pathway by which cutthroat trout migrated upward to North Two Ocean Creek then down Atlantic Creek to populate that side of the Continental Divide over 6,000 years ago.

Pacific Creek Road exits Grand Teton National Park and heads northeast, trending generally in the same direction as its namesake. After leaving the park, its surface quality diminishes somewhat, but not enough to bring one easily to Pacific Creek Campground on the Teton Wilderness Area boundary. If you seek tranquility, walk up the trail into the wilderness area a way and begin fishing. Bring plenty of potable water. The farther upstream you venture, the more likely your chance for solitude.

You will observe that the stream has pockets, riffles, runs, and occasional holes, and during summer months wet wading is not only practical but refreshing, unless a thundershower interferes. It may appear to be ideal for dry fly presentations, but you will find that the trout population is somewhat low compared to other regional streams. This means that you must cover a lot of water to encounter trout ranging to moderate size. Some holes will appear without fish and many will have only a few residents, so be persistent. Nevertheless, the beauty of surroundings as well as the isolation will make the visit here worth the effort.

SALT RIVER DRAINAGE

Surrounded by pastoral beauty, this river beckons the fly fisher to encounter its excellent Snake River fine-spotted cutthroat and brown trout population, along with a few rainbows.

Access: County roads off US Highway 89 to several public access areas
GPS Coordinates: 43.126479, -111.030891
Equipment: 5- or 6-weight system with floating and sink-tip lines; caddisfly, BWO, Golden Stone, PMD, Trico, and Yellow Sally patterns, and streamer, terrestrial insect, and traditional attractor patterns
Nearest facilities and services: Alpine and Afton (Wyoming), USFS Alpine Campground, USFS Stump Creek Guard Station rental cabin, Hansen-Silver Guest Ranch
Information resources: Wyoming Game & Fish Department; USGS Flow Station Gage 13027500; Alpine, Auburn, Etna, Sage Valley, and Thayne West USGS topographic maps
Salmonids present: Brown, rainbow, and cutthroat trout and Rocky Mountain whitefish

The Salt River originates in Wyoming's Salt River Range to the southeast of Star Valley. Traveling US Highway 89 through western Wyoming's Star Valley, especially north of Afton, the river comes into view as an enticing meadow stream meandering through private lands. Here and there it emerges from willow thickets to exhibit bends with undercut banks, side channels, and deep holes. The exception is the brief run through the section locally named The Narrows just above the village of Thayne, where the gradient increases for a few miles and aquatic insect life takes on the character familiar in riffle-and-run streams. In fact, around mid-June, when

The Salt River flows through pastoral Star Valley, which parallels the Idaho-Wyoming border. Take heed of Wyoming trespass laws when visiting to fish, and enjoy the brown trout that predominate in this river.

the river can be discolored from runoff, a Giant Stonefly emergence takes place, and fish respond to drifting adult imitations.

Surrounded by animal husbandry and agriculture, the Salt River beckons the fly fisher to encounter its excellent trout population. Access can be limited because of Wyoming's stream access and trespass laws, but there is a way around this in the form of 12 access easements along the river's course. These are signed, mostly from Highway 89, indicating county or state roads going to each. In total, they allow about 20 miles of bank and stream access from the Swift Creek confluence downstream to Palisades Reservoir.

The Salt is a relatively small river, and drift-boating is not practical above the town of Grover. Below, caution must be taken because of low clearance beneath bridges and necessary portages around several irrigation diversions. Guiding on the river can be arranged at Alpine, Wyoming. Pontoon boats are ideal for float-fishing this river, remembering that the landowner owns the stream bottom. Throughout its course through public fishing easements, the Salt River must be waded with caution because of its swift current and deep holes in many bends. Runoff usually leaves the Salt before adjacent rivers, and typical early-season aquatic insect emergences take place. Around The Narrows section there is a season-long restriction of using artificial flies and lures only. Snake River fine-spotted trout up to trophy size inhabit the river below Afton, and most of the larger brown trout inhabit the river below The Narrows.

A particularly pleasant time to fish this river is during mid and late summer when terrestrial insects flourish along the well-vegetated banks. Long, drag-free drifts of large grasshopper or attractor patterns along opposite banks and into the heads of pools can be productive. During this time, certain access areas can become relatively crowded with wading and floating anglers seeking trophy brown and cutthroat trout. Another excellent time to fish this river is during the autumn run of brown trout migrating to spawning areas above The Narrows and out of Palisades Reservoir. The river above Thayne closes to fishing during November and December to protect the spawning trout. Some of these migrants concentrate in the river below The Narrows, and presenting large streamers brings responses from fish that range to several pounds.

Several small creeks flow west out of the Salt River Range and on to the Salt River. Willow Creek, just south of the town of Thayne, shares a public access site with the Salt River and can be accessed from a rest area on Highway 89. Swift Creek flows through Afton to reach the river. Other than being a conveniently reached small stream above town, it is known for its prolific Gray Drake emergence. These tributaries provide spawning habitat and restore flow in the river during irrigation season, all helping to maintain the salmonid population.

Yellowstone River Drainage

CHIEF JOSEPH SCENIC HIGHWAY WATERS

The Clarks Fork of the Yellowstone River is the trunk stream in this land of small waters, and the breathtaking Chief Joseph Scenic Highway gives access to its upper reaches.

Access: Chief Joseph Scenic Highway from the Montana state line to the Shoshone National Forest east boundary
GPS Coordinates: 44.977825, -109.834079
Equipment: 3- or 4-weight system with floating and sink-tip lines; caddisfly, BWO, Golden Stone, Giant Stone, PMD, Trico, and Yellow Sally patterns, and soft-hackle, streamer, terrestrial insect, and traditional attractor patterns
Nearest facilities and services: Cody (Wyoming); USFS Dead Indian, Hunter Peak, and Lake Creek Campgrounds; Sunlight Ranger rental cabin; Hunter Peak Ranch
Information resources: Shoshone National Forest, Clark's Fork Ranger District Office; Cody Visitor Center; Dead Indian Meadows, Dillworth Bench, Elkhorn Peak, Geers Point, Hunter Peak, and Hurricane Mesa USGS topographic maps
Salmonids present: Brown, cutthroat, and rainbow trout and Rocky Mountain whitefish

Just traveling the Chief Joseph Scenic Highway (aka Wyoming Highway 290) is an adventure. At the upper end, Index and Pilot Peaks are in view, commanding the dense pine forest, accompanying mountains, steep canyons, and rushing water courses. Sunlight Basin, with its wild and scenic beauty, dominates the middle portion, while Dead Indian Pass, marking the basin's lower end, has forced an engineering marvel to be constructed in the form of a sinuous highway. Not far to the south and southwest, the Absaroka Wilderness hosts the headwaters of many streams in the area. Nearly equivalent to Beartooth Pass, just to the north, with respect to complexity if not elevation, it demands careful driving of a vehicle in good operating condition.

This impressive pass also marks the transition from the heavily forested Absaroka Range uplands to the near-barren high-desert plains of the Bighorn Basin. Excepting the Clarks Fork in its canyon, it's a land of small freestone streams suitable for lightweight systems and a few small stillwaters hardly worthy of being designated lakes. Three small streams stand out. Draining high country, each is a runoff stream usually clearing before mid-July. Each has a good caddisfly population supplemented by some mayfly species, but mostly midges, Golden Stoneflies, and some *Isoperla* species. From late July through September, terrestrial insects are important food items for resident trout.

Going downstream, Crandall Creek is first to be accessed. It is nearly all on public land, except for about a mile of private property just above the highway crossing. A trail beginning at the highway leads to the creek above the private land. With sources high in the Absaroka Range, it begins with some gradient, then flattens a bit before dropping into its canyon to meet the Clarks Fork just below the top of the canyon. Brook, cutthroat, and rainbow trout populate its waters, with rainbows predominating in its lower portions. Nearby, accessible 10-acre Swamp Lake offers fly and lure fishing for brook trout that formerly reached large sizes.

Here Crandall Creek shows storm-related discolor as happens on area streams flowing through unstable geologic formations. After a few days of storm-free weather, fishing usually returns to normal.

Brook trout introduced over one hundred years ago through political pressure thrive in many Greater Yellowstone Area waters. In these waters they have replaced native trout and grayling. JOHN JURACEK PHOTO

Nonmotorized boating, especially through use of floatation devices, is appropriate for encountering the colorful resident brookies that respond well to damselfly, scud, and leech patterns.

At the western base of Dead Indian Pass, first Sunlight Creek and then Dead Indian Creek drop to enter the Clarks Fork Canyon. Sunlight is the largest of the three creeks and flows for miles through private land and ranches upstream of the highway crossing. It is accessed by Sunlight Road 101. Two miles upstream of the crossing, Sunlight Falls forms a barrier to upstream movement of rainbow trout. Above the falls, brook and cutthroat trout share the stream. A Wyoming Game & Fish access is present partway up the private land, and about 6 miles above, the creek returns to Shoshone National Forest, where access is unrestricted.

High in the drainage, accessible by first a four-wheel-drive road and then a steep trail for a total of 3.5 miles of walking, the Copper Lakes are famed for hosting golden trout. For the hardy backpacking fly fisher, toting a floatation device to the lakes gives the best chance of encountering these trout. The goldens populate the small upper two lakes, while cutthroat trout populate the larger lower lake.

Adjacent just to the east of Sunlight Creek, Dead Indian Creek, the smallest of the three creeks, crosses the highway at the base of the pass sharing the same name. Trails access it above and below the highway. Rainbow trout predominate in lower reaches, with brook and cutthroat trout taking over in upper portions.

CLARKS FORK OF THE YELLOWSTONE RIVER

From high-country heaven to canyon country, diverse character and generous access through much of its upper and middle stretches make this an exciting destination.

Access: Upper river is adjacent to US Highway 212 and Chief Joseph Highway; middle portion in canyon reached only by Forest Service roads above the Crandall Creek confluence and trails; lower river reached via Wyoming Highway 120 to County Road 1AB (Wyoming 292) to Shoshone National Forest boundary and Morrison Road

GPS Coordinates: Dead Indian trailhead, 44.753429, -109417896; Reef Creek trailhead, 44.845739, -109.560242; Russell Creek trailhead, 44.787467, -109.422368; Morrison Road: 44.857176, -109.292774

Equipment: 5- or 6-weight system with floating and sink-tip lines; caddisfly, BWO, Gray Drake, Green Drake, Golden Stone, PMD, Trico, and Yellow Sally patterns, and soft-hackle, streamer, terrestrial insect, and traditional attractor patterns

Nearest facilities and services: Cody (Wyoming), several USFS campgrounds along US Highway 212 and Chief Joseph Highway, Sunlight Ranger rental cabin, 7D Ranch

Information resources: Shoshone National Forest, Clark's Fork Ranger District Office; Cody Visitor Center; Wyoming Game & Fish Department, Drainage Area 2 Office; Cody; Bald Peak, Chapman Bench, Dilworth Bench, Hunter Peak, Jim Smith Peak, Muddy Creek, and Windy Mountain USGS topographic maps

Salmonids present: Brown, cutthroat, and rainbow trout and Rocky Mountain whitefish

The Clarks Fork of the Yellowstone River is the first in Wyoming in which an in-stream water right was established. For the purpose of fly fishing, it can be divided

The author weighs the decision whether to fish with showers moving in on the Clark's Fork beneath Index and Pilot Peaks.

The river flowing through remote and dangerous Clarks Fork Canyon should be approached only with planning and precaution. Relative solitude will be found here, but expect some recreational boaters.

into three sections, each open the entire year to artificial fly and lure fishing only. With origins coming from numerous lakes in Montana's Beartooth Mountains, the upper section flows through a valley in a moderate gradient as scenic as any in the Greater Yellowstone Area. Next, the river flows through a steep canyon in near isolation. Finally, near the Shoshone National Forest boundary, it enters high desert to begin its curve through a wide arc to return to Montana and end in the Yellowstone River west of Billings. It seems best to discuss each section in turn because of differences in physical character and fly fishing approach.

The upper Clarks Fork is high-country heaven for the visiting fly fisher. At first it runs adjacent to US Highway 212 for miles. As this highway swings to the northeast to climb Beartooth Pass, the Chief Joseph Scenic Highway leaves to the southeast and provides the most access to the best fishing in the upper river. Index and Pilot Peaks signal that the upper end of Sunlight Basin, where fishing pressure is relatively light, is not far away. The nearly 20 miles of mostly moderate-gradient river here is not really suited for boat fishing, although an occasional kayaker can be encountered, so walk-in wade fishing is the name of the game.

Early-season runoff makes wading in deeper, swifter water dangerous, and the water seems never to warm enough for long periods of wet wading. All this adds up to cautious wading, especially when scenery can be so distracting. By mid-July runoff is usually finished, and the river is better suited for wading. Presentation efforts on pockets, holes, runs, and any soft water can now be tried with mid- or lightweight systems.

This part of the river is where I came to realize how versatile and effective the Humpy is as an all-purpose attractor. It remains one of my "go-to" patterns and is always present, traditional or blond, in my fly box when visiting Greater Yellowstone Area streams. The wild rainbows are not large, rarely reaching 18 inches, but they are eager, strong, and challenging in the fast-moving water. A few brook trout and Yellowstone cutthroat trout, whose numbers are reduced through hybridizing with rainbow trout, are also present. Up to now public land, in the form of Shoshone National Forest, is abundant, allowing access to most of the river. Camping sites, commercial and public, are plentiful in the basin. Near Crandall Creek, the transition from easily accessed water to that in a steep and dangerous canyon begins.

Now the river and highway become separated by the famed prominent canyon. The 20-mile canyon stretch is designated Wild and Scenic River, the first in Wyoming, beginning near the Crandall Creek confluence and is entirely within Shoshone National Forest. With waterfalls, eddies and backwaters, and boulder-strewn bottoms and banks, it is challenging to the utmost to fish. Kayakers relish its brawling waters and are frequently present. Some of these are also fly fishers. Getting to the water is difficult and at places dangerous. The river is most safely fished by going upstream from the lower end. A four-wheel-drive road extends a few miles up into the canyon, and trails lead into the canyon from Crandall, Reef, and Dead Indian Creeks. These do not provide easy walks, thus wading access in the canyon is limited and solitude is easily obtained.

Although the Clarks Fork is open to year-round fishing, snow blocks roads until mid-spring, then runoff makes visiting the canyon dangerous and fishing slow. Thus the season usually begins around mid-July, when the water in the canyon becomes somewhat safe for wading. As in the river above, traditional attractor patterns are effective. It is prudent to consider that direct sunlight does not penetrate this steep-walled and relatively narrow canyon. Therefore, time is required for its waters to warm to the point that insects become active, particularly on the south side of the canyon.

Below its canyon, the river changes character. Emerging from the canyon, it transitions to a more tranquil state. Here it slows and meanders a bit in the Bighorn Basin high desert to become more friendly in physical character to visit. A few swatches of state land below the forest boundary allow limited opportunities to walk in and wade, but private land dominates, with only four public access sites managed by Wyoming Game & Fish on 25 miles of river to the Montana state line. Thus float-fishing is the best approach. As with the upper river, the end of runoff signals the practical beginning of fishing season. Trout are larger although fewer than in the river above, and brown trout become a worthy quarry. Rainbow trout and Rocky Mountain whitefish are also present. High desert means plentiful terrestrial insects while the seasonal progression of aquatic insect emergences advances. By mid-September presenting large wet fly and streamer patterns becomes effective for encountering brown trout beginning their annual fall migration to spawning areas.

GREYBULL RIVER

The remote Greybull River in Shoshone National Forest offers tranquil small-stream fishing.

Access: West on Wyoming Highway 290 from Wyoming Highway 120 to the Shoshone National Forest boundary and Greybull River trailhead

GPS Coordinates: 44.109656, -109353547

Equipment: 4- or 5-weight system with floating and sink-tip lines; caddisfly, BWO, Golden Stone, PMD, Trico, and Yellow Sally patterns, and streamer, terrestrial insect, and traditional attractor patterns

Nearest facilities and services: Cody (Wyoming), USFS Jack Creek Campground, Fiddleback Ranch

Information resources: Shoshone National Forest, Greybull District Ranger Office; Wyoming Game & Fish Department, Drainage Area 2 Office; Cody and Meeteetse (Wyoming) Visitor Centers; USGS Flow Station Gage 06276500; Irish Rock and Phelps Mountain USGS topographic maps

Salmonids present: Brown, cutthroat, and rainbow trout and Rocky Mountain whitefish

Small and beautiful in its upper reaches, the Greybull River, with its smaller tributary Wood River, marks the southern end of Bighorn Basin streams we will discuss. Through its entire flow it is a freestone stream subject to runoff from the Absaroka Range peaks rising as high as 13,000 feet. Runoff is usually spent by July, and wading to fish above the forest boundary becomes less perilous. Near

The remote Greybull River in Shoshone National Forest offers tranquil small-stream fishing. Local fly shops provide the opportunity to fish the private land reach holding good numbers of brown trout. TIM WADE PHOTO

the Shoshone National Forest boundary, the river emerges from its steep mountain valley, where it flows in a northerly direction out onto the high desert and changes to an easterly course. A trail beginning at Jack Creek Campground parallels the river upstream for miles into the Washakie Wilderness.

As with many freestone streams, caddisflies and stoneflies predominate, although the late-summer Trico emergence can result in excellent fishing. Presenting dry flies of almost any type into plunge pools, pockets, and runs and in front of logjams brings responses from eager cutthroat trout ranging to midsize. Wading wet during summer months is practical and adds aerobic exercise to fishing. At times boulder hopping is necessary.

As with so many Greater Yellowstone streams on leaving national forest land, access changes from ample to difficult. Watching the river while traveling west of Meeteetse creates a longing to fish when the long, sinuous meanders come into view. It's a sight similar to that seen when traveling through ranches on Montana's upper Ruby River between its reservoir and the Deerlodge-Beaverhead National Forest boundary. Brown trout populate this water, joining the cutthroat for interesting fishing. Doing so on a walk-in basis is possible where ranchers and fly fishing retailers have access agreements in place. These locations are above diversions, resulting in generally good water conditions, but as with so many Greater Yellowstone rivers, the quality in lower reaches decreases due to diversion. Thus it is worth consulting with fly fishing retailers in Cody in order to obtain information on fishing these private tracts, where solitude and easier wading is guaranteed.

HOGAN AND LUCE RESERVOIRS

Popular with Cody-area fly fishers, but not many others. The short walk to Hogan makes carrying a floatation device easy.

Access: Wyoming Highway 120 to Park County Road 7RP to Luce Reservoir, then trail from Luce Reservoir parking lot to Hogan Reservoir
GPS Coordinates: 44.787277, -109256811
Equipment: 5-weight system with floating and intermediate lines; dragonfly, damselfly, midge, and Speckled Dun patterns, and leech, scud, streamer, terrestrial insect, and traditional patterns
Nearest facilities and services: Cody (Wyoming), Luce Reservoir Campground
Information resources: Cody Visitor Center; Wyoming Game & Fish, Drainage Area 2 Office; Bald Peak and Chapman Bench USGS topographic maps
Salmonids present: Cutthroat trout in Luce Reservoir; rainbow trout in Hogan Reservoir

On descending the east side of Dead Indian Pass on the Chief Joseph Scenic Highway, one can observe to the northeast two stillwater bodies in the middle distance. These are Hogan and Luce Reservoirs. The highway soon ends at the intersection with Highway 120. Going north about a mile on this road leads to the signed connecting County Road 7RP, which goes about 4 miles west to Hogan Reservoir's campground. This reservoir is managed for family fishing, where all terminal gear

Pelicans are a controversial presence due their taking of trout on many Greater Yellowstone waters. However, they also prey on rough fish. DAVE LETENDRE PHOTO

except live bait can be used. Yellowstone cutthroat trout are the quarry here, and they reach trophy size feeding on baitfish, leeches, midges, and scuds. The size of these fish and the presence of a campground make Hogan Reservoir popular and therefore at times heavily fished.

The Hogan Reservoir parking lot holds the trailhead to Luce Reservoir. The trail to Luce is only a quarter-mile walk, the end of which is a fly fishing reward. Only artificial flies and lures are allowed here, and the resident hard-fighting Kamloops rainbow trout grow to sizes exceeding 20 inches. Floatation devices can easily be packed up the trail, and they are ideal for fishing this brush-lined reservoir with about 30 acres surface area. Terrestrial patterns work well here, because the well-vegetated shoreline inhibits wading at Luce Reservoir, much to the joy of floatation device enthusiasts.

During midsummer the water in all area reservoirs tends to warm into the 60s, slowing daytime fishing activity, and Hogan tends to become quite weedy. With so many reservoirs undergoing weed growth, fishing channels between the weed beds is the preferred strategy. But the advantages of fishing early and late in the day improves chances for action, as well as offering a better chance of solitude.

MONSTER LAKE

This private lake has regained its fame as a producer of exceptionally large trout.

Access: Wyoming Highway 120 south from Cody to Nielson Road
GPS Coordinates: 44.398158, -108.980751
Equipment: 6- or 7-weight system with intermediate and floating lines: dragonfly, damselfly, midge, and Speckled Dun patterns, and leech, scud, streamer, terrestrial insect, and traditional attractor patterns
Nearest facilities and services: Cody (Wyoming), Monster Lake Ranch Resort
Information resources: Cody Visitor Center; Oregon Basin USGS topographic map
Salmonids present: Brook, brown, cutthroat, rainbow, and tiger trout

Privately owned but accessible Monster Lake is famed for producing large and vigorous trout. With five salmonid species present and each ranging to trophy size, the fun of fishing here is not knowing which is responding to your presentation.

As with eastern Idaho's Sheridan Reservoir, colorful stories abound of fishing in this pay-to-fish lake. Actually, two lakes make up the water on this private property. The one farther east, formerly known as Wiley Lake and now as Monster Lake, is the place of legend. Located about 10 miles south of Cody just off Highway 120, the new owners have restored fishing here to the fame it enjoyed in the 1990s. The full-service facilities of Monster Lake Ranch, including lodging, are concentrated at the east end of the smaller lake, Quick Lake, itself no slouch at offering good fishing. Here boats and equipment can be rented, guides hired, and lodging made. A reservation system applies, with details on all aspects of a visit available on the ranch website. Individual to corporate-size clients are welcomed. The only motors allowed on waters are electric, and drift boats and floatation devices are best suited for use on the nearly 200-acre lake. Guides are not required but are suggested, as using them minimizes time spent locating fish during your visit.

Fishing is year-round, with an ice-fishing season during winter. Fly fishing usually begins with April ice-out, but can occur earlier if this event takes place in March. The fishing can be particularly good right after ice-out, and it may also slow during the heat of summer. Fishing early or late in the day can be most productive any time of the season, especially in shallow water where there are good locations for wading. The season can extend into November, depending on the uncertainties of high-country weather. In addition to the size of the salmonids present, variety adds to the fun of fishing here. The presence of brook, brown, cutthroat, rainbow, and tiger trout make for an unusual diversity, and because of trophy sizes going into double-digit poundage, stout rods and strong leaders are required.

Nutrient-rich water is the basis for growing unusually large fish here. This combined with minimal pollution, a managed water level, and the catch-and-release ethic of fly fishers ensure the presence of large fish. The rich waters also support the abundance and variety of food forms. Scuds are so abundant that they coat waders, fins, and the bottom of boats. Weed beds that expand rapidly during warming weather shelter growing quantities of scuds as well as provide shelter for other life-forms. Quantities of leeches and minnows swim freely. Damselflies and dragonflies offer further variety, but midge populations likely provide the bulk of food. They too can coat waders, fins, surfaces of boats, and clothing during early-season blanket emergences.

All these food forms give clues on fly patterns and strategy for fishing this lake. If presenting patterns on sinking lines to simulate dragonfly nymphs, leeches, or minnows does not interest fish, a switch to smaller patterns to simulate scuds, damselfly nymphs, midge larvae and pupae, or Speckled Dun nymphs may be in order because fish here are always feeding on something. With this switch one must determine a retrieve of correct speed or an indicator at correct depth if fishing below the surface. It is all these options that makes fly fishing so interesting! Of course, there are times when weed growth comes close to ruling out certain presentations, and presentation and pattern selection become obvious when fish feed on or near the surface when insects emerge. And, yes, it is a bit expensive to fish here, and doing so is subject to schedule availability, but the potential rewards of a visit make saving resources to do so worth considering.

NEWTON LAKES
By Tim Wade
Special regulations on East Newton Lake make it a fly fishing favorite.

Access: Park County Road 7C off Wyoming Highway 120
GPS Coordinates: 44.541812, -109.117220
Equipment: 5- or 6-weight system with intermediate and floating lines; dragonfly, damselfly, midge, and Speckled Dun patterns, and leech, scud, soft-hackle, terrestrial insect, and streamer patterns
Nearest facilities and services: Cody (Wyoming), West Newton Lake Campground
Information resources: Cody Visitor Center; Wyoming Game & Fish Department, Drainage Area 2 Office; Cody and Goff Lake USGS topographic maps
Salmonids present: Brook, brown, cutthroat, and rainbow trout and splake

Just outside Cody, Wyoming, East and West Newton Lakes offer a superb example of governmental and private groups coming together to produce and maintain a high-quality fishing destination that is an important part of the local economy. When about 30 years ago the lakes and hosted fisheries were threatened by natural and man-made events, various private and public groups combined efforts to save them. This cooperation stands as an example of what can be accomplished by anyone and any organization, or combination of both, striving to maintain an excellent destination fishery.

East Newton's shoreline has places suitable for wading, but boating allows the entire lake to be fished. How the lake is sustained as an outstanding fishery is a model of how organizations can come together to benefit the recreational public.

Located 5 miles north of town on about a half square mile of public land, both lakes are former brood stock ponds now owned by the Wyoming Game & Fish Department. Currently sustained by the department as public fisheries, the recreation area is maintained and managed by a steering committee made up of members from concerned groups including the city of Cody, Trout Unlimited, the Absaroka Fly Casters, and Park County. Both lakes are protected by the Newton Lakes Endowment Fund, to which contributions are welcomed to sustain the lakes as a superb stillwater fishery and to manage the recreation area as a quality location. The fund's advisory committee is made up of the presidents of the local Trout Unlimited chapter and the Absaroka Fly Casters and another individual delegated from the steering committee.

West Newton Lake, slightly larger and deeper, with a powerboat limit of 15 horsepower, is natural and maintained as a family fishery where bait fishing is allowed. Cutthroat trout are the primary salmonids present, and the flies that work on East Newton Lake are also effective here. Large individuals are present and are sought by fly fishers. East Newton Lake, maintained by water pumped from the nearby Shoshone River, receives most attention from fly fishers due to its artificials-only regulations. Maintained as a trophy fishery, brown and rainbow trout are the major species, with some splake and brook trout present as well. Within these species individuals approaching 30 inches are present. Only artificial flies and lures are allowed as terminal gear, and the daily limit of one fish over 22 inches gives a solid clue as to the size of trout present.

East Newton Lake, also with a powerboat limit of 15 horsepower, is ideal for float tubes and pontoon boats, and stalking the banks can be effective to enjoy the many hosted salmonids over 20 inches. The fly fishing season begins with ice-out. Wade-fishing is popular at East Newton at that time, as the water level is usually low. The first few weeks after ice-out offer sporadic fishing, mostly due to the unpredictable spring weather in the foothills where the lake is located. April and early May offer sight-fishing to pods of bank cruisers and rainbow trout attempting to spawn. Low water can negatively impact fishing at this time, but when the annual midge emergence begins, the action starts.

Better fishing results when water is pumped into the lake from the nearby Shoshone River to bring it to full pool. Floatation devices become popular at this time, allowing better access to the trout that move to the edges of the emerging aquatic vegetation that will abound throughout most of the fishing season. Midges become the most important food source for trout during this transition period. Most of the other insects are not yet consistently active, while scuds, leeches, and minnows are predominantly secluded in the increasing cover provided by submerged vegetation. Large caddis pupa and Partridge and Olive Soft Hackle flies become effective for encountering big trout when a large caddisfly emerges during late-spring afternoons. By evening, skating large adult patterns results in more interesting surface fishing. This can go on for weeks and provides some of the most reliable dry fly action on the lakes.

By summer, extensive submerged and shoreline vegetation harbor vast quantities of aquatic and terrestrial insects, but at times during midsummer, warming waters can slow fishing a bit. Successful fishing now is close to shorelines as trout cruise weedy areas and shallows in search of the abundant insects, particularly during early mornings and evenings. When the lakes warm during summer, playing fish quickly and releasing them as thoroughly revived as possible becomes vital for their survival.

As days grow shorter with the onset of autumn, water temperatures cool and aquatic vegetation deteriorates. The masses of aquatic insects become increasingly active to seek cover in what remains of the vegetation and thus are a major prey for foraging trout. Scud, leech, and nymph patterns return to the effectiveness they offered in the early season. Shoreline wading once again becomes practical, as some drawdown can take place by late summer. Near the beginning of November, western Wyoming weather suggests that winter is just around the corner, and fishing from small boats becomes more comfortable than wading or fishing from floatation devices. This change in weather also signals the beginning of the fly-tying and armchair-fishing season, when locally the emphasis is on creating new patterns for enjoying the large fish that East Newton Lake offers to all fly fishers.

LOWER SHOSHONE RIVER

The "Lo-Sho" offers excellent seasonal fishing. It is best fished through boating because walk-in fishing is limited to public access areas.

Access: US Highways 14 and Alternate 14
GPS Coordinates: 44.534227, -109.064081
Equipment: 5- or 6-weight system with floating and sink-tip lines; caddisfly, BWO, and midge patterns, and soft-hackle, streamer, terrestrial insect, and traditional attractor patterns
Nearest facilities and services: Cody (Wyoming), 7D Ranch
Information resources: Cody Visitor Center; Wyoming Game & Fish Department, Drainage Area 2 Office; USGS Flow Station Gage 06282000; Cody, Corbett Dam, Shoshone Canyon, Ralston, and Vocation USGS topographic maps
Salmonids present: Brown, cutthroat, and rainbow trout and Rocky Mountain whitefish

The two Shoshone River forks above Buffalo Bill Reservoir, the North Fork of the Shoshone River and the South Fork of the Shoshone River, are well known in the fly fishing world. The North Fork flows along US Highway 14/16/20 from just inside Yellowstone National Park's east boundary downstream to Buffalo Bill Reservoir a few miles west of Cody, Wyoming. From the Shoshone National Forest boundary on upstream, access is abundant, except for minor interruptions from private land. Rainbow and cutthroat dominate its salmonid population, with some brown trout in the lower river above the reservoir and brook trout in upstream tributaries. The smaller south fork is just the opposite. On leaving the national forest boundary, access is difficult to find, other than four public access sites owned by Wyoming Game & Fish. These open about 5 miles out of around 30 miles of river to walk-in fishing. Both forks end in the reservoir formed in 1910. The reservoir is mostly the realm of deep trollers searching for trophy-size lake trout. In warmer weather, recreationists including water-skiers, windsurfers, and speedboaters dominate the surface until early September.

Below Buffalo Bill Reservoir, the term "working river" applies to the Shoshone. Yes, this seems harsher than the term "multiple use," but it is a fact that all activities using this river have played, for over a hundred years, second banana to its use by agriculture and animal husbandry. Throughout mid-spring and summer, flows are therefore erratic. So from January to the beginning of irrigation season, sometime in May, the lower Shoshone (locally known as the "Lo-Sho") offers streamer and big wet-fly fishing for those seeking large rainbow trout migrating to spawning areas, some cutthroats, and resident browns ranging to several pounds. On occasion midge emergences provide some dry fly fishing.

Walk-in wade fishing is practiced by only a few local anglers, and the number of float-fishers is small. Access, excepting steeper canyon areas, is relatively good around Cody, but diminishes to only three public access areas downstream to near Powell, Wyoming, below which fishing quality diminishes. Thus float-fishing is the name of the game this time of year in order to prospect banks with overhead cover, heads and tails of pools, runs, and soft water. The best option for success at this time is to contact local fly fishing retailers offering guide services, or to launch

The "Lo-Sho," as the lower Shoshone River is known locally, offers excellent seasonal fishing. It is best fished through boating because walk-in fishing is limited to public access areas. Between runoff and increased flow for agriculture and again at the end of the agricultural season are the best times to fish.

one's own boat so long as the owner and participants have a good knowledge of where to put in and take out. Between Cody and Powell there are two diversion dams that require a portage.

Demand for agricultural water ceases soon after the first of October, when clearing water in low and steady flows returns as storage in the reservoir takes place. The roles of rainbow and brown trout reverse, with streamer and big wet-fly fishing for migrating brown trout to large sizes being most popular. As in the early season, float-fishing results in the greatest success. Because October into early November can offer some excellent weather for fishing, the number of walk-in wade anglers as well as those boating can increase somewhat compared to the early season. A bonus this time of year are caddisfly and midge emergences which at times can be prolific. Between these two insects and some BWOs emerging, some good dry fly fishing is possible. But as November progresses, it becomes a good idea to bundle up and keep an eye on the sky.

Near the end of October 2016, an ecological disaster took place on the "Lo-Sho." Prior to making repairs on the Willwood Diversion Dam, about 12 miles downstream from Cody, water flow was lowered to expose damage. Massive silt beds that had accumulated through the 90-year life of the dam created a slurry that invaded the river below, likely smothering all fish and aquatic insect life for miles downstream at least to Mormon Dam, another diversion structure. Therefore, life in this portion of a major quality fishery has been terminated for the foreseeable future.

Wind River Headwaters

UPPER WIND RIVER

High-country angling at its finest, with short seasons, storms, striking scenery, and relatively small but eager salmonids.

Access: Off US Highway 26/287 within Shoshone National Forest boundary and through public access locations below
GPS Coordinates: 44.534227, -109.064081
Equipment: 5- or 6-weight system with floating and sink-tip lines; caddisfly, BWO, Golden Stone, PMD, Trico, and Yellow Sally patterns, and soft hackle, streamer, terrestrial insect, and traditional attractor patterns
Nearest facilities and services: Dubois (Wyoming), USFS Falls Campground, Longhorn Ranch Lodge and RV Resort
Information resources: Shoshone National Forest, Wind River District Ranger Office; Wyoming Game & Fish Department; USGS Flow Station Gage 06218500; Dubois, Esmond Park, Kisinger Lakes, Mason Draw, Torrey Lake, and Warm Springs Mountain USGS topographic maps
Salmonids present: Brook, brown, cutthroat, and rainbow trout and Rocky Mountain whitefish

Heading east on US Highway 26 over the nearly 10,000-foot-high Togwotee Pass, a traveler crosses the Continental Divide, descends the beautiful mountain country, and soon leaves Shoshone National Forest. Upstream of the forest boundary, the Wind River begins near Wind River Lake at the base of Sublette Peak. From the outlet, the river is little more than a brook. Ultimately this is the source of the fabled Bighorn River. Within the forest boundary it flows for about 15 miles and picks up tributaries to increase in size. One of these is the outlet of the nearby photogenic Brooks Lake.

The Wind River is another small freestone stream paradise, with tributaries coming from the Absaroka Range to the north and from the Wind River Range to the south. Brooks Lake itself is at 9,200 feet in elevation. Ice-out here is usually around first of July, when wading and float-fishing can begin. The high elevation and relatively scanty food supply for resident brook, cutthroat, lake, and rainbow trout here result in a short growing season. Fish rarely grow to more than a pound, but the lack of size is compensated by the stunning scenery the lake offers to anglers. Backcountry lakes are numerous in surrounding mountains, and outfitters based in Dubois, Wyoming, can be hired to access many of them.

Yellowstone cutthroat trout are native here, but in the river itself and in tributaries, rainbow and brook trout also reside. The farther downstream one proceeds, the more brown trout are encountered, some of which reach large size. Access to the river and its drainage is abundant within the Shoshone National Forest boundary because of the adjacent highway, but below the forest boundary the visiting fly fisher encounters mostly private land. The river gradient eases here, and just downstream from the Du Noir Creek confluence, seven public access fishing sites are present on the river down to the Wind River Reservation boundary. Outside of these, wading

The Wind River within Shoshone National Forest offers miles of easily accessible fishing, with much of the river beside the highway. Traveling downstream, brown trout increase in number but access diminishes as the river runs through private land.

the river is impossible without hard-to-come-by landowner permission, and float fishing is nearly impractical because of its rocky, shallow, and swift nature and the fact that the stream bottom is private land. Nevertheless, the river here is a significant brown trout fishery with a lesser population of rainbow trout. Before runoff begins and after it has ended, the river is suitable for wading, even within the town of Dubois.

The Sawmill Public Access at the edge of town includes wheelchair-accessible angler ports. These were developed and are maintained by the Dubois Anglers and Wildlife Group (DAWGS), a grassroots organization formed to protect the salmonid habitat and population of the upper Wind River drainage. In addition, DAWGS is spearheading efforts to establish a youth fishing pond at the downstream end of this access. The public access locations below town allow wading. The Wind River Reservation west boundary marks the farthest downstream point on the river that we address; however, the major tributaries and stillwaters discussed below also offer quality fishing with a better chance of solitude.

EAST FORK WIND RIVER
By Larry Lewis

Quality small-stream fishing thanks to the actions of a local group of citizens.

Access: North on Wyoming Highway 277 (East Fork Road) from US Highway 26/287 to Spence and Moriarty Wildlife Management Area and Shoshone National Forest
GPS Coordinates: 43.697119, -109.360289
Equipment: 4- or 5-weight system with floating and sink-tip lines; caddisfly, BWO, Golden Stone, PMD, Trico, and Yellow Sally patterns, and soft hackle, streamer, terrestrial, and traditional attractor patterns
Nearest facilities and services: Dubois (Wyoming), Bear Creek Campground, Lazy L&B Ranch
Information resources: Shoshone National Forest, Wind River District Ranger Office; Dubois, Castle Rock, East Fork Basin, and Rain Draw USGS topographic maps
Salmonids present: Brown, cutthroat, and rainbow trout and Rocky Mountain whitefish

Coming into the river from the Absaroka Range to the north, this is the largest upstream tributary to the Wind River. It, along with tributaries Bear Creek and the Wiggins Fork, hosts an abundant Yellowstone cutthroat trout population in the 10- to 16-inch range. Brown and rainbow trout and Rocky Mountain whitefish are also present.

The East Fork of the Wind River offers several miles of quality small-stream water. After runoff it offers season-long fishing with an aquatic insect emergence sequence and an abundant bankside terrestrial insect population. LARRY LEWIS PHOTO

Over the years, local fly fishers observed an apparent decline in trout populations in the East Fork drainage. Members of DAWGS took ownership of efforts to reverse the decline, and lobbied the Wyoming Game & Fish Department for stricter regulations and proposed habitat studies for the East Fork drainage. DAWGS promoted catch-and-release fishing, solicited public comments for supporting tighter angling regulations, and obtained agency support for funding habitat and fisheries studies. Concurrently, Trout Unlimited conducted telemetry studies of cutthroat trout movement throughout the drainage. As a result, catch-and-release for cutthroat trout and artificial-flies-and-lures-only regulations now apply throughout the entire East Fork drainage of the Wind River. Instream flow water rights now protect the East Fork's quality habitat and spawning potential from irrigation drawdown.

Upper reaches of the East Fork and its tributaries are in the Spence and Moriarty Wildlife Management Area and Shoshone National Forest. They can be fished before and after runoff and have a particularly good summer season when terrestrial insects are plentiful. Local fly fishers suggest traditional attractor patterns, dry and wet, any time after runoff leaves the stream. Care must be taken to observe signed Wind River Reservation land bordering the east side of the stream because a reservation permit is required for fishing there.

HORSE CREEK

By Leon Sanderson

Grass roots actions result in the return of a wonderful fishery as well as good runs of brown and rainbow trout from the Wind River.

Access: North on Wyoming Highway 285 (Horse Creek Road) from Dubois, Wyoming, to the Shoshone National Forest boundary
GPS Coordinates: 43.665495, -109.635137
Equipment: 4- or 5-weight system with floating and sink-tip lines; caddisfly, BWO, Golden Stone, PMD, Trico, and Yellow Sally patterns, and soft hackle, terrestrial, traditional attractor, and streamer patterns
Nearest facilities and services: Dubois (Wyoming), Horse Creek Campground, Longhorn Ranch Lodge and RV Resort
Information resources: Shoshone National Forest, Wind River District Ranger Office; Dubois, Five Pockets, and Ramshorn Peak USGS topographic maps
Salmonids present: Brown, cutthroat, and rainbow trout and Rocky Mountain whitefish

Flowing south, Horse Creek enters the Wind River as it flows through Dubois, Wyoming. It's not a large stream, but it is a contributor to the Wind River salmonid population. Brook, brown, and rainbow trout and a minor population of cutthroat inhabit the creek, with most mature fish eventually heading down to the river. Twelve miles upstream of Dubois, the creek flows through Shoshone National Forest land, with easy public access and a maintained campground.

Irrigation diversion limits productivity in lower Horse Creek, particularly during summer months. A few years ago, the physical condition of one diverting structure was in poor enough condition that it interfered significantly with fish movement in

The golden eagle (juvenile, left) is more likely seen in open country such as along the lower reaches of many Greater Yellowstone Area streams. It is the largest of the eagle family and can hunt over an area of nearly 100 square miles. RON MIZIA PHOTO

the creek. This led to another example of landowners, agency personnel, private citizens, and advocate organizations cooperating to help a fishery. DAWGS convinced local ranchers using Horse Creek water, Trout Unlimited Wyoming, Wyoming Game & Fish, the US Forest Service, the Wyoming Wildlife and Natural Resource Trust, and the Natural Resources Conservation Service to form the Horse Creek Project. The project, with Wyoming Game & Fish taking the lead role, first obtained funding from ranchers and public sources then went on to rebuild the degraded head gate and install in-stream rock veins to move some water to the diversion, thus eliminating the need for the annual in-stream construction of a push-up dam. The result is easier passage for resident trout around the structure to benefit the river below, fewer fish being entrained into the diversion, and within a few years, the return of a wonderful fishery as well as good runs of brown and rainbow trout from the river. DAWGS members continue to upgrade diversion structures and screen local irrigation ditches, as well as propose actions supporting the upper Wind River salmonid habitat and population.

JAKEY'S FORK

A chance to encounter large migratory trout in the spring and fall.

Access: US Highway 26/287 to Fish Hatchery Road
GPS Coordinates: 43.513425, -109.571292
Equipment: 4- or 5-weight system with floating and sink-tip lines ; caddisfly, Golden Stone, PMD, Trico, and Yellow Sally patterns, and soft-hackle, streamer, terrestrial, and traditional attractor patterns
Nearest facilities and services: Dubois (Wyoming), Trail Lake Campground, CM Ranch
Information resources: Shoshone National Forest, Wind River District Ranger Office; Wyoming Game & Fish Department, Lander Regional Office; Mason Draw, Simpson Lake, and Torrey Lake USGS topographic maps
Salmonids present: Brook, brown, cutthroat, and rainbow trout

The Wyoming Game and Fish Department has purchased several locations along rivers for public access. Some are ideal platforms for teaching fly fishing.

Coming into the Wind River from the Wind River Range to the south and a few miles downstream of Dubois, Jakey's Fork is a quality freestone mountain stream. There is a good springtime run of rainbow trout from the Wind River into the creek to spawn, but this stream is more famous for its late-autumn brown trout run out of the river that attracts anglers. Large individuals take part in both runs, even though it seems that many of the larger fish in the Wind River are below the Jakey's Fork confluence.

Jakey's Fork offers good fishing the entire season after runoff leaves (and before it begins). Caddisflies, midges, and stoneflies are the main insect fare for resident brown and rainbow trout, with terrestrial insects being an abundant food form in the summer, making patterns for them a must. Traditional dry and wet patterns are also effective here.

Some of the best water is on private land above the Dubois Fish Hatchery, where a guest ranch offers miles of good fishing in solitude for a price. Above this private land, a rough, steep barrier canyon within Shoshone National Forest keeps out brown and rainbow trout. Brook trout reside here, and Jakey's Fork, smaller than downstream and of high gradient, is a less attractive fishery. These trout are small but eager to take a fly, and they receive minimal fishing pressure. A sign at Fish Hatchery Road proclaims the small (a few hundred yards long) public fishing area with parking near the highway and at the hatchery.

TORREY, RING, AND TRAIL LAKES

A string of lakes in scenic country.

Access: US Highway 26/287 and Fish Hatchery Road to Trail Lake Road
GPS Coordinates: 43.513158, -109.568488
Equipment: 6- or 7-weight system with floating and full-sink lines; dragonfly, damselfly, midge, and Speckled Dun patterns, and leech, scud, and streamer patterns
Nearest facilities and services: Dubois (Wyoming), Trail Lake Campground, Ring Lake Ranch
Information resources: Wyoming Game & Fish Department, Drainage Area 2 Office; Torrey Lake USGS topographic map
Salmonids present: Brown, lake, and rainbow trout and splake in Torrey Lake; brown and rainbow trout and splake in Ring Lake; brown and rainbow trout, splake, and Rocky Mountain whitefish in Trail Lake

Like pearls on a string, a series of lakes about 8 miles southeast of Dubois, Wyoming, begin at the mouth of Torrey Creek Canyon. Torrey Lake is the farthest downstream of these picturesque lakes. The all-weather gravel road skirts its west shoreline, continues for about a mile to do the same at Ring Lake, and then goes another 2 miles to Trail Lake. From there it is no longer improved and continues

Torrey Lake is accessible from a southwest corner boat ramp and offers mostly trolling and shoreline casting for large trout. Springtime, especially soon after ice-out, is best for encountering these in trophy size.

Torrey Creek offers an attractive location to fish where it enters Trail Lake at the campground. It is an alluring meadow stream hosting brown and rainbow trout above the lake and is paralleled by a good gravel road allowing access through state land for a few miles.

up the canyon to end at the Trail Lake trailhead at the Shoshone National Forest boundary. It's scenic country with a mix of badlands and mountain majesty. Consult up-to-date weather forecasts before venturing onto these lakes.

Torrey Lake's shoreline is private land, and Ring Lake's is the same. Shoreline wading is possible on both and on Trail Lake. Torrey is the largest and deepest of the three lakes, with a surface area as large as the other two lakes combined. Its shoreline quickly drops off to depth, except at the outlet and the inlet. Torrey alone hosts lake trout, and they range to more than 2 feet in length. They are not easily encountered, as they reside in the deepest water most of the season. Using a lead-core line to sink large streamer patterns deep might result in some interest from them. They can be caught in shallow water soon after ice-out and again in late autumn through presenting large streamer and Woolly Bugger patterns.

Brown and rainbow trout and splake also inhabit Torrey Lake, and as with the lake trout, the browns and splake tend to reside in the cooler, deep water during the summer months. Each of these salmonids range in length to around 18 inches. They can be encountered through presenting streamer patterns in shallower water in the springtime and autumn, when waters are cooler. In the late summer, browns and rainbows can be encountered near the surface during a Speckled Dun emergence.

A boat ramp is located at the southwest corner of Torrey Lake just off Trail Lake Road. Its use is allowed by verbal landowner agreement. A fruitful early-season strategy is to launch a watercraft from this ramp then travel to the inlet to wade and present streamer patterns to large trout staging below to feed on items drifting into the lake.

It is impractical to navigate the short, shallow channel connecting Torrey and Ring Lakes. Punctuated by large boulders, it is mostly shallow water of an uneven bottom. Most of the Ring Lake shoreline is private land, but a primitive Wyoming Game & Fish campground and boat ramp is sited on the southwest shoreline, bordered on the east by the Torrey Creek inlet. Ring Lake Campground offers some shoreline fishing and also a primitive boat launch for access to the entire lake. It can be used as a base from which to try upstream waters of the Torrey Creek drainage, many of which offer solitude and scenery.

Lacking the extent of deep water present in Torrey Lake, lake trout are absent in Ring Lake. Brown and rainbow trout and splake reside here and are most active late and early in the season. Streamer and leech patterns presented with sinking lines are effective for encountering them. Because shallower water dominates this lake, summertime warming slows daytime fishing. Presenting damselfly patterns can be effective in June, and a good Speckled Dun emergence can bring trout to feed on the surface during mid and late summer evenings.

Trail Lake is about 2 miles up the road from Ring Lake. It is deeper and slightly larger than Ring. Ring Lake Ranch occupies land on the northeast corner, and most of the remaining shoreline is on public land as part of the Whiskey Basin Wildlife Habitat Management Area. A primitive Wyoming Game & Fish campground and boat ramp are located at the southwest corner, just off Trail Lake Road near the Torrey Creek inlet.

Rainbow trout and splake to moderate sizes inhabit Trail Lake. The brown trout here grow to the largest size in the three lakes, up to several pounds. One reason for this growth is the presence of Rocky Mountain whitefish, not present in the other two lakes, providing abundant forage. Early in the season, streamer and leech patterns fished near the shoreline are effective. By autumn, fishing for large brown trout can be best near the inlet. As with the other two lakes, fishing success slows during midsummer but improves by late summer into autumn. Some dry fly fishing can be enjoyed on Trail Lake during late summer because of a Speckled Dun emergence near shorelines. Otherwise, a return to presenting leech and streamer patterns is successful. Torrey Creek above the lake flows through a beautiful meadow holding willow thickets, which are few enough not to impede access to the stream. It's another example of a good fishery encased in surroundings so scenic to be distracting.

PART 5

FLY PATTERNS

The Greater Yellowstone Area hosts an unmatched number of renowned fly tiers and the number of new tiers here increases annually. Greater Yellowstone fly tiers, new, experienced, and renowned continue to create patterns for any fishing situation. Some of these, proven to be effective, are described below. You will find some for sale in retail businesses, while others you will not find outside of this book unless you visit the originator of the pattern.

A repeating theme emerges throughout this book with respect to aquatic and terrestrial insects and other food forms available to Greater Yellowstone salmonids. When selecting fly patterns to imitate the suite of common foods, I hesitate

Selecting the taking fly depends so much on experience and willingless to observe what food forms are available to salmonids. The feeling of accomplishment that comes from making the correct selection is one of the joys of fly fishing. JOHN JURACEK PHOTO

to recommend specific patterns and suggest that anglers put the "hype" aside and listen to common sense. Here are the two overwhelming reasons why: First, a proper presentation strongly trumps the requirement for a specific pattern. You can possess the most precisely tied and elegant flies available, but if not presented properly, they are less effective than properly presented but casually tied flies. Second, whether you can or cannot see a particular floating pattern on the water you intend to visit overwhelms the need for a specific fly. Regardless of the reputation of a pattern, how can you respond properly to a take if you cannot see that pattern on the water? When making dry fly selections, consider whether you can see a particular pattern on the water you intend to fish. Be sure your presentation skills, and your vision, are up to snuff before you assemble a dry fly pattern suite.

ARF Articulated Sculpin (Brown)

- **Hook:** #2-4 Daiichi 2451
- **Thread:** Black 6/0 Uni-Thread
- **Articulated shank:** 55-35 mm in diameter
- **Head:** Brown Fish-Skull Sculpin Helmet (small or large)
- **Tail:** Black-barred tan marabou
- **Butt:** Black barred tan marabou
- **Body:** Tan, brown, and dark tan Laser Dub
- **Flash:** Root beer Krinkle Mirror Flash
- **Collar:** Grizzly variant brown schlappen

Al Ritt makes several close wraps of brown saddle hackle fronted with several wraps of folded marabou hackle to form the tail and butt. He suggests that the hackle keeps the marabou from collapsing, giving the fly a more full profile. He stack-dubs the Laser Dub, leaving a space between each clump, and brushes the dubbing rearward. Folding the dubbing back will leave a full profile even with sparse amounts of dubbing. The sparse dubbing allows water to pass through the fly, resulting in a quicker sink rate. The flat head profile is intended to mimic sculpins and other bottom-dwelling baitfish. Al suggests allowing the fly to sink near the bottom before retrieving. Vary retrieves until finding one to which fish respond.

ARF Simple Stone

- **Hook:** #6-12 Tiemco 5262
- **Thread:** Orange 6/0 Uni-Thread
- **Underbody:** Nontoxic weighted wire, strips tied on either side of the shank
- **Tail:** Ringneck pheasant tail feather fibers
- **Rib:** Fine copper wire ribbed over dorsal stripe
- **Abdomen:** Brown stone nymph Dave Whitlock SLF dubbing
- **Dorsal stripe:** Ringneck pheasant tail fibers
- **Wing case:** Orange mottled bustard Thin Skin
- **Legs:** Barred or speckled brown soft-hackle fibers tied in flat over thorax and under wing case
- **Thorax:** Dark stone nymph Dave Whitlock SLF dubbing
- **Antennae:** Two ringneck pheasant tail fibers

To help keep the weighted wire along the sides of the fly, Al Ritt suggests cementing or securing them with Clear Cure Goo after wrapping them along the sides of the hook shank. This underbody keeps the profile of this fly as flat as possible to best mimic a stonefly. Stoneflies live as nymphs for several years before maturing into adults. This leaves the nymphs available to fish year-round, and typically multiple-year classes (sizes) are present. Because stoneflies do not swim, patterns for them should be presented with a dead drift close to the stream bottom.

Baetis Nymph

- **Hook:** #18-20 Daiichi 1140
- **Thread:** Black 8/0 UNI-Thread
- **Tail:** Dyed black pheasant tail fibers
- **Rib:** Fine silver wire
- **Body:** Tying thread
- **Wing case:** Small pearlescent Mylar
- **Thorax:** Peacock herl

With fly fishing experience ranging from California's Sierra trout streams to Montana's Bighorn River, Dorothy Zinky has good reason for calling this pattern her "go-to" fly for trout keying on BWO nymphs. According to Zinky, the fine silver wire rib should be spiraled tightly enough over the thread body to result in a segmented effect. She also states that the peacock herl used to form the body should be spiraled tightly around the tying thread then wrapped around the hook shank to form a more durable thorax. Any flat, narrow pearlescent Mylar product such as Flashabou can be used to form the wing case.

Baetis Upright Dun

- **Hook:** #16-22 Tiemco 206BL
- **Thread:** Olive dun 8/0 UNI-Thread
- **Tail:** Dun Coq de Leon fibers
- **Body:** Tying thread
- **Wing:** Blue Winged Olive EP Trigger Point Int'l Fibers
- **Thorax:** Brown-olive Ice Dub

As with all Blue Ribbon Fly patterns, this one by Bucky McCormick is easily tied, effective, and uses readily available materials. Tie in and splay a couple tail fibers, then wrap the body forward. Tie in Trigger Point Fibers for wings, and dub around the wings to form a thorax. Whip-finish and wait for inclement weather! *Baetis* emerge into tiny duns mostly during poor weather conditions, and on doing so their emergence is often so heavy that anglers have difficulty keeping track of their fly because so many insects are on the water. Bucky designed this pattern to be highly visible and easy to track, and to not require babysitting to keep afloat.

Bead Bunny

- **Hook:** #1/0-6 Daiichi 1720 (cut off bend when fly is completed)
- **Thread:** Black 140-denier Ultra Thread
- **Stinger hook:** #4 Gamakatsu Octopus
- **Bead:** 4 mm brass
- **Cone:** Large gold
- **Tail:** Root beer Krystal Flash
- **Connection:** 65-pound SpiderWire, on which are strung three faceted glass beads
- **Body:** Large tan crystal chenille
- **Wing:** Natural rabbit strip
- **Collar:** Natural rabbit strip spun in dubbing loop after hide removed

Paul Bowen's accomplishments in presenting streamers comes from decades of fly fishing experience and innovation at the tying bench. He has tried this pattern on many Greater Yellowstone streams after proving it on the South Fork reach. Proving it was easy because Paul, an award-winning tier, lives adjacent to the South Fork reach. He recommends presenting this weighted pattern using a floating line and stout 6-foot leader. Applying a jigging action to the retrieve after a dead-drift swing is a most effective presentation for fishing from the head of pools and runs through them. Swim and dead-drift it along overhead cover. Paul presents this pattern in shallower water, especially under low-light conditions.

Black Foam Ant

- **Hook:** #12-16 Daiichi 1140
- **Thread:** Black 8/0 UNI-Thread
- **Body:** Black drawer liner foam
- **Indicator:** Orange, red, white, or yellow foam
- **Hackle:** Light or dark dun dry fly saddle or neck

Vic Loiselle noticed that drawer liner foam (available from big box hardware stores) could be compressed just like any foam offered in fly shops, thus his foam ant. Flying ants are more commonplace than most anglers realize. Such renowned fly fishers as René Harrop, Mike Lawson, Boots Allen, and Dr. Joe Burke encounter ant falls at various times of the season. Perhaps ants do not receive the same respect as grasshoppers, but they should because their presence spans at least the same time of the season as hoppers. To do hoppers one better, ant falls in large numbers can take place almost anywhere on the water thanks to our dear friend wind.

Boom's Crawfishy

- **Hook:** #12 Mustad 9671
- **Thread:** Brown 70-denier Danville Flymaster Plus
- **Bead:** Coffee ⅛-inch lucent tungsten
- **Tail:** Pheasant tail fibers over tan chickabou
- **Claw:** Light olive Super Floss tips split and painted red
- **Body:** Ice blue brown Arizona Diamond Dubbing
- **Hackle:** Soft brown saddle

The presence of crawfish is an indicator of good water quality. A high level of dissolved oxygen and dissolved bicarbonate is also required for their presence. They are bottom-dwellers and feed on living and dead animals and on certain plants. Shawn (Boom) Bostic grew up in the southeastern United States, where waters host crawfish of diverse species in abundance. On relocating to eastern Idaho, he brought knowledge of their habits and effectiveness of their imitations to taking gamefish. After observing them in certain Greater Yellowstone waters, he created this pattern for young crawfish. He presents it deep in waters that host them. Shawn offers that this pattern tied with olive as the dominant color is also effective.

Bow Tie Midge

- **Hook:** #10-22 Tiemco 200R
- **Thread:** Black 8/0 UNI-Thread
- **Rib:** Fine copper wire
- **Body:** Black Frog Hair dubbing
- **Wing case:** White Thin Skin
- **Wings:** White poly yarn

Tim Wade created this popular pattern in the early 1990s, and it has undergone variations by many tiers since then. He uses a Tiemco 200R hook because it has the correct weight to allow the pattern to lie flat in the surface film. Midge emergences occur nearly year-round on waters in the Cody, Wyoming area. These vary in size depending on species, thus Tim offers this pattern in a broad size range. Locally it has proven effective on stillwaters such as East Newton, Luce, Monster, and Swamp Lakes as well on all regional rivers.

Callibaetis Parachute

- **Hook:** #8-20 Daiichi 1560
- **Thread:** Gray 8/0 UNI-Thread
- **Tail:** Speckled gray Whiting Tailing Fibers
- **Wings:** Mallard flank fibers, divided parachute, looped wonder-wing style
- **Body:** Muskrat belly fur dubbing
- **Hackle:** Grizzly, parachute style
- **Head:** Tying thread

This pattern is Gretchen Beatty's and her husband Al's go-to mayfly imitation. Gretchen developed it to be an easily tied parachute pattern using materials in plentiful supply. The Beattys are sure to include it when planning visits to stillwaters in the Greater Yellowstone Area as well as any stillwater where Speckled Dun activity is expected.

CDC Parachute Emerger

- **Hook:** #12-18 Daiichi 1167 Klinkhammer
- **Thread:** Black 8/0 UNI-Thread
- **Rib:** Extra fine gold Ultra Wire
- **Tail:** Turkey tail fibers
- **Abdomen:** Turkey tail fibers
- **Parachute post:** Fluorescent chartreuse Float-Vis
- **Thorax:** Olive Super Fine dubbing
- **Hackle:** Blue dun CDC

Cliff Sullivan is a central California resident with ties to Idaho and the Greater Yellowstone Area. When fishing his favorite streams in the area during family visits this is his go-to pattern. He fishes it in various sizes and colors to simulate an emerger, a low-floating dun, or even a spinner. To hackle the pattern, he removes CDC fibers from the stem, places them in a dubbing loop, and then closes the loop.

Next he spirals the loop containing the fibers around the base of the parachute post, ties the loop off, and whip-finishes to complete the fly.

CDC Yellow Sally

- **Hook:** #14 Dai-Riki 300
- **Thread:** Tan 3/0 Danville Waxed Monocord
- **Egg sac:** Dubbed red rabbit fur
- **Body:** Yellow nylon yarn
- **Hackle:** Light dun dry fly saddle or neck
- **Underwing:** Three natural CDC feathers
- **Wing:** Elk body hair

Doug Gibson created this pattern in the "Mormon Girl" style; that is, with a red egg sac and yellow body to simulate an egg-laying adult. This term originated in Utah in the days when stoneflies in Wasatch Front streams emerged, mated, and laid eggs in uncountable numbers, attracting trout to vigorous feeding. The brilliant colors of the Yellow Sally stoneflies with red egg sacs reminded anglers of the colors in the gala dresses young Mormon women fashioned for social events, thus the fly-tying term "Mormon Girl." To ensure that the fly lies flat and convex, Doug pulls back on the CDC feathers when tying them in together to form an underwing. He offers that with use, the nylon yarn body gains a segmented appearance.

Cuttnip Scud

- **Hook:** #10-12 Tiemco 2499SP-BL
- **Thread:** Fire orange 8/0 UNI-Thread
- **Beads:** Three pearl clear 10/0
- **Dubbing:** Rust or light olive seal or chopped goat
- **Tag:** Tying thread

My friend Robert Phillips is known to some in the fly-tying world as "Britt" Phillips. Fishing slower-moving (think spring creeks!) and still waters, no pattern outfished this one when presented around submerged vegetation. Britt named his creation Cuttnip Scud from the "semi-Latin" *Cutthroaticus scudasarus catnipus,* a favored cutthroat trout food.

Thread three beads onto the hook, and place it in a fly-tying vise. Form a thread dam behind the rear bead. Double half-hitch (DHH) the thread, and bring it forward over the rear (third) bead. DHH the thread here to lay a narrow thread base. DHH again and bring the thread over the middle (second) bead. DHH again, then apply a sparse amount of dubbing. DHH again and bring the thread to the front of the first bead. Apply a sparse amount of dubbing here, then tie off at the hook eye.

CW's Coq de Leon Caddis

- **Hook:** #14-20 Tiemco 102Y
- **Thread:** Olive 16/0 Veevus
- **Egg sac:** Ball of light olive Antron dubbing
- **Body:** Tan turkey biot
- **Underwing:** Two tan CDC feathers
- **Overwing:** Medium pardo Coq de Leon fibers removed from stem and stacked
- **Hackle:** Whiting Farms cree or speckled badger
- **Thorax:** Medium olive Antron dubbing
- **Head:** Tying thread

Begin Chris Williams's searching pattern by tying a thread base on the back half of the hook. Apply a small amount of olive Antron dubbing to the thread, rub it into a ball, slide it to the hook bend, and secure it in place with a thread wrap to form the egg sac. Tie in a tan turkey biot, notch forward, wrap it forward, and tie it off about two-thirds the way up the hook. Tie in two matched CDC feathers, concave sides up, forming wings extending to the end of the egg sac. Clip several Coq de Leon fibers from a hackle, stack them to even the tips, tie them in with tying thread waxed by the tier, and secure them with wraps. Tie in the hackle, dub the thorax, and palmer the hackle through it. Tie off, clip excess hackle, and whip-finish.

CW's Half & Half CDC Green Drake Emerger

- **Hook:** #10-11 Tiemco 2487 or 212Y
- **Thread:** Brown 14/0 Veevus for nymphal part, olive 14/0 Veevus for hatching dun
- **Tail:** Three brown turkey biots
- **Rib:** Clear UTC Round Rib
- **Body:** March Brown Antron dubbing with turkey biots pulled over and ribbed with brown tying thread
- **Hackle:** Whiting cree, dun, grizzly, or speckled badger
- **Wing:** Two matched goose CDC feathers
- **Thorax:** Olive Super Fine dubbing

Chris Williams created this pattern to imitate the dun leaving the wing case. Cover the hook shank with brown tying thread, and tie in the tail biots. Separate biots with thread wraps, and wrap thread forward without trimming biot butts. Return thread to the rear, and tie in a Round Rib strand. Add Antron dubbing to thread and wrap forward to shank midpoint, then back to tails. Pull turkey biot butts over top of dubbing, and secure with forward thread wraps. Wrap Round Rib over dubbing and biots, forming a sheath. Dub small thorax, half-hitch thread, and trim all material. Make olive thread base over front hook half. Tie in two CDC feathers, hook shank length, with convex sides opposing. Tie in hackle behind wings. Apply olive dubbing to thread, and wrap forward to wings. Wrap a few hackle turns behind wings. Form thread head in front of wings. Tie off, and trim hackle at bottom.

Diamond Hair Shad

- **Hook:** #2-20 Gamakatsu SC15
- **Thread:** White 6/0 UNI-Thread
- **Bottom:** Pearl/green Arizona Diamond Hair (ADH)
- **Top:** Successive peacock ADH , light silver ADH, and silver minnow ADH
- **Molded eyes:** Silver 3D eyes in proportion to hook size

Turn hook upside down in vise after attaching thread. With thread just behind the eye, tie in a small clump of pearl/green ADH at its midpoint. Fold the rear-facing part to the front, and tie down. Turn hook upright in vise. Tie in a small clump of peacock ADH just behind the eye. Fold the rear-facing part to front, and tie down. Tie in a small clump of light silver ADH just behind pearl/green ADH. Fold the rear-facing part to the front, and tie down. Tie in a slightly larger clump of silver minnow ADH just behind light silver ADH. Fold the rear-facing part to the front, and tie down. Add a drop of superglue and trim thread. All materials are now tied down with the tips facing forward. Turn hook upside down in vise and pull the pearl/green ADH clump back, then glue it to the hook shank. Turn the fly upright in vise and pull all materials on top back, adjusting them to form head. Apply nail glue to either side of head, attach 3D molded eyes to either side, and recoat with nail glue to finish this fly by John Rohmer.

Do-Rite

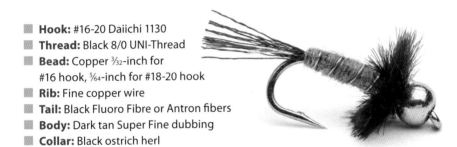

- **Hook:** #16-20 Daiichi 1130
- **Thread:** Black 8/0 UNI-Thread
- **Bead:** Copper ³⁄₃₂-inch for #16 hook, ⁵⁄₆₄-inch for #18-20 hook
- **Rib:** Fine copper wire
- **Tail:** Black Fluoro Fibre or Antron fibers
- **Body:** Dark tan Super Fine dubbing
- **Collar:** Black ostrich herl

Buddy Knight offers this simple pattern from his friend Steve Densley. Buddy and Steve are both proponents of using tightly wrapped ostrich herl in place of chenille. They anchor the tail material, whether Antron fibers or Fluoro Fiber, along the entire shank of this fly in order to minimize the chance of them being pulled out. They also suggest using four or five turns of rib to secure the body and tail even further. Buddy and Steve suggest using this pattern as a dry dropper or under an indicator.

Dorothy's CDC Dun

- **Hook:** #16-20 Daiichi 1190 (barbless), size to match natural insect
- **Thread:** 8/0 UNI-Thread, color to match natural insect
- **Tail:** Pair of Microfibetts tied in to make a V
- **Body:** Turkey biot dyed to color matching natural insect
- **Wing:** Natural post-style CDC
- **Hackle:** Sparse dry fly quality saddle, tied parachute style around post

California girl Dorothy Zinky fishes as many Greater Yellowstone Area waters as she is able. Throughout the season, she may be seen trying her luck during any seasonal mayfly emergence. She particularly seeks out trout responding to smaller mayfly species. Realizing the need to minimize her time at the tying vise when a good mayfly emergence is in progress, she created this omnibus pattern by changing hook size and materials colors. It's another of her go-to patterns, and she ties it mostly in size 18 down into the 20s. She recommends that the hackle be sparse, meaning that a single turn of hackle is sufficient.

Drake's Drake

- **Hook:** #10-12 Daiichi 1130
- **Thread:** Olive dun 8/0 UNI-Thread
- **Tail and thorax:** Mallard flank pulled in reverse and trimmed out
- **Wing:** Four yellow TroutHunter dun CDC feathers
- **Side wing dressing:** Dyed bright yellow mallard flank
- **Abdomen:** Olive Super Fine dubbing
- **Hackle:** Dyed dark dun rooster neck

Ben Byng ties this pattern using a classic style for the body and tail. It's a takeoff of the standard Catskill 2 feather fly popularized on western waters years ago by Dick Alf as the "hatch matcher" style but originated by Harry Darbee. Ben's adaptation with heavy wings and profile gives more body, better visibility, and improved floating properties in moving water. That makes it a great candidate for such streams as the South Fork reach or the Madison River, when Green Drake duns can be drifting by on fast-moving water. Ben also suggests tying this pattern on a European-style Czech nymph hook.

Foam Black Stone

- **Hook:** #4 Daiichi 730
- **Thread:** Orange 6/0 UNI-Thread
- **Tail:** Pair of dyed black goose biots
- **Rib:** Dry fly saddle hackle counter-wrapped with fine gold wire
- **Body:** Black closed-cell foam
- **Underwing:** White poly yarn
- **Wing:** Elk body hair
- **Hackle:** Brown dry fly saddle hackle
- **Head:** Black foam strip folded back toward rear
- **Legs:** Black-and-white Sili Legs

Logan Cutts created this pattern for use during the Giant Stonefly emergence on any water. The emergence on the Henry's Fork is one of his favorites. Waters such as Box Canyon below Island Park Dam and the reach from the Warm River to Ashton Reservoir can become crowded during this event, but Logan points out that there are locations on this famed river where crowding is minimal during "The Hatch." These include the Hatchery Ford, Bear Gulch, and Coffee Pot areas. At times he uses black Sili Legs instead of black-and-white when tying this pattern.

Foam Humpy

- **Hook:** #10-16 Daiichi 1190 (barbless)
- **Thread:** Black 70-denier UNI-Thread, color matching shellback
- **Tail:** Natural deer hair
- **Body:** Tying thread wraps to conceal butt ends of tail fibers and the shellback foam
- **Shellback:** Black 3 mm closed-cell foam strip, color of choice
- **Wings:** Natural deer hair, upright and divided
- **Hackle:** Grizzly dry fly quality saddle hackle

There may be other versions of this pattern around, but Gregg Messel uses his with success on several area streams, including the Boulder River and the Ruby River. With various colors of components, it can be tied to be a traditional Humpy to resemble a beetle as shown above, or an ant, horsefly, or one of several mayfly species. It's a terrific floater, highly visible, and more durable than traditional versions tied with a deer or elk hair shellback. In addition to all these assets, it is easily tied. Gregg suggests his Foam Humpy for use on all streams, especially those with a broken surface.

Fonda Fly

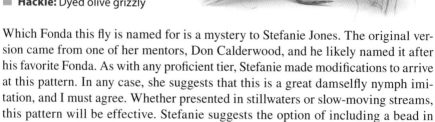

- **Hook:** #10-12 Tiemco 5210
- **Thread:** Black 8/0 UNI-Thread
- **Tail:** Dyed olive grizzly marabou
- **Body:** Olive brown Ice Dub
- **Hackle:** Dyed olive grizzly

Which Fonda this fly is named for is a mystery to Stefanie Jones. The original version came from one of her mentors, Don Calderwood, and he likely named it after his favorite Fonda. As with any proficient tier, Stefanie made modifications to arrive at this pattern. In any case, she suggests that this is a great damselfly nymph imitation, and I must agree. Whether presented in stillwaters or slow-moving streams, this pattern will be effective. Stefanie suggests the option of including a bead in proportion to the hook size, and putting a few strips of Krystal Flash or Flashabou in the tail. She also brushes out the body for a "buggier" appearance.

Fred's Fox Squirrel Nymph

- **Hook:** #10 Mustad 9671
- **Thread:** Tan 6/0 UNI-Thread
- **Bead:** 5/32-inch gold
- **Tail:** Grouse hackle fibers
- **Rib:** Single gold Krystal Flash fiber
- **Body:** Red fox squirrel nymph abdomen Whitlock SLF dubbing
- **Thorax:** Natural hare's ear dubbing
- **Hackle:** A few turns of grouse collar

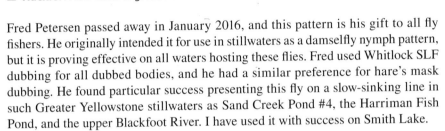

Fred Petersen passed away in January 2016, and this pattern is his gift to all fly fishers. He originally intended it for use in stillwaters as a damselfly nymph pattern, but it is proving effective on all waters hosting these flies. Fred used Whitlock SLF dubbing for all dubbed bodies, and he had a similar preference for hare's mask dubbing. He found particular success presenting this fly on a slow-sinking line in such Greater Yellowstone stillwaters as Sand Creek Pond #4, the Harriman Fish Pond, and the upper Blackfoot River. I have used it with success on Smith Lake.

Gib's Stonefly Nymph

- **Hook:** #6 Dai-Riki 710
- **Thread:** Black 135-denier Danville's Flat Waxed Nylon
- **Antennae:** Pair of duck biots
- **Tail:** Pair of duck biots
- **Body:** 1/4-inch-wide strip of black #23 double-sided Scotch electrical tape
- **Hackle:** Black saddle
- **Wing case:** Three pieces from same material used for body

Doug Gibson created this pattern as a dropper to be fished under a large dry adult stonefly imitation, but it can also be dead-drifted solo along a stream bottom. He prefers using the electrical tape identified above rather than bicycle tire inner tube strips because of its elasticity, thinness, and double-sidedness. When using a strip to form the body, Doug diagonally cuts its back end to help taper the rear of the body when tied in and wound forward. He cuts a series of forked wing cases in a tape strip, and ties in three sequentially over the front third of the body. Next he wraps hackle around the bases of the three wing-case segments and trims the hackle away before tying the fly off. To give this fly a more natural appearance, Doug bends the hook shank.

GK's Spruce Moth

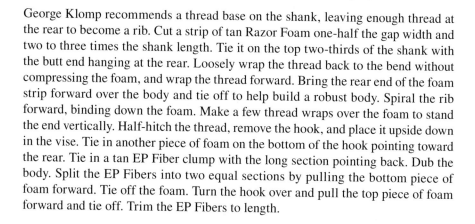

- ▨ **Hook:** #12 Daiichi 1190 (barbless)
- ▨ **Thread:** Wood duck 70-denier UTC Ultra Thread
- ▨ **Rib:** Tying thread
- ▨ **Body:** Tan Razor Foam strip
- ▨ **Wing:** Tan EP Fibers

George Klomp recommends a thread base on the shank, leaving enough thread at the rear to become a rib. Cut a strip of tan Razor Foam one-half the gap width and two to three times the shank length. Tie it on the top two-thirds of the shank with the butt end hanging at the rear. Loosely wrap the thread back to the bend without compressing the foam, and wrap the thread forward. Bring the rear end of the foam strip forward over the body and tie off to help build a robust body. Spiral the rib forward, binding down the foam. Make a few thread wraps over the foam to stand the end vertically. Half-hitch the thread, remove the hook, and place it upside down in the vise. Tie in another piece of foam on the bottom of the hook pointing toward the rear. Tie in a tan EP Fiber clump with the long section pointing back. Dub the body. Split the EP Fibers into two equal sections by pulling the bottom piece of foam forward. Tie off the foam. Turn the hook over and pull the top piece of foam forward and tie off. Trim the EP Fibers to length.

Grayson's PMD Emerger

- **Hook:** #12-18 Tiemco 200R
- **Thread:** Tan 8/0 UNI-Thread
- **Shuck:** Sparse orange Z-Lon fibers
- **Body:** Yellow Krystal Dub
- **Wing:** Dyed gray TroutHunter CDC
- **Head:** Brown Krystal Dub

Overdressed flies are common these days. Having been in the fly fishing retail business for decades, Todd Lanning realizes that overdressing adds nothing to the pattern's effectiveness. In fact, in some cases it hinders a pattern by not correctly imitating the natural. Fully dressed bodies for adult caddisfly and certain mayfly dun patterns are good examples. Through his lengthy experience fly fishing the Henry's Fork in Harriman State Park, Todd realizes that the adult and emerger forms of many aquatic insects have slender bodies and wings delicate enough that only sparse and elegant materials are needed to imitate them effectively. This pattern, named for his son Grayson, is a good example of how a pattern should be tied to imitate a natural where finicky trout are concerned.

Grumpy Frumpy

- **Hook:** #10-16 Tiemco 102Y
- **Thread:** Red 70-denier UTC Ultra Thread
- **Tail:** Brown Z-lon trimmed to gap length
- **Underbody:** Camel Evazote foam
- **Body:** Four-strand yellow rayon floss
- **Wing:** White polyyarn
- **Hackle:** Two cree saddle hackles
- **Legs:** Fine white round rubber legs

This is Clark (Cheech) Pierce's favorite version of his multipurpose attractor pattern. Tie in the tail fibers along the shank to extend a gap-width length to the rear. Do the same with a gap-width piece of Evazote with the long end extending to the rear. Cover the Evazote on the shank with turns of floss. Pull the long end of Evazote over the top, back to front, forming a shellback. Trim the Evazote at an angle, a little behind the eye, to minimize the bump. Tie in polyyarn over the Evazote tie-off point such that a small amount extends to the rear and the majority extends to the front. Tie in, shiny side forward, and wind two cree saddle hackles together. Use tying thread to prop the McFlylon upward and trim to be slightly longer than the hackle. Whip-finish and tie off. Reattach tying thread at the body midpoint, royal the body with red tying thread, and tie in rubber legs Madam X style, and whip finish. Stretch the legs then mark them as you see fit with a Sharpie, and trim them to a bit longer than the hackle.

Hackle Stacker Variant

- **Hook:** #10-16 Daiichi 1130
- **Thread:** Olive 8/0 UNI-Thread
- **Shuck:** Olive Antron
- **Body:** Dark olive Flex-Floss, Wonder Wrap, or natural stripped peacock herl
- **Post:** Olive Flex-Floss
- **Hackle:** Olive dyed dry fly quality grizzly saddle hackle
- **Thorax:** Olive UV2 Fine and Dry, mixed with olive UV2 Ice Dub

Ned Long taught Linda Windels how to tie this fly the year before he died. She has made a few changes that work better for her style of tying. Her Green Drake version is pictured above. She relates: "I didn't know who he was when I met him [Ned], but I could tell right away that he was exceptional. He spent at least an hour with me making sure I had the procedure down pat. I fish it as an emerger, treating only the hackle. It rides low in the water and floats like a cork. I tie it as a Green Drake, Gray Drake, Brown Drake, *Callibaetis*, PMD, and others. Even though it is a variation, I wish I could let Ned know what a great fly it is and how much I appreciate the time he spent working with me."

Hairball Emerger

- **Hook:** #8-14 Daiichi 1160
- **Thread:** Olive 6/0 Danville's flat waxed nylon for hairball; yellow 12/0 UNI-Thread for remainder of fly
- **Hairball:** Yellow over olive stacked deer hair
- **Tail:** Five or six wood duck flank feather fibers
- **Rib:** Medium copper wire
- **Body:** Brown-olive dubbing
- **Hackle post:** Pearlescent Larva Lace or Super Floss
- **Hackle:** Dyed olive dry fly quality Whiting grizzly tied pullover style around hackle post

About a year into developing this fly, the light came on in Steve Potter's brain: Tie the hair ball in first, then complete the rest of this fly. This way it goes together easier and takes less time to complete. The Hairball Emerger has proven to be a productive pattern when used during a Green Drake or Hex hatch. The Quigley Cripple is one of Steve's favorite patterns, but he observes that in larger sizes, it tends to drop a bit in the water column. Through using the deer-hair ball and Ned Long's pullover style of hackling, this pattern in any size sits perfectly in the water. In particular, Steve recommends trying it on the surface on quiet water or in lakes and reservoirs.

Hi-Vis Horror

- **Hook:** #6-12 Tiemco 200R
- **Thread:** Fluorescent orange 6/0 UNI-Thread
- **Tail:** Butts from deer hair used to form the body
- **Underbody:** Tying thread wraps to cover shank
- **Body:** Deer hair cross-wrapped with tying thread
- **Underwing:** White polypropylene or Magic Wing
- **Wing:** Natural deer hair
- **Legs:** White/black speckled Sili Legs or round Tarantula Legs
- **Indicator:** Fluorescent orange egg yarn
- **Head:** Bullet style from deer hair

This pattern evolved from Tim Wade's original Horror pattern in order to improve visibility on streams with rough surfaces. Such streams are numerous in the Cody,

Wyoming, area, where so many originate in the Absaroka Range and have higher gradient. Particularly when float-fishing such streams as the North Fork of the Shoshone River, the main stem Shoshone River, and the lower Clarks Fork of the Yellowstone River, highly visible patterns are required for observing a strike. Tim wraps the entire shank of the hook with fluorescent orange thread before tying the deer hair body so that the fly's visibility to fish is retained as the body degrades from multiple strikes.

HNL Caddis Emerger

- **Hook:** #14 Tiemco 2457
- **Thread:** Tan 8/0 UNI-Thread
- **Rib:** Fine gold wire
- **Body:** Amber angora dubbing
- **Wing case:** Black and tan Thin Skin
- **Emerging wing:** Trimmed pheasant aftershaft feathers
- **Head:** Brown angora dubbing

In the Greater Yellowstone Area, caddisfly species are more numerous in moving water than in stillwater. Nevertheless, caddisflies can be an important food form in stillwaters. The caddisfly pupal stage swims up through the water column to emerge on the surface, and it is this action that attracts salmonids to feed on it. Gerry "Randy" Randolph recommends beginning with a slow retrieve of this pattern then increasing it incrementally until a rate is found that simulates that of the natural insect emerging in the water column. Stillwater caddisflies appear to emerge mostly during afternoon hours, and this time of day Randy uses a floating line and long leader to present this pattern in water not more than 4 to 5 feet deep.

Ida-Know

Hook: #12-16 Mustad S60-3399A,
size to match natural
Thread: Olive 8/0 UNI-Thread
Body: Olive EZ Magic-Dub
Underwing: Natural dun TroutHunter
CDC puff
Hackle: Natural grouse tied
soft-hackle style
Head: Small amount of tan dubbing

Kieran Frye ties this pattern for his favorite Idaho waters to be a low-riding emerger. On presentation it will stay briefly on the surface. When it saturates with water, allow it to swing in the current. When it begins to rise at the end of the swing, hold on because that is the most likely time for a hit. With the numerous mayfly species available, the variation in color and size of this pattern is almost unlimited. It can also be used as a caddisfly pupa rising through the water column. Be sure to tie the CDC puff underwing in at the top of the hook bend.

Jacklin's October Caddis Soft Hackle Emerger

Hook: #6-10 Mustad #S80-3906
Thread: Black or burnt orange
70- or 140-denier UNI-Thread
Rib: Medium or fine copper wire
Body: Burnt orange wool yarn
Thorax: Cyclops copper bead
Hackle: Oversize partridge flank feather

In the Greater Yellowstone Area, the October Caddis begins emerging in late August then peaks in the fall. During a recent September visit to the Yellowstone River in the park, resident cutthroat showed no interest in large dry caddis imitations for Bob Jacklin and a friend. But when they presented this pattern wet-fly style to simulate emerging caddis, the cutthroat really showed interest. The fish seemed most attracted when a short retrieve with some rod-tip action brought the fly upward through the water column. Bob thinks that the fly is attractive because of the motion from the oversize partridge hackle. This hackle, tied in front of the copper bead, comes "alive" when an up-and-down action is applied with the rod tip. Bob also has success presenting this fly to migrating brown trout in the Madison River and the South Fork reach.

KG's Spring Creek CDC Emerger

- ▓ **Hook:** #14-16 Dai-Riki 125
- ▓ **Thread:** Light Cahill yellow 8/0 UNI-Thread
- ▓ **Shuck:** Yukon orange Arizona Simiseal over 3-4 Coq de Leon fibers
- ▓ **Rib:** Rust 6/0 UNI-Thread, doubled
- ▓ **Abdomen:** Tying thread with pheasant tail fibers over back and ribbed in place
- ▓ **Wing case/wing:** Two medium dun CDC puffs
- ▓ **Thorax:** PMD Super Fine dubbing
- ▓ **Legs:** One PMD dyed CDC puff

Kelly Glissmeyer is the At the Vise column editor for the Federation of Fly Fishers' *Fly Fisher* magazine. The day before one of his deadlines, he was preparing a pattern to submit for his upcoming column. When nearly finished, he realized that he had already submitted it the previous year, so he stayed at the tying vise, burning midnight oil. After a dozen or so attempts, he came up with this pattern, which was satisfying enough to be published in his column. Kelly is a proponent of fishing the many Greater Yellowstone spring creeks, and this pattern is his gift to other such enthusiasts.

Kiss Streamer

- ▓ **Hook:** #6-10 Tiemco 200R
- ▓ **Thread:** White 6/0 UNI-Thread
- ▓ **Body:** Pearlescent Flat Diamond Braid
- ▓ **Beard:** Butt end of Diamond Braid
- ▓ **Wing:** Sparse white hackle fibers

A proponent of easily tied flies, Tim Paxton begins the Kiss (Keep It Simple Stupid) Streamer by tying in the Diamond Braid body just behind the hook eye and spiraling this material around the hook shank to the bend, then back to the beginning just behind the eye to form a tapered body. He folds the butt end underneath the shank and ties it in at that position. He paints the butt red with a Pantone pen and then clips it to length, completing the beard. Next he ties in sparse white hackle fibers to form a wing extending to the hook bend. He builds the head up with tying thread, applies lacquer, and allows it to dry. He then paints on the eyes and the gray head stripe, and applies the final lacquer head. If you prefer, Tim allows this fly to be called "Screaming Streamer!"

Linda's Gray May

- **Hook:** #10-14 Dai-Riki 300
- **Thread:** Gray 8/0 UNI-Thread
- **Tail:** Three fibers of dark dun hackle from Whiting Tailing Pack
- **Abdomen:** Dyed gray stripped peacock herl
- **Thorax:** Adams gray UV-Dub mixed 1:1 with Callibaetis Ice Dub
- **Post:** White McFlylon
- **Hackle:** Dry fly quality grizzly saddle hackle

"Hi Linda: When getting flies together for your visit here, be sure to include at least a dozen size 10 gray mayflies. There's a hatch of gray drakes on the river now, and the trout are all over them." This is what a guide related to Linda Windels just before her yearly trip to a Montana guest lodge. She didn't have any size 10 gray mayflies in her boxes, so she quickly came up with this pattern that turned out to be so successful that clients and guides alike were asking her to tie some for them. She thinks the slender body and the thorax dubbing made the difference in fishing success.

Little Green Caddis

- **Hook:** #16 Daiichi 1560
- **Thread:** Black 8/0 UNI-Thread
- **Abdomen:** Fluorescent green micro chenille
- **Thorax:** Natural gray ostrich herl
- **Hackle:** Starling feather

Buddy Knight is a veteran stillwater fly fisher. His years of fishing and guiding on public and private Utah stillwaters is nearly unparalleled. This is his pattern for a stillwater caddis in the pupa stage that he has encountered over the years. First, he quickly passes a half-inch-long piece of micro chenille through a flame to form a tapered body. He ties this piece on top of the hook shank at the halfway point to extend about a quarter of an inch beyond the hook bend. At the tie-in point for the micro chenille abdomen, he ties in the ostrich herl and tightly winds it forward to form the thorax. With care, he ties in a usually fragile starling feather to hackle this fly. He presents it dead drift under an indicator with enough weight to sink it to near the bottom.

Macrame Hopper

- **Hook:** #8-12 Daiichi 2220
- **Thread:** Yellow 70 denier Uni-Thread
- **Body:** Yellow macramé yarn braid
- **Wing:** Lacquered and compressed pheasant church window feather
- **Head:** Deer or elk body hair
- **Legs:** Yellow or red round rubber legs tied Madam X style

Mike Andreasen is the quintessential stillwater fly fisher and fly tier. He is a sought-after presenter on stillwater fly fishing as well as the author of two informative books on the subject. Like all creative fly tiers, his talent extends to patterns for all waters, and this pattern is a great example. To taper the body, Andreasen pulls on the macramé section while melting the butt end with a propane pocket lighter. He then slides the hook through the macramé piece and ties it down on top of the front third of the shank, leaving the remainder as a detached body. After the body is secured, he ties in the pheasant feather wing, forms the body hair bullet head, and ties in the legs on either side at the base of the bullet head. The result is Mike's favorite pattern for meadow streams.

Mosquito Hawk

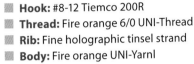

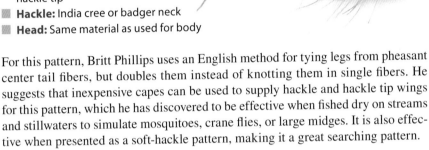

- **Hook:** #8-12 Tiemco 200R
- **Thread:** Fire orange 6/0 UNI-Thread
- **Rib:** Fine holographic tinsel strand
- **Body:** Fire orange UNI-Yarnl
- **Legs:** Two pairs knotted pheasant center tail fibers, two fibers per leg
- **Wings:** India cree or badger hackle tip
- **Hackle:** India cree or badger neck
- **Head:** Same material as used for body

For this pattern, Britt Phillips uses an English method for tying legs from pheasant center tail fibers, but doubles them instead of knotting them in single fibers. He suggests that inexpensive capes can be used to supply hackle and hackle tip wings for this pattern, which he has discovered to be effective when fished dry on streams and stillwaters to simulate mosquitoes, crane flies, or large midges. It is also effective when presented as a soft-hackle pattern, making it a great searching pattern.

Mother's Day Caddis

- **Hook:** #12-18 Daiichi 1180
- **Thread:** Black 8/0 UNI-Thread
- **Body:** Opaque olive Razor Foam
- **Wing:** Light dun mottled Web Wing
- **Hackle:** Medium brown rooster saddle hackle

On most Greater Yellowstone rivers, from the end of April to the middle of May is time for a blanket caddisfly emergence that trout gorge on. This cabin-fever-breaking event is the so-called Mother's Day Caddis hatch, and its intensity and time varies from stream to stream depending on such factors as water temperature, weather, and elevation. Timing is required for successful fly fishing because, as with blanket midge emergences on stillwater, fish feed heavily for a time and then become almost dormant. Vic Loiselle created this pattern years ago and still enjoys its effectiveness, even well after the Mother's Day Caddis hatch. Vic suggests that when this fly is completed, soak it in Loon Hydrostop for around 20 minutes, then let it dry about 24 hours. Doing so ensures it will be buoyant for a long time on the water.

Natural Vixen

- **Hook:** #14-18 Daiichi 1130
- **Thread:** Charcoal 8/0 UNI-Thread
- **Tail:** Tips of pheasant tail fibers used to form body
- **Rib:** Fine gold Ultra Wire
- **Body:** Pheasant tail fibers
- **Thorax:** Natural hare's ear dubbing
- **Wing:** Pearlescent midge Krystal Flash
- **Hackle:** Partridge tied soft-hackle style

Christy and Mike Carlson, owners of Pioneer Anglers, Alpine, Wyoming, specialize in fly fishing the Greys River and Salt River drainages. This is the basic pattern of Christy's Vixen series. None of its components are dyed, thus the use of "Natural" in its name. The near-pristine Greys River is a superb example of a stream made for dry fly or emerger presentations. This pattern has proven ideal there as a season-long emerger by varying only its size to match the emerging natural insect. For use on the less-pristine Salt River, Christy recommends fishing this pattern deeper through use of split shot clamped to the leader. Another favorite is Christy's purple version of this pattern, which uses a peacock herl body, purple UV Ice Dub thorax, and dyed purple grizzly hackle.

One Feather Wet Fly

- **Hook:** #10-16 Dai-Riki 070
- **Thread:** Black 8/0 UNI-Thread
- **Rib:** Pearl Krystal Flash strand
- **Body:** Olive Antron dubbing
- **Wing:** Brown Hen hackle tip
- **Hackle:** Remainder of hen hackle used to form wing

Creativity is the name of Scott Sanchez's game, and his pattern is another example of applying the versatility inherent in hen hackle. Besides hook and thread, Sanchez uses only three components in tying this fly. After tying in the hackle tip to lie flat over the body, he holds the remaining hackle firmly upright while stroking the fibers rearward past the stem. He then wraps a few turns of hackle, and its fibers flow rearward. Sanchez offers that various colors can be used when tying this pattern without impacting its attraction to trout. That's a hint that it is effective for simulating various emerging aquatic insects when presented properly. A good way to do so is to swing it in the current of a medium-size stream.

Orange Butt Platinum

- **Hook:** #12-16 Daiichi 1530
- **Thread:** Black 6/0 UNI-Thread
- **Tail:** Strands of fluorescent orange yarn
- **Body:** Dyed lilac Angora rabbit yarn
- **Hackle:** Soft brown hen hackle tied wet-fly style

After tying in the fluorescent orange yarn fibers, cut them to form a tail extending no farther than the hook bend. Dyed lilac Angora rabbit is hard to find, so Mike Andreasen makes his own using Rit Dye. After dubbing the angora yarn, Mike twists it tightly to form a segmented-appearing body on being wrapped around the hook shank. After wrapping the yarn around the shank, he strokes it with Velcro or gently with a dubbing rake to free fibers that move in water to give a lifelike appearance. He suggests working this pattern at depth through holes and runs where it can simulate a caddisfly pupa or an emerging mayfly. In stillwaters this pattern is known for being a superb scud imitation.

Pheasant Tail Mayfly Cripple

- **Hook:** #12-22 Dai-Riki 320
- **Thread:** Olive 6/0-16/0 (depending on hook size) UNI-Thread
- **Tail and abdomen:** Natural or dyed olive or yellow pheasant tail fibers
- **Rib:** Fine copper or gold wire
- **Thorax:** Amber Super Fine dubbing
- **Wing:** Gray or white synthetic fibers, such as EP Fiber or Widow's Web
- **Hackle:** Ginger or grizzly dry fly quality saddle hackle

This is Satoshi Yamamoto's omnibus mayfly emerger pattern. He proved its effectiveness on the famed spring creeks in the Yellowstone Valley south of Livingston,

Montana. By changing size and color it can simulate a low-profile emerging or cripple stage of any mayfly species living in the Greater Yellowstone Area. It is effective when fished by itself in any water type, but in larger sizes it also functions as a visible pilot fly for a small nymph pattern suspended at any level in the water column.

PQ Green Drake Emerger

- **Hook:** #10-12 Tiemco 2303
- **Thread:** Rust/brown 8/0 UNI-Thread for abdomen and rusty dun Coats & Clark Dual Duty All-Purpose thread for thorax
- **Trailing shuck:** Amber Z-Lon
- **Tail and abdomen:** Three rust ostrich herls
- **Rib:** Fine gold wire
- **Hackle:** Olive dry fly quality saddle hackle, tied Hacklestacker style
- **Thorax:** Green Drake olive, light olive, and chartreuse CDC, combined with dubbing loop
- **Wing:** Natural CDC
- **Legs:** Natural CDC trimmed wing butts

Howard Cole's "PQ" comes from Andy Puyans's pontoon CDC style and Bob Quigley's Hacklestacker technique. He forms the tail and the abdomen with three ostrich herls tied in at the hook midpoint. Gold wire ribs the abdomen, is tied off, and is whip-finished. Rusty dun sewing thread secures two CDC plumes extending over the hook eye. After secured, move the tying thread behind the wing and tie in the rusty dun sewing thread back to the abdomen. Install hackle and wind around thread. Figure-eight the dubbing loop around the wing butts to stand them horizontal to the hook shank and form the thorax. Pull the hackled thread forward over the top of the thorax, Hacklestacker style. Tie off and move the tying thread in front of the wing, standing it up and angling back. Whip-finish and trim the wing butts about a hook-gap length, forming pontoons.

Pullover Hackle Dun

- **Hook:** #14 Gamakatsu S10S
- **Thread:** Black 8/0 UNI-Thread
- **Tail:** Cream Microfibetts
- **Abdomen:** Light olive dyed turkey biot
- **Post:** Olive Super Floss
- **Hackle:** 10 to 16 wraps of cree dry fly
- **Thorax:** Gray olive Super Fine dubbing

The pullover hackling technique is performed by placing tension on an elastic material such as Super Floss or even a rubber band, the rear end of which is attached just forward of the hook shank midpoint. The elastic material is essentially a horizontal post, and tension (by stretching) can be applied to it with such means as an extended body or a gallows tool. The hackle stem is tied onto the shank, and the fly body (abdomen and thorax) is tied in. The hackle is then spiraled toward the rear of the post and tied off. Tension is released from the hackled post, and it is brought forward over the fly body and secured just behind the hook eye. This pattern is one of many that Cliff Sullivan ties in this manner. He recommends it for imitating mayfly duns and spinners on spring creeks and slow-moving streams. Vary color and size to simulate the natural insect.

Queen Hecuba

- **Hook:** #10 Daiichi 1160 Klinkhammer
- **Thread:** Burnt orange 8/0 UNI-Thread, doubled
- **Shuck:** Light amber Antron fibers
- **Rib:** Doubled tying thread
- **Body:** Tan Super Fine dubbing with a slight amount of black Super Fine added
- **Thorax:** Strip of thin packing foam under body dubbing
- **Hackle:** Light ginger saddle
- **Wing:** Tan snowshoe hare foot fibers

Hecuba timpanoga, also known as the Great Red Quill or the Summer Drake, populations are usually minor and limited to quality-water streams having moderate gradient, riffles, and pools with silt bottoms. Being a large insect, they receive the attention of trout when emerging during late summer and early autumn evenings. When asked to donate a pattern for a recent Jackson Hole One Fly event, Dave

Brackett offered this emerger that he created and named Queen Hecuba. He had presented it with much success to large Snake River fine-spotted cutthroat trout rising during a late summer afternoon from the Snake River near the South Bridge below Jackson. The foam strip thorax underwrap adds buoyancy to this pattern.

Randy's TC Damsel

- **Hook:** #10-12 Daiichi 1710
- **Thread:** Tan 8/0 UNI-Thread
- **Tail:** Tips of tan hen neck feathers
- **Body:** Clear Thin Skin sheath over pale yellow dubbing
- **Legs:** Partridge neck hackle fibers
- **Wing case:** Brown Thin Skin
- **Eyes:** Monofilament tippet material melted to shape
- **Gills:** Clear Thin Skin

Gerry "Randy" Randolph is a stillwater fly fishing specialist who frequently targets sunken vegetation, which is a sure host of numerous food forms sought by salmonids. During a damselfly emergence, this is his favorite pattern to present just under the surface over vegetation with a floating line and long leader. Before applying the clear Thin Skin strips to the fly, he paints the edges with a Magic Marker, orange for the body and brown for the gills.

Ribbed Stonefly Nymph

- **Hook:** #6 Dai-Riki 135
- **Thread:** Tan 8/0 UNI-Thread
- **Weight:** Lead-free .015-inch-diameter wire
- **Tail and antennae:** Brown goose biot pairs
- **Rib:** Brown medium UTC vinyl rib
- **Body and thorax:** Dark brown Super Fine dubbing
- **Legs:** Dark brown hen saddle hackle
- **Wing case:** Brown ¼-inch-wide Scud Back
- **Head:** Brown 3/0 UNI-Thread

This is Brian Morishita's all-season stonefly nymph pattern. He is sure to carry it when visiting most Greater Yellowstone streams. By changing color and size, he can simulate the nymph stage of any stonefly in these streams. Before dubbing the body and thorax, tie in the hen saddle and butt end of the wing case, both on the hook shank at the location for the rear of the thorax. After dubbing and then ribbing both of these, bring the Scud Back segment over the top of them and tie in place, then trim the excess to form the wing case. Form the head with brown thread wraps over the tying thread used to tie off the front of the wing case. Apply a layer of Clear Cure Goo to the wing case and cure to dryness using a UV curing light.

Shameless Hussy

- **Hook:** #4-6 Dai-Riki 700
- **Thread:** Red 6/0 UNI-Thread
- **Body:** White UNI Glo Yarn
- **Wing:** Fluorescent red rabbit strip
- **Beard:** Red Krystal Flash fibers

When Joni Tomich is not planning or participating in concerts, she creates flies and ties them commercially and completes orders for her line of furled leaders. Unlike similar Matuka-style patterns, this fly's wing stays free in order to impart more motion on a retrieve. Joni offers that allowing the wing to be exposed to sunlight for several minutes increases its brightness. She created this pattern for stillwaters but is eager to try it in moving waters, especially during the early season and later when brown trout are migrating.

Simi Seal Leech

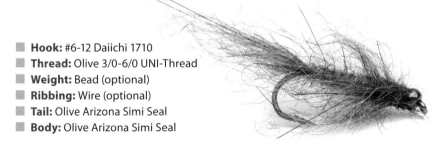

- **Hook:** #6-12 Daiichi 1710
- **Thread:** Olive 3/0-6/0 UNI-Thread
- **Weight:** Bead (optional)
- **Ribbing:** Wire (optional)
- **Tail:** Olive Arizona Simi Seal
- **Body:** Olive Arizona Simi Seal

John Rohmer created Arizona Simi Seal because mohair is a versatile, useful material for leeches, buggers, streamers, and crayfish patterns. He added nylon and Mylar for flash, producing a durable, easily used material that has proven itself on many patterns. Tied in different colors, John's Simi Seal Leech is taken as a baitfish, dragonfly nymph, or even a crayfish. An optional bead imparts a jigging motion to the fly.

Pull pinch of Simi Seal for the tail and tie the middle in above the barb. Fold the forward-facing end back over the thread wraps and tie down, completing a tail. Tie in ribbing with the thread hanging just in front of the tail. Apply dubbing to cover the thread from the hook shank to bobbin tip. Hold the thread, dubbing, and bobbin tip between the index finger and thumb. Wrap all three up the hook shank. The material tightens around the thread with every wrap. Wrap up and back over the shank, forming desired body shape. Repeat to cover shank. Tease out fibers with Velcro stick. Apply ribbing, whip-finish, and re-tease.

Soft Hackle March Brown Emerger

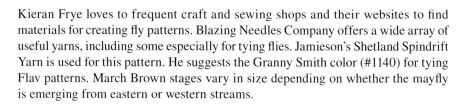

- **Hook:** #12-16 Mustad C53S
- **Thread:** Brown 8/0 UNI-Thread
- **Tail:** Three or four cock ringneck pheasant tail feather fibers
- **Body:** Scotch broom Jamieson's Shetland Spindrift Yarn (#1160)
- **Thorax:** Pumpkin Krystal Flash Chenille
- **Hackle:** Light dun or golden straw Whiting Brahma hen

Kieran Frye loves to frequent craft and sewing shops and their websites to find materials for creating fly patterns. Blazing Needles Company offers a wide array of useful yarns, including some especially for tying flies. Jamieson's Shetland Spindrift Yarn is used for this pattern. He suggests the Granny Smith color (#1140) for tying Flav patterns. March Brown stages vary in size depending on whether the mayfly is emerging from eastern or western streams.

Stub Tail Caddis

- **Hook:** #8-20 Daiichi 1560
- **Thread:** Brown 72 or 140-denier UNI-Thread depending on hook size
- **Tail:** Trimmed hair remaining from the wing
- **Body:** Natural muskrat belly fur dubbing
- **Rib:** Tying thread
- **Wing:** Stacked then folded blond elk hair
- **Head:** Folded blond elk hair

On trying this pattern for a number of streams, Al Beatty found he created a "killer fly." He ties the stacked elk hair onto the top of the hook shank with the tips facing forward and butts to the rear. He dubs the body over the tied-in elk hair, then uses the tying thread to rib and secure the body in place. Next, he folds the tips of the elk back to the rear to form a wing. Tying this off forms the head. Al recommends that after trimming the "stub tail," clip the trimmed fibers off the bottom of the tail so the pattern lies flat in the water. This fly's construction allows the tier to use less material in the wing and still produce a high-floating pattern.

TD's Adult Crane Fly

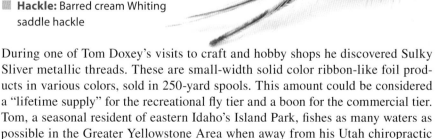

- **Hook:** #12-14 Daiichi 1270
- **Thread:** Tan 8/0 UNI-Thread
- **Rib:** Light gold Sulky Sliver Metallic Thread (#145-8003)
- **Body:** Cream Super Fine dubbing
- **Legs:** Two or three cemented strands of ringneck pheasant tail fibers, each side
- **Wings:** Small Whiting Coq de Leon saddle hackle fibers
- **Hackle:** Barred cream Whiting saddle hackle

During one of Tom Doxey's visits to craft and hobby shops he discovered Sulky Sliver metallic threads. These are small-width solid color ribbon-like foil products in various colors, sold in 250-yard spools. This amount could be considered a "lifetime supply" for the recreational fly tier and a boon for the commercial tier. Tom, a seasonal resident of eastern Idaho's Island Park, fishes as many waters as possible in the Greater Yellowstone Area when away from his Utah chiropractic practice. A dry fly enthusiast by choice, he enjoys tying and presenting such patterns throughout the season. He suggests giving this pattern a gentle twitch as it drifts along moving waters.

Todd's C&S Emerger

■ **Hook:** #10-16 Daiichi 1550
■ **Thread:** Black 8/0 UNI-Thread
■ **Bead:** Gold, sized to hook
■ **Tail:** Pair of dyed black duck biots
■ **Body:** Tapered of purple floss
■ **Thorax:** Fine red crystal chenille
■ **Legs:** Orange and brown barred Sili Legs
■ **Wing:** Silver Widow's Web or Thin Skin strip

Todd Smith created this all-purpose emerger pattern for both walk-in wade and float fishing, and it has proven effective for both. "I've used it with effect at depth, but especially when trout are taking caddis or mayfly emergers near the surface. In that case, I tie it with a clear glass bead rather than a gold bead and present it on a floating line," he offers. He also suggests switching to body and thorax colors that appear to match those of the emerging insect.

Triple Down Streamer

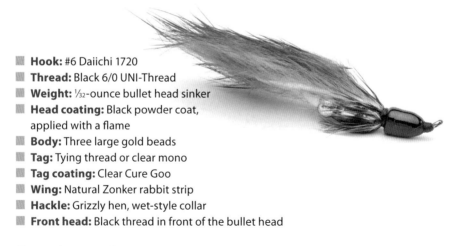

■ **Hook:** #6 Daiichi 1720
■ **Thread:** Black 6/0 UNI-Thread
■ **Weight:** ⅟₃₂-ounce bullet head sinker
■ **Head coating:** Black powder coat, applied with a flame
■ **Body:** Three large gold beads
■ **Tag:** Tying thread or clear mono
■ **Tag coating:** Clear Cure Goo
■ **Wing:** Natural Zonker rabbit strip
■ **Hackle:** Grizzly hen, wet-style collar
■ **Front head:** Black thread in front of the bullet head

Since Al Beatty discovered this pattern, it has become one of the Beattys' go-to streamers. With a bullet head and three brass beads, it quickly drops in the water column to the "fish zone." Present it on a sinking line in still water or on a sink-tip line in streams. Note that the hook point, barb, and bend puncture the rear end of the Zonker strip tied in on the underside of the shank. The hook-point-up design also keeps the fly out of most underwater snags, a much-desired property for a deep-running pattern.

Trolling Fly

⫸ **Hook:** Gaelic Supreme 8XL Mike Martinek's Carrie Stevens Streamer Hook
⫸ **Thread:** Black 6/0 UNI-Thread with red or orange band of 6/0 in head
⫸ **Body:** Gold Mylar tinsel
⫸ **Belly:** Mixed orange and purple bucktail
⫸ **Underwing:** Five or six dyed orange ostrich herls
⫸ **Wing:** Magenta or lavender over orange Whiting American saddle hackles
⫸ **Wing veiling:** Whiting medium pardo hen saddle hackle
⫸ **Cheek:** Lemon wood duck flank under optional jungle cock eye
⫸ **Throat:** Lavender or magenta schlappen fibers

Whiting medium pardo rooster and hen saddles are beautiful to behold. They are, however, too delicate to form feather-wing streamers by themselves. Thus I use them to veil such material as Whiting American hackle in colors light enough not to hide the unusual pardo markings. Colors such as lavender or magenta, or even orange, pink, or yellow, maintain these markings. In the Rangeley style, I build the left and right sides of the wing–that is, the wing, wing veiling, and cheek components—first. Then I build the body, belly, underwing, and throat on the hook. Last I tie in the wings, far side before facing side. Using an intermediate line, I troll this fly slowly from my floatation device to simulate a minnow.

Twist Nymph Variant

- **Hook:** #8-12 Tiemco 2499SP-BL
- **Bead:** Copper tungsten, in proportion to hook size
- **Weight:** A few turns of 0.015-inch-diameter non-lead wire
- **Thread:** Black 8/0 UNI-Thread
- **Body:** Three strands of peacock herl with peacock black Ice Dub in a thread loop
- **Dubbing cement:** Mousetrap glue

This is Bill Liebegott's variation of Gary LaFontaine's original Twist Nymph. It is his nymph pattern of choice when presenting flies European style with a Tenkara rod. In this manner, he has caught an uncountable number of salmonids. He ties this pattern on a Tiemco 2499SP-BL in sizes 8 to 12 because he prefers a wide gape on the hook. He uses mousetrap glue for coating the thread prior to twisting the peacock herl and touch-dubbing the peacock black Ice Dub to the thread loop. He tapers the body to medium length and thickness. Bill says that if he were limited to only one fly pattern, this would be his choice.

UPS No Hackle

- **Hook:** #16 Tiemco 100
- **Thread:** Dark brown 70-denier UNI-Thread
- **Wing:** Cut from packaging foam sheet
- **Tail:** Dark brown moose mane hairs
- **Body:** Mahogany dyed turkey biot
- **Thorax:** Chocolate brown dubbing
- **Marker:** Delta brown Chartpak

Sumi Sakamaki observed the thin delicacy of packaging sheeting used by United Parcel Service (UPS) and considered that mayfly dun wings could be cut from it. She cuts wings to shape, ties them upright and divided onto the hook shank just behind the eye, then paints them with the delta brown marker for the Mahogany Dun pattern pictured above. She proceeds to finish the fly tail first, then the biot body, and finally the dubbed thorax. She offers that the unpainted foam can also be used to form spinner wings, painted cream for PMD dun wings or smoky gray for BWO dun wings. She finds this material forms a durable wing that holds its shape after landing several fish. Sumi recommends using the Mahogany Dun version of this pattern on slow-moving stretches of river, where trout usually feed on these drifting insects.

BIBLIOGRAPHY

Allen, Boots. *Snake River Fly Fishing*. Portland, OR: Frank Amato Publications, 2010.

Back, Howard. *The Waters of Yellowstone with Rod and Fly*. New York: Lyons Press, 2000.

Brooks, Charles E. *Fishing Yellowstone Waters*. New York: Nick Lyons Books, 1984.

———. *The Living River*. New York: Nick Lyons Books, 1979.

Diem, Kenneth L., and Lenore L. Diem. *A Community of Scalawags, Renegades, Discharged Soldiers and Predestined Stinkers: A History of Northern Jackson Hole and Yellowstone's Influence, 1872–1920*. Moose, WY: Grand Teton Natural History Association, 1998.

Green, Dean, H. *History of Island Park*. Ashton, ID: Island Park–Gateway Publishing, 1990.

Konizeski, Dick. *The Montanans' Fishing Guide*. Vol. 2, 3rd ed. Missoula, MT: Mountain Press Publishing, 1977.

Lawson, Mike. *Fly-Fishing Guide to the Henry's Fork*. Mechanicsburg, PA: Stackpole Books, 2012.

Marcuson, Patrick E. *Fishing the Beartooths*. 2nd ed. Guilford, CT: Lyons Press, 2008.

———. *The History and Present Status of Golden Trout in Montana*. Helena, MT: State of Montana Department of Fish, Wildlife and Parks, Fisheries Division, 1984.

Pierce, Steve. *The Lakes of Yellowstone*. Seattle, WA: The Mountaineers, 1987.

Retallic, Ken. *Flyfisher's Guide to Wyoming: Including Grand Teton and Yellowstone National Park*. Gallatin Gateway, MT: Wilderness Adventures Press, 1998.

Rubinstein, Paul, Lee H. Whittlesey, and Mike Stevens. *Yellowstone Waterfalls and Their Discovery*. Englewood, CO: Westcliffe Publishers, 2000.

Schiess, Bill. *Fishing Henry's Lake*. Jerome, ID: 3KB Productions, 1997.

USDA Forest Service. *Motor Vehicle Use Map, Gallatin National Forest*. May 15, 2014.

Varley, John, and Paul Schullery. *Yellowstone Fishes: Ecology, History, and Angling in the Park*. Mechanicsburg, PA: Stackpole Books, 1998.

Whittlesey, Lee H. *Yellowstone Place Names: A Montana Historical Society Guide*. Helena, MT: Montana Historical Society Press, 1988.

INDEX